PATTY MILLS
BEYOND BASKETBALL

BOTI NAGY

Published by Wilkinson Publishing Pty Ltd
ACN 006 042 173
PO Box 24135 Melbourne, VIC 3001, Australia
Ph: +61 3 9654 5446
enquiries@wilkinsonpublishing.com.au
www.wilkinsonpublishing.com.au

© Copyright Boti Nagy 2024

All rights reserved. No part of this publication may be reproduced, stored in a retrieval system or transmitted in any form by any means without the prior permission of the copyright owner. Enquiries should be made to the publisher.

Every effort has been made to ensure that this book is free from error or omissions. However, the Publisher, the Authors, the Editor or their respective employees or agents, shall not accept responsibility for injury, loss or damage occasioned to any person acting or refraining from action as a result of material in this book whether or not such injury, loss or damage is in any way due to any negligent act or omission, breach of duty or default on the part of the Publisher, the Authors, the Editor, or their respective employees or agents.

Title: Patty Mills Beyond Basketball (2024)
ISBN: 9781922810618

A catalogue record for this book is available from the National Library of Australia.

Cover and internal design by Spike Creative Pty Ltd.
Printed and bound in Australia by Ligare Book Printers.

For Yvonne and Benny

Thank you for giving us

this gift named Patrick

Contents

Chapter 1: Gael Force Wins 9

Chapter 2: The Indigenous Trail Blazer 37

Chapter 3: A Time for Tigers 64

Chapter 4: The Tower of London 80

Chapter 5: The Spur for San Antonio 101

Chapter 6: Forever the Champion 116

Chapter 7: Bala Lazza and the World 132

Chapter 8: Putting the Boots into Wellington 144

Chapter 9: The Rock Doesn't Break 161

Chapter 10: I Go to Rio 175

Chapter 11: Reach for the Stars 193

Chapter 12: A Very Big Year 208

Chapter 13: A World of Hurt 225

Chapter 14: Gold Vibes Only 246

Chapter 15: Our Dreamtime Team 269

Chapter 16: A Very Different Role Model 284

Chapter 17: Changing of the Guard 304

"Sport has the power to change the world. It has the power to inspire. It has the power to unite people in a way that little else does. It speaks to youth in a language they understand. Sport can create hope where once there was only despair. It is more powerful than government in breaking down racial barriers."

Nelson Mandela

CHAPTER ONE
GAEL FORCE WINS

Seasoned Network 7 sports reporter Mel McLaughlin was barely containing her own tears as she turned the microphone toward a relieved, emotional and exhausted Patty Mills. The Australian men's basketball team, known globally as "the Boomers" — a male kangaroo, its image perhaps best recalled worldwide as a caricature on a yellow flag wearing boxing gloves and preparing to fight above its weight — finally had broken the glass ceiling. Australia's men's team at last had won a medal at an Olympic Games and, most appropriately, at the delayed 2020 Tokyo Games of 2021.

First competing in basketball as the host nation of the 1956 Melbourne Olympic Games but only as an international minnow, Australia failed to qualify for the 1960 Rome Olympics but made it through the most arduous of pre-Olympic campaigns to reach the 1964 Tokyo Olympic Games. That was the Olympic tournament at which Australia first planted its flag, an overtime pre-Olympics loss to international superpower Yugoslavia signalling the intent of these suntanned part-timers. The first Indigenous man to represent Australia at an Olympic Games, the late, great Michael Ahmatt, was a cornerstone of that 1964 team which covered itself in glory by beating Korea, Mexico and wildly-supported host nation Japan to claim ninth placing.

It was at a basketball coaching clinic conducted by Ahmatt in far north Queensland where another Indigenous superstar, Danny Morseu first encountered the sport of basketball. Morseu was bound for a career in rugby until the wizardry of Ahmatt's entrancing ball skills and infectious, joyous love for the game turned him to the round ball. Two Olympic representations (1980 and 1984) followed, rugby merely a memory. Patty Mills once told Uncle Danny he planned to better his record and in Tokyo, as now a four-time Olympian, Mills had more than achieved that ambition. But with that historic first-ever bronze medal around his neck after leading Australia to an epic 107-93 playoff win over Slovenia, that Indigenous circle from Tokyo-to-Tokyo also was complete.

"We've been waiting for this moment for a long time," Mills replied to McLaughlin's heartfelt congratulations. "You know it's taken a lot of experiences, a lot of ups, a lot of downs for us to get over the hump and it's our culture at the end of the day. It's our Australian culture, our Aussie spirit. It's the boys being able to hang together and understand the meaning of what it means to represent your country and how deep the layers go.

"And now that we've made it over the hill, this is the standard now of Australian basketball for men, and we take nothing less. We say that, you know, 'gold vibes only' is the standard and we don't accept anything less, from on the court, off the court, all of our preparation and it pays off in the long run. I don't know whether to cry, laugh, smile… (I'm feeling) a lot of emotions.

"I think where we've been able to build our Boomers culture is understanding the lay of the land. It goes far beyond basketball and for us it's always (about) giving back. Where we've been able to build our Boomers culture to this point is being able to understand where we come from, where we see the future, living in the present and who we represent. Our names are Boomers for a reason and for us to be able to give back to our nickname is where we started this campaign.

"There's many different layers and we were able just to dig deep and find all of those and really touch everyone. For us older guys, we've been through a lot. For the young boys, the new boys that have come into this, they really understand now what it means to be a Boomer and hopefully the rest of the country does as well now."

Mills' performance in the bronze medal playoff arguably was the greatest single game played by anyone wearing the green-and-gold of an Australian men's basketball team. There have been myriad great performances by Boomers greats across the ages, from Ahmatt to Les Hody, to Eddie Palubinskas, to Ian Davies, to Phil Smyth, to Larry Sengstock, the master Andrew Gaze and all the way to Andrew Bogut and Joe Ingles. But Mills was in another stratosphere as he loaded the Boomers – and the nation – onto his shoulders, producing a game for the ages, and for all ages.

His 42 points and nine assists in that clinical erasure of Slovenia was as outstanding a single-game performance as any by anyone wearing the hallowed green-and-gold, and also an Olympic record as the highest individual score in a medal playoff since Dr James Naismith's sport of basketball first was introduced to the Games in 1936. As a nation, Australia has enjoyed some fine Olympic accolades, with first Eddie Palubinskas in 1976, then Ian Davies in 1980, Andrew Gaze in 2000 and Mills in 2012 leading the Games tournament in scoring.

No other country can boast having four players achieve that. Brazil's scoring machine Oscar Schmidt led the Games scoring in 1988, 1992 and 1996 and Spain's perennial Pau Gasol did it in 2004 and 2008. But for all those achievements, nothing comes close to winning the bronze medal and Patty absolutely guaranteed Australia would do it.

He had 26 points at halftime, then knew as Slovenia would focus on him in the second half, he could draw defenders and dish the ball for others. Fortuitously, his long-time partner-in-prime, Joe Ingles, was knocking down outside shots to go with his international career-best eight defensive rebounds from his team-high total of nine. And Mills' nine assists were every bit as valuable as his 16-point second half.

Patty Mills, bala extraordinaire, the uncrowned but clearly King of Australia that fateful day in Tokyo, made every one of his countrymen proud, no matter their background or back story. "Aussie! Aussie! Aussie!" morphed into "Patty! Patty! Patty!" even though he was far more pleased and happier with the result than of his immense and immeasurable contribution to it.

"We represent the past, the present and the future that's coming in," an elated but drained Patty told McLaughlin. "They'll know," he added, referencing the work done by players such as Andrew Gaze and Andrew Bogut across this Boomers journey that began 65 years earlier in Melbourne. "We're only here because of all of them, right back to the Tokyo team that first came over here. You know, we were able to touch base with them and understand who was on that team and what they were able to do. So it's guys like Andrew Gaze and Andrew Bogut, and uncle Danny Morseu, and the great Ahmatt... from Day One it's all of these people that we went and touched and made sure we revisited where this Boomers programme started."

Mills, of course, is the personification of what it is to be a Boomer, and more, what it means to be an Australian. Reuniting with Ingles as an Olympian for the fourth time and with Brian Goorjian, the coach from their original Games campaign together in Beijing, he took Australians everywhere along on a thrilling, emotional, exhilarating and ultimately glorious journey. So where to now for that bronze medal?

"It's time to bring an Olympic medal home," he said, his voice trembling with the emotion and realisation of the achievement. "Back to our country, Australia, so I can hang it up at mum and dad's house."

"Mum and dad's house" these days is on the Sunshine Coast but it is far from where their journeys began. Patrick Sammy Mills' father Benny is a Torres Strait Islander. Torres Strait separates Australia's Cape York Peninsula from Papua New Guinea. His mother Yvonne is an Aboriginal

Australian, the daughter of a white man and an Aboriginal woman. After they separated in 1949, as part of the "Stolen Generations", Yvonne and her four siblings were taken from their parents. "Stolen Generations" was a programme enacted by Australian federal and state government agencies and church missions; a misguided and disastrous policy of assimilation by force. Mills has said learning of his mother's past was a turning point in his understanding of his identity as an Indigenous Australian. But his family history also makes him uniquely qualified as a spokesman and ambassador for *all* Australians.

While he no longer recalls when he first learnt of his mother's kidnapping by government authorities at the age of two or of her bizarre treatment simply because her skin was dark, Patty Mills was someone who never required a teacher or a textbook to understand the horrific details of the Stolen Generation. He had a living record of it at home in a loving mother who not only endured it but who dedicated her life to improving the lot and lives of other Aboriginals. In fact Yvonne Haynes met Benny Mills while working for the Government in Canberra at improving conditions for Indigenous Australians.

The couple married and started up the Shadows Basketball Club in Canberra as an opportunity for predominantly Aboriginal, Torres Strait Islander and African kids to play basketball on the south side of Canberra. It was where Patty Mills would take his first steps on a journey to basketball immortality, fulfilling a destiny denied many great Australian Olympic teams that laid the foundation for what is "Boomers culture".

The Boomers for decades were considered a nation of battlers, part-timers fighting well above their weight class when faced with the might of international teams at Olympic Games and FIBA World Championships. FIBA is basketball's global governing body and before Mills arrived on the scene, Australia's best finishes were fifth placings at its World tournaments in Bogota, Colombia in 1982 and in Toronto, Canada in

1994. A podium finish was little more than a pipe-dream then, Australia generally considered a realistic chance to fall somewhere between fifth and eighth if everything went well. Change began in 1987 ahead of the 1988 Seoul Olympic Games when then Boomers coach Adrian Hurley gambled on three youngsters to join national sporting hero Andrew Gaze in taking the team to unprecedented heights.

Talented young centre Luc Longley would go on to win three NBA World Championships as a starter with the Chicago Bulls of Michael Jordan, Scottie Pippen, Dennis Rodman, Ron Harper, Toni Kukoc and Steve Kerr. Muscular forward Andrew Vlahov would captain Stanford University in what was then the Pacific-10 Conference (now Pac-12), leading the Cardinals to the 1991 NIT (National Invitation Tournament) championship, three-times named the college's Best Defensive Player and also its Most Inspirational. As captain of the Perth Wildcats in Australia's NBL (National Basketball League), he first won the League's Rookie of the Year award, then three championships, accumulating awards throughout his career. And centre/power forward Mark Bradtke saw action in the NBA with Philadelphia 76ers and remains the NBL's all-time leading rebounder, a League MVP (Most Valuable Player) and a three-time championship winner, twice with Melbourne Tigers and additionally with Brisbane Bullets.

Hurley's gamble on the three tyros, scholarship-holders at Canberra's prestigious Australian Institute of Sport, also was supplemented via consecutive Australian tours by the World No.2 ranked super-powered Soviet Union team. While the Boomers were unable to take a single match off the USSR in either the 1987 or 1988 series, they eventually forced an overtime game and drew progressively closer.

Heading for the Seoul Olympics, Hurley's Boomers were more confident of their prospects then any Australian team previously off to a major international tournament. The Aussies opened by beating Puerto Rico. Intragroup losses to the Soviets and No.3 ranked Yugoslavia were erased by further wins over Central Africa and Korea, upsetting Spain catapulting Australia into the final four and a semi final berth. The semi loss to Yugoslavia meant the Aussies were playing off for the bronze medal for the first time, most likely against an opponent they now knew intimately, the Soviet Union.

Except the Soviets did not read the script, scoring a major Olympic Games upset by ousting the USA in the other semi final. It was a reality check for USA Basketball, acknowledging the rest of the world had caught up and the Americans no longer simply could send the elite of their college players if they expected to return with the gold medal they believed was their birthright. USA's demise in Seoul ignited the birth four years later of the greatest assembly of basketball talent ever seen, the "Dream Team" and the entry into the Olympics of professional NBA players. The USSR's stunning semi final win and ultimate success in claiming the 1988 gold medal, irrevocably changed American perceptions of international basketball. With the advent of NBA pros from 1992 onward, the door also opened for players such as Luc Longley, Patty Mills, Joe Ingles, Andrew Bogut, Aron Baynes, Matthew Dellavedova and David Andersen to wear the Boomers' green-and-gold.

That final USA team comprised of college stars and soon to be NBA pros such as David Robinson, Dan Majerle, Stacey Augmon, Danny Manning, Charles D Smith, Hersey Hawkins, Charles Smith, Mitch Richmond and J.R. Reid, were appalled and embarrassed at their own failure to bring home gold. Totally focused and determined to return with at least some sort of consolation prize in the bronze medal, the Americans slaughtered Australia 78-49. It remains a memorable breakthrough fourth place for Australia but that medal podium still seemed light years away. The good news no-one even knew at the time? Patrick Sammy Mills was born a month earlier.

Heartache slowly became the Boomers' constant international companion. It was back to sixth place at the Barcelona Olympics four years later, where Michael Jordan, Charles Barkley, Earvin "Magic" Johnson, Larry Bird and Co dominated Games headlines as the USA's untouchable "Dream Team" of megastar NBA athletes. Again, unbeknown yet but significantly in suburban Canberra, a four-year-old Patty Mills had taken up basketball as a primary passion.

Four years later at Atlanta's 1996 Olympics, Australia again would shock the world, storming through Korea, Puerto Rico, Brazil, Greece, losing to Yugoslavia but upsetting Croatia to make it to the tournament semi finals. The USA then flexed its muscles again and the Boomers, missing the injured Luc Longley throughout this campaign, were back again in a bronze medal playoff. International rival and sometime nemesis Lithuania, with exceptional centre Arvydas Sabonis, stood in Australia's way. And the 221cm, 132kg Sabonis was substantial in Lithuania's tight 80-74 win.

Rarely did Australia need Longley more than in that one game, Boomers players and officials now confident in their ability to secure a coveted medallion at the 2000 Olympic Games on home soil in Sydney, Australia. And it wasn't a "quiet confidence" either, players openly declaring Sydney would see an end to the near-miss medal misery. The Boomers boasted seven players with some degree of NBA experience, Hurley's 1988 gamble on his tyro trio of Longley, Vlahov and Bradtke about to bear fruit. It also would be the international farewell of Australia's most beloved and decorated basketballer, Andrew Gaze.

Gaze became basketball's historic first-ever flag-bearer for the Australian Games team and if ever a storied career deserved a fairytale finish, his was it. But the tournament could not have started more poorly, NBA superstar Steve Nash carving up the Boomers to lead Canada to an opening night upset over the host nation. A second night loss to

Yugoslavia and the talk for Australia no longer was of medalling but of making it past the intragroup rounds.

Loading the Boomers onto his back, Gaze led the way in victories over Russia, Angola and Spain, a great sense of relief accompanying Australia's advance to the quarterfinals. Once more Gaze dug deep to personify the Boomers spirit as Australia beat Italy 65-62 to yet again reach the semi finals. France, which last won a silver medal at an Olympic Games in 1948, looked a very beatable prospect in that penultimate round. However it proved exactly the opposite, the Frenchmen on a mission, inflicting Australia's heaviest loss of the Olympics, a decisive 24-point rout.

Four years earlier with the heartbreak of the bronze medal loss in Atlanta, Lithuanian centre Arvydas Sabonis was the difference, Luc Longley unavailable. Now in Sydney the Aussies would be playing Lithuania again for bronze, this time the visitors without Sabonis but the Boomers with Longley. *Except they would not be.* In the process of being downgraded into another playoff for bronze, the Aussies lost Longley to a knee injury late in that seminal semi final and he was in street clothes as the Boomers succumbed 71-89. A 12-year-old Patty Mills watched the Sydney Olympics on TV mesmerised, though less by what he saw of the Boomers and more by Aboriginal sprinter Cathy Freeman lighting the cauldron and then, during her victory lap after sensationally winning the 400 metres, carrying both the Southern Cross and the Aboriginal flags.

The overwhelming despair and disappointment of Sydney 2000 for the Boomers took Australian basketball years to recover. In 2002, it failed to qualify for the FIBA World Championship, the only occasion that occurred since competing for the first time in 1970. At the 2004 Athens Olympics and with master NBL coach Brian Goorjian at its helm and Australia's exciting potential new hero, 213cm (7-ft) centre Andrew Bogut making his Games debut, the Boomers only could muster wins over Angola and New Zealand. Bogut was the star of Australia's gold medal success at the 2003 FIBA Under-19 World Cup and named MVP of the tournament. His teammates included other exciting young future Olympians such as Brad Newley and Damian Martin. But in Athens, losses to Greece, USA, Puerto Rico and Lithuania left the Boomers well shy of the quarterfinals.

Two years later and still under Coach Goorjian at the FIBA World Championship in Japan, Australia beat only Brazil and Qatar. Defeated by Turkey, Greece, USA and Lithuania, it again was a far cry from the quarterfinals. On the plus side, a set of circumstances were conspiring in the Boomers' long-term favour, while a new breed of young Australian players such as Bogut, Newley and Martin also were starting to make their mark.

Scott Pendlebury was an outstanding young basketball player from Sale in Victoria, representing Vic Country as a junior and showing sufficient talent to be offered a scholarship to the Australian Institute of Sport in Canberra. It only took Pendlebury a few weeks at the AIS to realise Australian Rules Football was his true passion and calling. He quit the Institute to focus on football and never had cause to regret that decision, going on to become the games-played record-holder for the Collingwood Football Club, arguably the best-known and supported AFL team in the world. He also was one of the club's longest-serving captains and won the Norm Smith Medal – as the MVP or best-on-ground of the AFL grand final – while leading Collingwood to its 2010 premiership.

Pendlebury's vacated scholarship in the 2005 AIS squad was awarded to one Patty Mills, an exhilarating 183cm (6-ft) combination guard who also had to make a decision between basketball and a burgeoning Australian Rules football career. When he did, the course for basketball in Australia was forever and definitively altered. But he wasn't the first

Mills to win an AIS scholarship. His uncle Sammy Mills, his father Benny's brother, has the distinction of being the first Indigenous basketball player at the Institute, attending on scholarship in 1983.

By January 2006 as a 17-year-old, Patty Mills was winning the prestigious RE Staunton Medal at the Under-20 Nationals in Perth. It was a watershed year, without question, Andrew Bogut tipping it off as Australia's most successful NBA draft pick when selected at No.1 by the Milwaukee Bucks ahead of the 2005-06 season. Then Australia's senior women's team, the Opals, won the gold medal at the FIBA World Championship. Yet unobtrusively, 2006 truly would be Patty's year.

He attended the Australian Junior Camp in his home town of Canberra at the beginning of 2006 and as a key player on Australia's junior national men's team, helped beat New Zealand to qualify for the 2007 FIBA World Championship for Junior Men. In April he was a member of the World Select Team that competed against the USA National Junior Team in the Nike Hoop Summit in Memphis, Tennessee. The USA, with one of Mills' future NBA teammates at Brooklyn Nets, Kevin Durant, scoring 20 points, won 109-91. Mills scored eight points and dished a game-high six assists. A huge learning experience, it also showed Mills where he stood amid the world's best young talent.

Playing for the AIS team in the South East Australian Basketball League – Australia's No.2 elite competition behind the NBL and the No.1 interstate competition across winter – Mills was named the 2006 Australian Youth Player (Under-21) of the Year. He averaged 18.1 points and 3.9 rebounds per game against teams laden with off-season NBL and Boomers regulars, plus a host of quality American import players. He steered the AIS to a 16-10 regular season record, finishing the season third in the SEABL for assists, averaging 4.37 per game.

In July, he was named the 2006 Junior Male Player of the Year at Basketball Australia's annual Junior Basketball Awards, and the "most promising new sports talent" at the 2006 Deadlys Awards. The Deadlys Awards honour Aboriginal and Torres Strait Islanders' achievements in sports, music, entertainment and community. In addition to receiving the Deadlys Award, Mills was named the 2006 Australia Basketball Player of the Year and the National Sportsperson of the Year by the NAIDOC (National Aborigines and Islanders Day Observance Committee).

Yet despite this sudden rush of recognition and avalanche of justified accolades, possibly the piece de resistance for Patty in 2006 was his selection as the youngest athlete in the 22-man extended Australian Boomers squad ahead of that year's FIBA World Championship. While he did not win selection for the championship in Japan, it was a further disastrous campaign by the Boomers and the time was ripe for change.

Outstanding for the Emus, Australia's Under-19 men's team which competed at the 2007 FIBA Under-19 World Cup, Mills was fast-tracked into the Boomers that year. The Emus were desperately unlucky at the Worlds in Novi Sad, Serbia, Mills quarter-backing the team to an impressive 8-1 tournament win-loss record. Its only loss unfortunately was in the quarterfinal to Brazil, relegating Australia to the fifth-to-eighth-place playoffs. Mills led from the front with a game-high 21 points at 53 per cent, adding three assists and two steals as the Emus spanked Argentina 83-59 to secure fifth place. Patty averaged 14.9 points, 4.6 assists and 2.8 rebounds in announcing his arrival on the international scene.

Boomers coach Brian Goorjian took note. A week after the Junior Worlds concluded, Goorjian seconded Patty onto his touring Boomers team and in his senior Australian debut against Austria in Bormio, Italy, Mills saw 23 minutes of action. Goorjian's "point guard of the future" had 11 points, a rebound and a steal in the 84-63 international "friendly" win, part of Australia's preparation for its best-of-three Oceania Championship against New Zealand later that month. The Oceania Series winner automatically qualified for the 2008 Beijing Olympic Games.

"Patrick was our best player and that has made people happy but it has made people nervous too," Goorjian said post-game. "We have four guys on tour for the point guard spot in a 14-man squad, but we'll only play 12 against New Zealand so somebody has to go." It was Adam Gibson who missed the cut on this occasion, naturalised 196cm American Darnell Mee at the time looking likely to follow in the footsteps of the more recent Aussie citizens who started their life as imports before representing their adopted country; players such as Cal Bruton (1986 Worlds), Leroy Loggins (1992 Olympics) and Scott Fisher (1996 Olympics, 1998 Worlds).

Mee, an NBA shooting guard at Denver Nuggets before winning two NBL championships with Adelaide 36ers as their point guard, also was a five-time winner of the league's best defensive player award. FIBA rules allow every national team the option of suiting one naturalised player. Mee was playing in the NBL for Cairns Taipans after naturalising in 2006, but at 36 when selected for the Boomers, his best days were in the rearview mirror. And to suggest he had the same "burning passion to play for Australia" as his predecessors in that one sanctioned naturalised player role would be overstating it in the extreme.

"Growing up in the United States, your goal is to make it to the NBA," Mee said. "That's the target for every young basketball player in the US. Here (in Australia), representing your country at an Olympics is the goal." Making millions of dollars playing in the NBA made far greater sense to young basketball aspirants than representing the United States at some distant international tournament very few Americans cared about or even knew about. Mee was never a reluctant potential Boomer, but equally not dismayed by the prospect of omission.

It was two "new faces," a couple of veterans and some tenacious defence which steered Australia to its 79-67 win over New Zealand for a 1-0 lead in the Oceania Championship. David Andersen already was an Aussie Olympian, but in notoriety was lagging in Andrew Bogut's NBA shadow.

Andersen stepped out with 20 points and his presence in the keyway made it easy for Sam Mackinnon — relishing the Boomers' captaincy — to also thrive with 18 points and seven rebounds.

Another veteran, Glen Saville, also was devastating for 16 points on 5-of-7 shooting, including a perfect 3-of-3 from beyond the three-point arc. But it was another genuine new face, promoted Emus guard Patrick Mills, who made the biggest impression with his lightning quickness after Darnell Mee collected two early fouls. Trailing 25-31 five minutes out from halftime, Mee swished a three-pointer and Mackinnon drove to the hoop to bring the crowd of 6,053 at Melbourne's Vodafone Arena to life.

Down 35-36 inside the last two minutes from the interval, Mackinnon tied it from the free throw line before Brad Newley fed Saville for one of his long-range trifecta. A Mackinnon steal opened the floor for a Newley dunk and when Saville scored off a quick steal, Australia had compiled an 8-0 run to be 43-36 ahead. "That little flurry gave us the lead," Goorjian said. "There was no doubt our defence was the difference in the two teams." Patty Mills had seven points in 18 minutes to stand out among the point guard candidates. His fellow member of Australia's "future force" Brad Newley added four. Mee contributed five points and no assists.

Ahead of Game Two in Sydney, Goorjian warned against complacency. "Anytime you're in this situation, if you're down one game, in the first 10 minutes of Game Two you come out swinging," the Boomers coach predicted. "They (NZ) have got a team that would be pretty good in that form. If we were going to win this series, at some point we were going to face that and I'm sure it will be in the first half of Game Two." Prepared for the onslaught in Sydney, Australia started with a flurry of its own to lead 25-17 at the close of the first quarter. The Tall Blacks responded with a withering 25-16 second period to take a one-point lead into halftime.

Sights firmly set on a 10th consecutive Olympic Games appearance, the Boomers sank the series with an exceptional 28-9 third quarter in a blistering 52-25 second half. If their defence was exemplary in Game One, it was at a whole other level in the 93-67 Game Two rout, Australia clinching the series 2-0 to earn its berth to Beijing. Mills delivered 17 points, behind only leading scorer and dual-Olympian Sam Mackinnon on 18. He also dished three assists. Mee scored 11, with two assists. Although he appeared a step slow and off the pace in Game One, it was largely his third quarter defensive example which set up the domination.

But with CJ Bruton's likely return for Games team consideration and Mills now a certainty, Mee's Olympic prospects looked shot. The energy and excitement Mills generated through the Oceania Championship left no doubt he would be on the plane to Beijing. "I just thought there was so much at stake and we carried such a responsibility," Goorjian said. "The game (in Australia) needs the Boomers to go to the Olympic Games. Our game needs this right now especially, and this was the most vulnerable team in my time."

As if on cue responding to Goorjian's observation, New Zealand's Tall Blacks clinched the "dead rubber" in Brisbane. A New Zealand team boasting the multi-talents of Tall Blacks legends such as Kirk Penney, Pero Cameron, Craig Bradshaw, Dillon Boucher, Phill Jones, Mark Dickel, Paul Henare, naturalised Casey Frank and Mika Vukona had indeed posed a major threat to the Boomers' hopes of advancing. Ultimately though, other than Newley leading Australia with 14 points, it was a meaningless result, the Boomers on their way to another Olympic Games and likely with several new young faces in a "changing of the guard". Could it mean a changing of fortune too?

There was no question Patty Mills would make his Olympic basketball debut in the Boomers' team for the Beijing Games of 2008. The trajectory of his game and his career were self-evident. After his 2006 emergence as a future force in the game, he was recruited into the U.S. college basketball system to Saint Mary's College at Moraga in California, about an hour and a quarter south-west of the state capital of Sacramento. It was a programme boasting at least one player from Australia every season since Randy Bennett became head coach in 2001.

Andrew Bogut's MVP performance for Australia gold medal-winning Emus at the 2003 FIBA Under-19 World Cup was a further catalyst. When the Melbournite subsequently was setting records at the University of Utah, it additionally informed the U.S. there were other recruitable potential game-changing players Down Under. "Everyone then was asking: 'Where did this Andrew Bogut come from?' He came from the AIS," Mills told ESPN's Thomas Neumann. "So then all the college scouts came to the AIS for the next couple years, trying to find the next Andrew Bogut. I definitely wasn't a 7-foot-1 big white guy."

Bennett's ongoing relationship with Marty Clarke, head coach of the AIS's men's basketball programme, turned into a mutually agreeable one, the institute almost becoming a direct pipeline to St Mary's. And one of Bennett's assistant coaches was David Patrick, who played NBL at the Canberra Cannons from 2000–02 as CJ Bruton's back-up point guard. Patrick also was an Australian under-22 rep, and additionally figured prominently in the Gaels' heavy recruiting from the AIS. Growing up in Canberra, Mills was a ballboy for the Cannons. It was where he originally met Patrick, whose presence at St Mary's was a big factor.

The list of past, present and future Aussie basketball greats to attend the college is extraordinary, from Adam Caporn to Daniel Kickert to Mills, Matthew Dellavedova, Jock Landale, Clint Steindl, Mitch Young, Lucas Walker, Matt Hodgson, Ben Allen, Carlin Hughes, Kyle Clark, Jordan Hunter, Tanner Krebs, Alex Ducas, Kyle Bowen, Jock Perry, Emmett Naar, Alex Mudronja and Dane Pineau. Bennett's goal, albeit among many others, was to produce an Australian Olympian out of his programme. In Patty Mills, he achieved his goal, Dellavedova and Landale ultimately following suit.

St Mary's school records now are dominated by its Australian content. The most career points record is held by Dellavedova, with Kickert at Number 2. Landale owns the "most points in a single season" record and career field goal accuracy, Emmett Naar most career and single season assists totals. Dellavedova also has compiled the most made three-point field goals and highest free throw percentage at the school, Naar with the single season record. Additionally Dellavedova in 2012 and Landale in 2018 were named the West Coast Conference Player of the Year.

The sixth Aussie signed by the college, Patty Mills was the first though to truly make a profound impression at the school and in the West Coast Conference. In his freshman season, the first of four years of college eligibility comprised of freshman, sophomore, junior and senior years, he was named 2008 WCC Newcomer of the Year. He was a two-time First Team All-WCC selection in 2008 and 2009, and still holds St Mary's record for career steals. What makes that astonishing is that he declared for the NBA draft after his sophomore season which means he only had two seasons to set a steals mark others have not beaten across four years of eligibility. Even more amazing, in his sophomore season, he missed nine games with a broken hand.

Bob Cousy is revered in the United States as one of basketball's most outstanding point guards, winning an NCAA championship at Holy Cross and six NBA championships spearheading the Boston Celtics. The "Bob Cousy Award" is for the top point guard in college basketball across the nation and its myriad conferences. Patty Mills was a finalist for the award in 2008 and 2009. He didn't just knock quietly on the door of St Mary's and WCC basketball, he flung it open and left it wide enough for

Dellavedova and many others to successfully follow him through.

One of the ultimate basketball accolades after prolonged exceptional service to a programme is for that college, team or club to retire a sportsperson's playing number, the uniform raised into the rafters of the home venue, so hallowed and revered as to never again be worn. Before Patty Mills' arrival at St Mary's, the college retired the #31 of Tom Meschery, who completed his playing career with the Gaels in 1961. Mills' #13 now also hangs in the rafters at the Gaels' home court of McKeon Pavilion, along with only one other. That belongs to Matthew Dellavedova, his #4 also no longer in circulation.

"Clearly, Patty Mills is one of the elite student-athletes this programme has ever seen," coach Randy Bennett said ahead of the uniform retirement ceremony in 2015. "Patty is one of the college's greatest ambassadors and provides visibility for Saint Mary's every time he steps on the court. He is the most high-profile recruit the programme has ever signed, had two great seasons at Saint Mary's and made a significant impact on our programme. Through his play on the court, the success we had as a programme and his international experience at the Olympic Games, he provided a great deal of visibility to Saint Mary's during his college career.

"As great of a player Patty is, he is even a more special person. To this day, he completely embodies the ideals of Saint Mary's College and truly appreciates the opportunities and experiences Saint Mary's provides him." And he achieved all of this in just two seasons before declaring for the NBA draft.

"It is such a privilege that Saint Mary's is retiring my number," Mills said at the time. "This is an unbelievable honour and one of the most prestigious recognitions I've ever received. From the day I got there, I knew Saint Mary's would always be my home away from home. My memories of playing at McKeon Pavilion are awesome. To this day, it is still one of my favourite places to play. But, it is the memories of friends and family that I've made on and off the court that I will cherish for life."

Mills was in the starting five for all 32 games of his freshman season and set the school's (then) scoring record for points in a season. He scored 37 points in a Gaels win over highly rated Oregon University Ducks in a nationally televised match. Going into it, the Ducks were ranked #11 in college basketball across the nation, making it an epic win for the small Californian college. Mills shot 10-of-20 from the floor, with four triples and stroked 13-of-14 from the free throw line. He also enjoyed five assists and two steals, his 37 points a record for a freshman at St Mary's and the sixth best individual return in its history.

"If Mills plays that way every night, he's a pro," Oregon coach Ernie Kent predicted, also favourably comparing him to San Antonio Spurs star — and future Mills teammate — Frenchman Tony Parker. Kent was not the only coach to be dazzled by Mills' standout game.

"That performance against a quality team is great for Patrick, big for St Mary's… and huge for the Boomers," Australia's national coach Brian Goorjian said, Mills still to also win accolades as the Most Valuable Player at the Rainbow Classic and Shamrock Office Solutions Classic tournaments.

As a sophomore, Mills started in the first 20 games of the season, leading the Gaels to a number 18 national ranking before suffering his broken hand injury at Gonzaga. Out for nine games, he returned in time for the annual WCC Championship in Las Vegas. He led the Gaels to consecutive postseason appearances for the first time in the programme's history. And in a pair of high-profile postseason home games, Mills steered St Mary's to consecutive victories over future Golden State Warriors superstars Klay Thompson (Washington State) and Stephen Curry (Davidson) before dropping a quarterfinal game at San Diego State in the 2009 National Invitation Tournament.

"He brought a swagger to our programme that we, we didn't have it," Bennett reflected. "That's just kind of how he is. He came in as a, he's just got a supreme confidence about him… I think his third or fourth game of his career he had 37 (points) against Oregon. That's what he did. We were on the map a little bit but he really put us on the map. But ever since he came through here, our leadership has been outstanding. I think he set the bar up there pretty high. He's a good NBA player, he's a better person."

Australia's most successful coach in its domestic National Basketball League, Brian Goorjian, again held the reins for the Boomers at the 2008 Beijing Olympics. Athens in 2004 had not gone well but he only had David Andersen, Andrew Bogut, CJ Bruton, Matt Nielsen and Glen Saville returning from that team. His only other experienced Olympian was Chris Anstey who made his Olympic debut with the Boomers in 2000 at the Sydney Games. The wiry 213cm Anstey missed Athens selection, out injured with torn ligaments in an ankle.

Andersen, a 211cm forward/centre who was building a hugely successful resume through Europe and the NBL, claiming an extraordinary 12 championships across the Euroleague, Spain, Italy, Russia and Australia, also spent 2009–11 in the NBA, logging time with Houston Rockets, Toronto Raptors and New Orleans Hornets (now Pelicans). Bogut was Australia's historic first NBA #1 draft pick, the 213cm rock solid centre eventually winning a championship with Golden State Warriors in 2015.

Livewire playmaking guard Bruton was on his way to joining only a handful of players to win six NBL championships, claiming crowns at Sydney Kings, New Zealand Breakers and Brisbane Bullets. He also was named the Larry Sengstock Medallist as the MVP of the Grand

Final Series in the Breakers' 2012 championship. Matt Nielsen and Glen Saville both led their NBL clubs — Sydney Kings and Illawarra Hawks respectively — to championships, each claiming the Larry Sengstock Medal. Neilsen also won league MVP honours in 2004 before playing in Greece, Lithuania and Russia.

Anstey won three NBL championships, and two Larry Sengstock Medals in the course of them. He also won the league's MVP award twice, spent 1997–2000 in the NBA with Dallas Mavericks and Chicago Bulls, before extended pro stints in Russia and Serbia. At the time, he was a big man rarity, perhaps the blueprint for taller athletes who could not only thrive close to the basket but deliver daggers from long range. Many saw him as "Australia's Kevin Garnett."

Clearly Goorjian's five returnees from Athens and one from Sydney for the Beijing campaign all boasted a strong pedigree. Patty Mills was making his mark at St Mary's College when he was selected as only the third Indigenous men's basketball player to represent Australia at an Olympic Games, following in the footprints left by Michael Ahmatt and his uncle Danny Morseu.

A 198cm forward, Brad Newley was another tyro now firing in Europe, his career taking him from the NBL to Greece, Turkey, Lithuania and Spain. Newley too would play an integral part in the development of the Boomers' culture, as would his former schoolmate in Adelaide, Joe Ingles. The 203cm shooting guard was still in the throes of steering South Dragons to an NBL championship before also plying his trade in Europe, Israel and ultimately the NBA with Utah Jazz.

David Barlow was a 205cm forward who already had three NBL championships and the 2006 FIBA World Championship campaign under his belt, power forwards Mark Worthington and Shawn Redhage rounding out the team. Bunbury-born 203cm Worthington played college basketball in the US and was the closest Australian basketball had to a second coming of Andrew Vlahov, the Perth Wildcats' four-time Olympian. Nebraska-born Redhage naturalised after settling in Australia first as an import in the secondary SEABL competition before thriving at Perth, integral in the Wildcats winning four NBL championships.

On paper, Goorjian appeared to have a medal round contender but sadly, the game is played on wood. Australia was no match for Croatia in its Games opener, losing 82-97. Neilsen led the Boomers' scoring with 13 points, Barlow with 12, Bogut 10 and Patty Mills nine points in 19 minutes. Mills shot at 50 per cent and scored his only three-point attempt.

Next up against Argentina and future San Antonio Spurs teammate in the NBA, Manu Ginóbili, Mills cut loose for 22 points at 53 per cent to lead all scorers. The Boomers had lost 91-95 to Argentina in the final of the prestigious Diamond Ball Tournament in the week leading up to the Games, Mills with 14 points in 16 minutes. But while Australia had cause to now fancy its chances in Beijing, Ginóbili scored 21 points to pace the eventual bronze medalling Argentines to a handy 85-68 victory, built on a match-winning 23-11 first quarter. Patty Mills, however, now formally had announced his arrival on the senior international stage.

In a 106-68 rout of Iran, he added a further 15 points at 50 per cent, including 4-of-6 three-point baskets, with an equal game-high five assists, matched by Mark Worthington and CJ Bruton. Newley led the scoring with 24 points but just as it appeared the new breed was ready to take the spotlight, the pivotal match with Russia loomed.

Australia opened brilliantly to lead 27-16 at the end of the first quarter. The Boomers then built on that with a 22-17 second period for a 49-33 halftime buffer. This was not the Boomers of two decades earlier, nursing their lumps after two years of on-court lessons from the Soviet Union team. This was a team ready to win and did so in stunning fashion, 95-80. But this was Goorjian's "old guard" who stepped up, Andrew Bogut and CJ Bruton both with 22 points, David Andersen and Matt Nielsen

11 apiece. Mills played 28 minutes for six points and Newley 35 for nine, both more important in this one for their defence and secondary complimentary roles in the victory. Joe Ingles never left the bench, the first and only time he would not see action in an Olympic game.

It was a very similar story as the Boomers once more set tongues wagging, hammering sometime nemesis Lithuania 106-75, Bogut again with a game-high 23 points, Newley 16, Mills and Anstey 13 each. Opening with a withering 28-14 first quarter, the Boomers set a tone for what was to follow by backing that up 27-15 in the second. This was over at halftime, but the spectre of whether Lithuania produced its best effort hung over the result. Lithuania had already won the group, entering the match with the Boomers boasting an unassailable 4-0 win-loss record. It presented the coaching staff with an opportunity to rest key players. For Australia, it meant a 3-2 win-loss record and fourth place in the group at the end of intrapool play. The Boomers were advancing to the quarterfinals and top eight. The only drawback?

The group's fourth-placed team was drawn to play the rival group's top team and that was the unbeaten USA. The Americans boasted Kobe Bryant, LeBron James, Dwyane Wade, Carmelo Anthony, Dwight Howard, Chris Paul, Chris Bosh and Jason Kidd. If the admittance of NBA players into the Olympic Games of 1992 gave the world the unprecedented success story of the "Dream Team," America's superstars this time dubbed themselves as the "Redeem Team."

Four year earlier in Athens, an athletic and talented USA team but one which lacked proper balance and inside/outside strengths, succumbed 73-92 to Puerto Rico in its Games opener. It was a "Stop the Presses" upset. The tournament's hot favourites then outlasted a plucky Greece 77-71, managed to keep Australia at arm's length 89-79, before losing again, this time to Lithuania 94-90. Losing a game in intragroup play was unprecedented. Losing twice was simply embarrassing for the world's

No.1 basketball superpower. It whacked Angola 89-53 to advance to the quarterfinal stage with a 3-2 record.

In what once would have been viewed as unbelievable, it finished its intragroup play in fourth place for a match-up with the rival group's top team, Spain. Summoning its best performance of the tournament, the USA beat the Spaniards 102-94, moving on to the semi finals, the win restoring its self-assuredness, the Americans once more believing in their own invincibility. It was a cocky mistake. Facing an Argentine team boasting fearless and super-talented players such as Manu Ginóbili, Luis Scola and Andres Nocioni, the Americans again ran into a massive roadblock, beaten 89-81. Argentina continued on to defeat Italy in the gold medal playoff, the USA collecting the bronze consolation after beating Lithuania 104-96.

Three losses by the USA at an Olympic Games was beyond humiliating. From the 1936 Berlin Games when the sport first was introduced on the Olympic stage, the USA had only lost twice. Once was in the highly contentious 1972 Munich Olympic Games gold medal final to the USSR, still the most controversial finish to a basketball game in the sport's storied history. The other was in the 1988 Seoul Olympic semi final, again against the Soviets, a loss so significant it led to the admission of NBA players by Barcelona in 1992.

Three losses by the USA at an Olympic Games was unthinkable. Yet in Athens it happened. Four years later in Beijing, no less a superstar than Los Angeles Lakers' Kobe Bryant was leading the Americans in their quest for redemption and restoration of the USA's reputation. They were taking no prisoners either, sweeping past China, Angola, Greece, Spain and Germany by a collective 161 points, or by an average winning margin of 32.2 points, before setting their quarterfinal sights on the Boomers.

Worse for Australia was the fact the Americans were fully aware of the pluck and feisty nature of the Boomers, having played them in a warm-up "exhibition friendly" in Shanghai as part of both teams' Games preparation. In Shanghai, the USA had smashed Canada by 55 points, Turkey by 32, Lithuania 36 and Russia by 21 before running into Brian's burgeoning Boomers. Typically, Australia refused to take a backward step, Patty Mills personifying the prevailing attitude with a coast-to-coast drive, taking the ball the length of the floor to score. His speed, skill and quickness with the ball saw him blow past reputable NBA defender Chris Paul as if the latter was a statue mired in molasses.

After one quarter, the USA eked out a 22-19 lead, the second quarter also starting on Australia's terms before LeBron James cut loose. Mixing his powerful physical presence with sublime finesse, James enjoyed a 9-0 run of his own within a 12-0 American outburst that swept them from 26-25 to 38-25. Ahead 44-29 at halftime, the now customary opposition fadeout was to be expected, Australia's big men in some foul trouble and the Boomers already without Andrew Bogut, who did not play due to an ankle sprain. A quiet fadeout would not have surprised anyone.

Wrong. The Boomers' symbol is the boxing kangaroo and they came out punching, a 13-2 run bringing them to 42-46 before USA coach Mike Krzyzewski was forced to call a time-out with 6:01 left in the third period. The USA was leading 48-44, the significance of Coach K's time-out call massive. When the fabled USA Dream Team of the NBA's greatest players of the era swept all before them in Barcelona 16 years earlier, coach Chuck Daly did not call a single time-out in the lead-up games or the tournament-proper. Krzyzewski was a young assistant coach on that hallowed team, indisputably the greatest assemblage of basketball talent in the history of the sport. The goal of his 2008 "Redeem Team" was not only to win gold but reclaim the USA's place as the world's most dominant master of the sport.

In their four previous exhibition friendlies in Shanghai, Krzyzewski had not called a time-out, clearly hoping to emulate Daly's feat in

Barcelona. Australia had forced him into one in an exhibition, the television commentary crew very aware of it and also marvelling at the Boomers, labelling this by far the most competitive match of the USA's five exhibitions. The Aussies won the quarter 26-21 to trail 55-65 with a period to play. In its other warm-up matches, the USA won the third quarter in every one, and by 10 or more points.

Threatening to cause an upset, the Boomers were down 61-69 midway through the final quarter and even closer when rookie Joe Ingles came off the bench and swished a three-pointer for 64-71. Mills enjoyed a personal purple patch too, scoring after seizing an offensive rebound – not an easy challenge when you're 178cm (5ft-10in) masquerading as 183cm but against USA, definitely stuck in the land of the giants. Mills next drew a charging foul out of Chris Paul in midcourt, the NBA playmaker fouling out on the call. And on the next play, Mills stuck a baseline jumpshot to finish with 13 points, Australia eventually beaten — but certainly not bowed — 87-76. In fact it was the closest game the USA had against any opponent in the lead-up or at the Games until it beat Spain by 11 points in the gold medal match.

It was against this backdrop the Aussies lined up against the white-hot favourite USA Redeem Team for their quarterfinal in Beijing. While the Americans now were alerted to what they could expect, the Boomers also had the confidence that if they could keep their turnovers down, hit the boards hard and run their offences crisply, they could compete. The first quarter saw the USA hold a 25-22 lead as Mills drove hard to the hoop for a tough basket, additionally drawing a foul from Chris Paul. Mills missed the bonus free throw but at 24-25 after one, Australia was very much alive in the contest.

It was a little less so by halftime when, trailing 43-52, the Boomers gave up a transition three-pointer to Deron Williams right on the interval buzzer. A timely reminder to play every minute to its conclusion, it left Australia 12 points in arrears as it entered the second half, the USA fully primed this time for the potential onslaught. With Kobe Bryant alight and on his way to a game-high 25 points at 63 per cent — his tally including four three-pointers — the margin quickly blew out into the 20s. The USA's 34-18 third period made it 89-61 with a quarter left. Effectively, Australia's Olympic Games campaign was at an end.

Bowing out to the USA 85-116 was no disgrace, the Americans fulfilling what they believed was their destiny and continuing on to claim the gold medal. But as they wrapped up the victory over Australia, it was Patty Mills and Joe Ingles, two of the players who would form the backbone of the Boomers' culture and relentless quest to break the Olympic medal drought, who stood out.

Mills led Australia with 20 points, two assists, three steals and no turnovers in 29 minutes, frequently schooling well-established NBA star Chris Paul, his performance doubtless hastening his intent to leave St Mary's early for the bright lights of the world's greatest basketball competition. The only collegiate player competing at the Games and the youngest Olympic basketball player ever from Australia, he averaged a team-best 14.2 points coming off the bench. Andrew Bogut was next with 12.7 points per game.

Ingles absolutely announced himself to the NBA, making the most of his 10 minutes of court time. The young Joe stunned the USA by swishing a rapid-fire 11 points on a perfect 4-of-4 shooting. He could not have made a bigger impression in such minimal time, his tally including a wicked 3-of-3 three-pointers and his other field goal a soaring slam dunk over the game's biggest name of the era, Kobe Bryant. The groundwork was laid, Ingles another piece of the team's cultural core — alongside sure-fire returnees such as Bogut, Mills, Andersen and Newley — announcing his arrival in no uncertain terms.

St Mary's still has Australian ballers heading there, though many universities now routinely recruit players from Down Under. The Gaels boast a slight advantage with newcomers. "They all know Patty. They all know Delly," Coach Bennett said.

"It's just a place that feels like your home away from home," Mills says. "That's definitely what it was like for me."

CHAPTER TWO
THE INDIGENOUS TRAIL BLAZER

Regarded as a conquering hero upon his arrival back at Saint Mary's College, Patty Mills had fulfilled the dream of head coach Randy Bennett of producing an Australian Olympian. Four years later in London, Bennett would experience the ultimate thrill as two of his alumni — Mills and Matthew Dellavedova — would start for the Boomers in their next Olympic campaign. But having proven himself at the Olympic Games and, importantly, showed he could get the better of a seasoned NBA pro such as Chris Paul, Mills was ready to take the next step along his basketball journey.

In April 2009, he declared himself available for the NBA draft in June, most likely forsaking the final two years of his college basketball eligibility in the United States. Concluding his second season with the Gaels averaging career highs of 18.7 points, 4.0 assists, 2.6 rebounds and 2.5 steals per game, it was worth taking the gamble and rolling the dice. Wisely though, he informed a teleconference with Australia's media arranged by Basketball Australia from Saint Mary's that he would not sign with an agent ahead of the draft. That meant he could return to college if he was not selected.

"It's a win-win situation for me," Mills said. "If I don't get all the feedback that I want or need, I come back for my third year (of college)." As long as they had not employed an agent, players who declared their availability for the NBA draft also could withdraw beforehand, thereby retaining college eligibility. The 30 players selected in the first round of the draft on June 25 at Madison Square Garden were guaranteed three-year contracts.

"It was a tough decision to come across... sitting down with my family and coach," Mills said. "I really need to push myself and challenge myself to the next level, test the waters and get the feedback." With no NBA destination in mind, Mills was open-minded about what the future might hold. "I will come across them in the next few weeks," he said. "We'll sit down and sort out the teams. Right now, I have to work on my conditioning, my basketball. These are the things I am worrying about at this point. I still have another semester left (at St Mary's) and I am doing the best I can to finish them off. I have never been in this situation, I'm new to it all... learning how to handle the off-court distractions as well as my work on court."

Mills plastered his dreams as a kid on his wall, including making the Australian Emus, playing American college basketball, going to the Olympics and playing in the NBA. "I wrote that a number of years ago now," he said at the time. "But I have stuck to it." When the opportunity to attend the Australian Institute of Sport in his Canberra hometown first emerged, Patty still was as adept at Australian Rules football as basketball.

From a young age he showed superior agility and was tough as nails on the sporting field, blessing him as a multi-sport talent. As an Aussie Rules footballer, he was an All-Australian under-15 star for the NSW/ACT team at the 2004 national championship. His exquisite football skills earned him the best-and-fairest award—won by Geelong AFL captain Joel Selwood the previous year—and All-Australian honours at those 2004 national championships. At 17, he was offered a contract by the powerhouse Sydney Swans to play AFL but instead seized the opportunity to pursue his basketball passions, while always retaining his love for football.

But Patty was barely 10 when he was already throwing behind-the-back passes for his Shadows team at Woden Basketball Stadium in Canberra on a Friday night or Saturday afternoon, the ageing tin facility so typical of basketball venues across Australia. Freezing cold in winter, a la famed Albert Park Stadium in Melbourne, Forestville Stadium in Adelaide, Perry Lakes in Perth or a dozen other staple venues, it would be steaming hot in summer, patrons swapping winter blankets for sitting in pools of their own sweat. When Mills was toting the number 13 royal blue, red and yellow Shadows uniform though, fans would flock to see this extraordinary competitor carving it up on court.

This was Patty Mills, a son of the Kokatha people of Koonibba, South Australia and the Dauareb and Komet tribes of the Murray Islands in the far east of Torres Strait, north of Cape York Peninsula, Queensland, and south of the island of New Guinea. Nagi Island is the home island of the Mills family. "This is where my grandfather lived, Sammy Mills, my great, great grandfather Frank Mills, and even further back, James Mills," Mills told a documentary by his long-time NBA club San Antonio. That goes some way toward explaining why Patty's full name is Patrick Sammy James Mills. "This is where my long line of family come from, Nagi Island."

Wongai Court is located on Thursday Island in the Torres Strait. "This is not only where I played as a kid but where a lot of family played on this court," Mills said. "It's a good reminder about obviously what I do now but, you know, where I come from and, I guess in a sense, where it started." Patty's parents Benny and Yvonne played basketball in their youth and taught him the game. "I like to say I got all my moves from my mum," Patty says, "and my dad just fine-tuned them."

Madison Square Garden is as hallowed a venue for basketball as Wimbledon is for tennis. The 2009 NBA Draft officially was underway there on June 25 when league commissioner David Stern read out the first pick. Blake Griffin was heading to the Los Angeles Clippers. James Harden went at #3 to Oklahoma City Thunder, Ricky Rubio at #5 to Minnesota Timberwolves, before a slightly built little guard named Steph

Curry was selected at #7 by Golden State Warriors. DeMar DeRozan went to Toronto and the Raptors at #9, Jrue Holiday at #17 to Philadelphia 76ers. The first round of 30 players was selected and NBA deputy commissioner Adam Silver substituting for Stern at the podium as the draft continued, Patty Mills still waiting for his name to be called.

"With the 55th pick in the 2009 NBA Draft, the Portland Trail Blazers select Patrick Mills from Canberra, Australia and Saint Mary's College in California, and he's here tonight," Silver finally declared, a roar emerging from the crowd. Mills rose to embrace his delighted father Benny and equally thrilled mother Yvonne before making his way to the stage. As he did, ESPN analysts were full of praise for him.

"Patrick Mills is a magician, plays the guitar and he's also the only collegiate player to compete at last year's Olympics—he played for Australia," the host informed viewers before throwing to draft analyst Jay Bilas. "What do you like about his game Jay?"

"He's got great speed and quickness," Bilas said. "Yeah, he's good off the dribble, he can get by defenders and put you into help. He's explosive off pick-and-roll situations, he's a streaky shooter (and) a solid back-up point guard in the NBA. Honestly I'm surprised that he didn't go a lot higher in this draft. I thought he would be a late first round pick, (or) pretty early in the second round. I think this young man can play in the NBA."

How right he would prove. And just like that, Patty Mills was in the greatest and richest basketball competition in the world, something to which every Indigenous youth in Australia now also could aspire. He became the first Saint Mary's player since 1983 to be drafted, and the highest pick from the college since 1961. First though came a minor setback as Mills fractured the fifth metatarsal in his right foot during an NBA Summer League practice session on July 9. Successful surgery on July 13 led to the rehabilitation process, Mills still generously listed as 6ft-1in on Portland's 2009–10 roster. He was the shortest player on a team which would include future teammates at San Antonio Spurs, Nicolas Batum and LaMarcus Aldridge.

Mills headed home for treatment of his right foot at the Australian Institute of Sport in Canberra. Assigned to Portland's NBA Development League hybrid affiliate the Idaho Stampede on December 29 after completing his rehabilitation, his first game there produced the headline "Points stampede as Mills 'kills' in debut". Patty opened this next phase of his career with a 38-point, 12-assist double in a sizzling 133-109 win over the Reno Bighorns at Reno Events Centre. Coming off the bench for Idaho, he played 36 minutes against the Bighorns, his 38 points delivered at 52 per cent and including 7-of-10 three-pointers and 5-of-6 free throws.

Within a week of being dropped to the Stampede to "find his legs and run into form", Mills was recalled to Portland's NBA roster, appearing in 10 games with the Trail Blazers during his rookie season. Patty averaged 2.6 points in a paltry 3.8 minutes, scoring a season-high 11 points in 13 minutes of court-time in Portland's last match of the regular season against the Golden State Warriors. "That game against Golden State was probably my best one and the more opportunity I get, the more comfortable I feel," Patty said. The groundwork here was being laid for a much longer NBA career.

Basketball Australia faced a dilemma in the wake of the Beijing Olympic Games. It was unwritten BA policy at the time to appoint its senior national coaches for two "Olympic cycles", meaning an eight-year run at the helm. Adrian Hurley inherited the Boomers' reins from 1984 Los Angeles Olympics coach Lindsay Gaze, steering Australia's fortunes at the 1986 FIBA World Championship in Madrid, 1988 Seoul Olympics, 1990 FIBA World Championship in Buenos Aires and concluding his run with the 1992 Barcelona Olympic campaign. His assistant coach, Barry

Barnes, then became Boomers boss for FIBA World Championships in 1994 in Toronto and 1998 in Athens, with the 1996 Atlanta Olympics and 2000 Sydney Olympics his two Games campaigns.

Brian Goorjian coached Australia over the next two Olympic cycles, starting with the Athens Games and closing with the Beijing Olympics, a FIBA Worlds in between in Japan in 2006. The Boomers having missed qualifying for the 2002 World Championship meant Goorjian had a case for a longer run in the role, his appointment originally in the aftermath of that minor disaster. The problem was Australia's international performances were not at the level of his domestic NBL success and there was a new incumbent in Brett Brown.

American-born Brown coached North Melbourne Giants to the 1994 NBL championship over Adelaide 36ers and was assistant Boomers coach to Barry Barnes through the Atlanta and Sydney Olympic campaigns. Australia played off for a bronze medal at both Games. Under Goorjian, it missed the quarterfinals in Athens and was seventh in Beijing. Brown was Barnes' international assistant coach for 132 games, including the two World Championships, However as BA debated the merits of its two leading candidates, Goorjian coached the South Dragons to the NBL championship — his sixth — following previous title runs at South East Melbourne Magic (1992–1996) and Sydney Kings (2003–2004–2005). His NBL success rate was at a remarkable 70 per cent from more than 700 games coached.

Brown, 48, took NBL Coach of the Year honours in 1994, coached 278 games in the league at a 54 per cent success rate and drove North Melbourne back to the grand final series against Perth Wildcats in 1995. Prior to that, he was an assistant coach to Lindsay Gaze at Melbourne Tigers before landing the Giants' head coach role from 1993–98. He coached Sydney Kings from 2000–2002 after a brief stint at the San Antonio Spurs. Married to Anna, an Australian, they had three children

Julia, Laura and Sam. Brown took his family back to San Antonio and worked for the NBA's Spurs after departing from Sydney, Goorjian stepping in as the Kings' new coach and winning three straight NBL championships.

Finally on March 31, 2009 and after much warranted debate, BA appointed Brown through to the 2012 London Olympic Games, with the FIBA 2010 World Championship his entrée to the main course. "I've known Brett for a long time. He's a great coach and a good person and I wish him every success with the national programme," Goorjian graciously said.

Brown knew exactly what Australia wanted—a medal. "I don't make any bones about it," he said. "It has to be our goal. It has been the goal of every coach coming through the programme. I don't back-pedal from that. The world's getting better. I'm very aware of the world stage but I don't want the players coming into the programme thinking anything else (other than winning a medal)."

Highly respected in Australia, Brown also received a ringing endorsement from San Antonio head coach Gregg Popovich, whose coveted and cosmopolitan Spurs programme had won three NBA championships during Brown's presence there. "Brett Brown has been paramount to the success of the San Antonio Spurs over the past decade and I am confident his technical and people skills will be well received by the team and organisation," Popovich opined.

Brown immediately brought in as assistant coaches, Melbourne-born Andrej Lemanis, a former NBL player now in his fourth year and in the middle of a serious rebuild as head coach of the NBL's New Zealand Breakers, and Marty Clarke, at the time running the men's programme at the Australian Institute of Sport. Clarke was across all the new faces of the nation's burgeoning young talent. His staff settled, Brown prepared for the first challenge of his reign, a three-match series in Perth, Melbourne and Adelaide against Argentina — the Olympic gold medallist in Athens and bronze medallist in Beijing. This would act as part of the Boomers' selection and preparation for the 2010 FIBA World Championship in Turkey in September.

It quickly became apparent at the Boomers' training camp in Perth in June that the team Argentina was sending to play Australia would not include NBA stars such as Manu Ginóbili or Luis Scola, the latter leading the scoring later at the 2010 Worlds. Without the drawcards, the focus instead shifted to the Australian public having its chance to see in live action players such as Patty Mills, Brad Newley, Joe Ingles and Nathan Jawai, together wearing the green-and-gold. Jawai was the quintessential "gentle giant" and the first Australian Indigenous player drafted to the NBA when he was taken with the 41st pick by Indiana Pacers in 2008.

At 209cm and 130kg, "Big Nate" was an imposing figure on-and-off the basketball court. He debuted under mentor and coach Aaron Fearne for Cairns Taipans in the NBL's 2007–08 season, winning the league's Rookie of the Year award, named MVP of what then was an annual All Star game, and selected in the NBL's All Second Team. His ascension to the NBA was the natural next step, even though Indiana traded him to Toronto Raptors for Jermaine O'Neal. In 2009, he was traded to Dallas Mavericks before being sent to Minnesota Timberwolves where he had arguably the best game of his NBA career, scoring a team-high 16 points and grabbing six rebounds in a 93-116 loss at Portland Trail Blazers, Patty Mills' home at the time.

Born in Sydney, Jawai grew up in the small township of Bamaga, north of the Jardine River and only 40km from the tip of Cape York Peninsula. An Indigenous Australian of Torres Strait Islander descent, before a string of injuries cut him down, Nate often revealed the potential to be an incomparable Australian centre player and keyway powerhouse. In 31 NBL games for the Taipans, he averaged 17.3 points, 9.4 rebounds and 1.9

assists per game, with 28 and 18 his season highs for points and rebounds respectively.

Shy with strangers but with warm eyes which clearly reflected a mischievous streak, we first met at the post-match function after the 2008 All Star game. Only a half hour or so earlier, he had the crowd at Melbourne's State Netball and Hockey Centre in raptures, pairing 24 points with 12 rebounds to lead the Aussie All Stars to a 146-141 win over the NBL's World All Stars, a team comprising the league's best imports. But after throwing down monster dunks, he now was sitting quietly by himself with a plate of food from the buffet, trying to be inconspicuous. Of course that was impossible but he was quite the contrast from his on-court persona. Nate was so friendly, so polite, our casual conversation made me a lifelong fan. The series against Argentina would give him the chance to press his claims for World Championship selection.

"We want to be stone-cold candid to the Australian public (about Argentina) that we don't know whether it's their C-team, or is it their D-team, because we do know it's not their A-team," Brown fearlessly admitted of the touring national side. "Our approach to it is, it's June, let's play some games. Right from the get-go, their people were very honest the likelihood of Argentina's NBA guys coming was remote."

Argentina's head coach Sergio Hernandez and the bulk of the nation's past medal-winning teams were not on the touring roster. "Sergio did explain this team coming out would be more of a development-type squad," Brown confirmed, unfazed because he now had an opportunity against lesser opposition to establish the foundation of how his Boomers would play. "We're trying to build a team," he said.

"We've done our homework, we've done our due diligence and we want to play with the core group. Other than the mystery of availability, such as Andrew Bogut being out with injury, we have a fair idea of who we want. I see this as a fantastic environment and opportunity. We've got a bunch of new guys and I've already had a couple of pleasant surprises in Alex Loughton and Steve Markovic."

Brown said Argentina had not risen to its No.1 international status by accident and while he remained uncertain of the level of talent on the visiting team's roster, the lack of big-name players was not hugely important. "I'm not hung up on that," he spruiked. "Argentina is a basketball powerhouse. It produces good players, great players. Time will tell about the level of talent in this team. It's a proud basketball nation and FIBA rates them No.1 in the world for a bunch of different reasons. They have 54 million people in their country, have a strong domestic competition and even without their NBA guys, we expect them to be very competitive.

"We want to win, no doubt about it. We put on the green-and-gold and we come to win. The big picture is trying to set the stage for what we want to get done in August. From a coaching perspective, trying to see if the defence, particularly, is at a standard that we're trying to get to."

Beijing Olympics forward Mark Worthington was slated to miss the series opener in Perth but scheduled to play in the Melbourne and Adelaide legs. "Nathan Jawai has had a six-week break rehabilitating an ankle injury so he's only practising one session of two at the moment," Brown said. "But he'll be playing too." Patty Mills would be as well, and he was another player crowds should flock to see, the coach maintained. Mills' reputation already was growing.

Australia's team for the Argentina series featured only four Olympians from Beijing, namely Patty Mills, South Australian pair Brad Newley and Joe Ingles, and Mark Worthington. Nathan Jawai was joined by other notable "bigs", 216cm Luke Nevill and Ben Allen whose previous stops were at US colleges. Alex Loughton and Steve Markovic both returned from playing in Europe and impressed at Brown's training camp, as did Perth Wildcats' championship playmaker Damian Martin and Gold Coast Blaze's multiple NBL champion guard Adam Gibson.

Emerging youngsters with international potential, Hugh Greenwood and Jason Cadee continued their rapid rise into senior ranks. But the landmark selection decision was pairing Patty Mills and Nate Jawai. The twin selections of the NBA duo marked the historic first occasion an Australian senior men's team suited two Indigenous players.

It took until 7:21 was left to play in the fourth quarter of the second match in the three-game series for Brown to feel a little of the heat of his hot-seat as national men's coach. Having thrashed what turned out to be Argentina's "C-team" 97-58 in Perth in the series opener, and ahead 53-27 at halftime of the second game in Melbourne, Australia was cruising. A 12-0 start to the third quarter gave the Boomers a whopping 38-point lead and tour organisers were worrying if anyone would show up in Adelaide for the third game the following night.

And then it finally happened. Despite the fact most of its personnel on this tour would disappear without trace from the international scene, Argentina suddenly started to play with some level of abandon, hitting shots and riding the hot hand of Carlos Schattmann. It went 19-24 in the third period — its best quarter of the tour to date -—then opened the last quarter with an 8-0 outburst, prompting Brown to call his first time-out of necessity. Ultimately Australia prevailed 85-71 after Argentina closed to within 12, but Schattmann finished with a game-high 24 points which included 7-of-10 second-half three-pointers. Joe Ingles, Brad Newley and Patty Mills led Australia's scoring.

Argentina's leading scorer from game one, Nicolas Romano finished with 15 points while also drawing the ire of Joe Ingles as Argentina's questionable holding, grabbing and feigning contact drew growing irritation. Ingles' unsportsmanlike foul inside the last five minutes when he bumped a typically quick-to-tumble Romano, had Melbourne fans hooting the play, likening it to international soccer shenanigans. Ingles downplayed the incident in laconic fashion, saying: "It's all good."

Actually though, it wasn't all good for the Aussies because Brown made it clear before the first shot in the series was even fired that chipping his desired defensive principles into stone was a priority. The match opened much as the first closed, the Boomers led by Mills and in full flight and highly entertaining. The Argentines again looked like boys facing men. Patty Mills was far too quick and slick for them, Brad Newley was a force, and Luke Nevill and Alex Loughton opened the game with dunks.

Ingles threw another one down on the break and though fans had to wait until 3:33 in the second quarter, Nathan Jawai's two-handed special slam was, once again, the stand-out. Damian Martin, still building his reputation as a defensive specialist, pushed his world championship selection claims with tremendous hustle and 11 first-half points on a perfect 4-of-4 shooting, including 3-of-3 threes. Yet after that 12-0 start to the third quarter, Australia was outscored 19-12 the rest of the way, then manhandled 25-8 in the final period.

Basketball Australia and its tour organisers were no doubt secretly high-fiving and figuratively jumping for joy when the Argentinians finally showed some fight and grunt. After all, its acting national coach Nicolas Casalanquida hadn't done them any favours by candidly admitting none of his touring players would be any chance of selection in Argentina's team for the world championship in Turkey from August 28–September 12. (Not that anyone who saw their dismal display in Game One in Perth was in much doubt about that anyway.)

Brown, while unhappy at his team's inability to stop the haemorrhaging, still was pleased the second hit-out revealed flaws and areas to which he now could attend. "I feel like it was a reality check and an opportunity," he said. "In probably a twisted way, I see it as a fantastic opportunity. We had nine turnovers in the fourth period and went long stretches without scoring." But the form of Mills and Jawai had to excite even the most ambivalent fan, suggesting a promising crowd for Adelaide's Clipsal Powerhouse venue the next night. At least that was what tour official and four-time Boomers Olympian Andrew Vlahov was predicting.

"Adelaide has the most knowledgeable basketball fans in the country and I'm sure they'll be out in force to support the Boomers," he said. Perth's crowd at Challenge Stadium for the series opener drew 4,482 fans and the second game had a 3,500 "sell-out" at Melbourne's State Netball and Hockey Centre.

The teams arrived in Adelaide and in my capacity as basketball writer for the state's daily newspaper *The Advertiser*, I headed to their hotel to conduct a few prearranged interviews. The key one was with Patty Mills and Nathan Jawai, our Indigenous history-makers, big Nate greeting me with a grin and embrace like a long-lost brother. Patty had his hair cut super short, was unshaven but full of mischief and fun as Nate introduced me to his "little brother". Both young men were polite, funny, quick to smile and immediately endearing. But as Indigenous men, both took the fact they were sharing this opportunity and responsibility to represent Australia together very seriously, anxious to present themselves as role model material.

"It's important to put yourself out there (into rural communities) so the young Indigenous and Australian kids can see you and hear from you in person," Mills said, the awareness of his responsibility already apparent. The popularity of the dynamic young playmaker already was growing nationwide, many of his matches at St Mary's College televised live via FOX-TV on its ESPN channel and his every NBA game with Portland Trail Blazers had fans glued to their sets, hoping to catch a glimpse of him. His sideline antics were a feature of Blazers games, the "reverse-goggles" with the ends of his thumb and first finger together to form an oval around his eyes, and the remaining three fingers outstretched, was his supportive signal for three-pointers teammates scored.

Jawai, 23 at the time, also enjoyed a legion of followers after winning the NBL's 2008 Rookie of the Year award and hitting the NBA with Minnesota Timberwolves. "It means a lot to me to be part of history with Patty," he said. "I only found out the other day. We played together at the Institute of Sport and hopefully we can make it to an Olympics together to make history there too." Sadly, that never would come to pass, though both men already were abundantly across their importance to kids of all colours.

Mills did not dwell on returning to the NBA and Portland, selection to the Boomers' team for the FIBA World Championship now his primary focus. "I've come to learn in the professional business, there's not a lot you can control off the court," he said of his NBA future. "But I can focus in on the (Worlds) campaign for the Boomers."

A good performance in Turkey was sure to illicit memories of his Beijing Olympic Games and open doors for the avid supporter of the AFL's Adelaide Crows. His favourite player at the time, not entirely surprisingly, was Adelaide's AFL games-played record-holder and dual Norm Smith Medallist as the best player on the ground in the grand final, Andrew McLeod. The silky smooth McLeod is an Indigenous footballer born in Darwin. "My all-time favourite though, was Tony Modra," he happily declared of the Crows' high-marking, goal-kicking centurion.

Fans at Adelaide's Clipsal Powerhouse venue wanted a show and Patrick Mills gave them one. The biggest crowd for the Australia-Argentina series of 4,997 revelled in Mills' second ever match at the venue as his Boomers completed the three-game sweep 90-72. His first was two years earlier when he had fans enraptured as he dominated an international friendly with Iran. "I love playing in Adelaide," Mills said. "I've got a lot of friends and family here and it's such a great atmosphere."

Boomers games in Adelaide were rare at the time and appearances by players of Mills' calibre even more so. That is why when he went off for 32 points at 60 per cent, including 5-of-9 three-pointers, and was forever the most dynamic player on the hardwood, the contest always remained interesting and entertaining. And even despite the final 18-point margin, it was the tightest of the three-match series and could have been much closer but for Sebastian Vega's free throw shooting.

The Argentine forward was clumsily fouled by Brad Newley on a three-point hope shot, a mere two minutes left and Australia ahead 83-72. Vega makes all three free throws and it's an eight-point contest with ample time left. Instead he aborted the trifecta, Newley sank back-to-back baskets and, fittingly, Patty Mills drained a triple for the final scoreline. The Aussies had one final defensive stand to go, the siren sounding with the ball in Mills' safe hands.

He frustrated and embarrassed the Argentinians all match and when he was dealt with unnecessarily harshly by a clearly aggravated Matias Nocedal in the open court with four minutes left, all 10 players on the floor came rushing in to the heated exchange. Boys will be boys. Mills was a sensation, Newley confirmed his status as a mainstay of the new generation and guard Steve Markovic, identified earlier by Brown as having been impressive during training camp, was another to blossom.

Argentina led 23-18 at the first quarter break before Nate Jawai tipped in his own miss to start the second period scoring. Damian Martin then struck a step-back three-pointer and inside a minute, Argentina's lead was erased. Joe Ingles, another member of the Boomers' new breed, and Mills helped bumped the run to 10-0. But from midway through the second period, the game turned into the Patty Mills Show. He buried a jumpshot, then consecutive triples, the fans now in full supportive voice.

With 21 points by halftime and Australia massaging a 48-40 lead, Mills gave everyone a glimpse of something to come, 11 years later.

Newley's three-pointer closed the half, the South Australian forward finishing with 14 points. Not surprisingly, Damian Martin and Steve Markovic played their way into the Boomers team for Turkey and the FIBA World Championship where the Boomers' group included Angola, the *real* Argentina, Germany, Jordan and Serbia.

In July, CJ Bruton, at 34, announced his retirement from international basketball, leaving the door wide open for Patty Mills to take the Boomers' point guard reins, with another prospect to grab up his understudy role. "We have another good point man in Stephen Markovic," Brown said. "I see (NBL playmakers) Damian Martin and Adam Gibson more as two-men (off guards)." Point guards, combo (combination) guards or two men, suddenly Brown had numerous options up his sleeve. It was in the big-man area he was troubled, Andrew Bogut suffering horrific injuries to his arm after crashing to the floor almost horizontally in an NBA match for Milwaukee Bucks. It was the quintessential "see it once, never want to see it again" look-away type of landing. And beefy 208cm NSW centre Aleks Maric was cooked after an exhausting season in Serbia.

Enter Aron Baynes, a new face soon to become another of the new breed of Boomer and an important piece in the ongoing medal quest. Baynes, 24 and 208cm, grew up in Mareeba, far north Queensland and found his way to basketball as a teenager, abandoning rugby league along the way. By 2004, he was attending the Australian Institute of Sport before accepting a college scholarship at Washington State University in 2006. From college, he was recruited to play professionally at Lietuvos Rytas in the Lithuanian Basketball League.

At 212cm, David Andersen was the tallest player in the Boomers team for the 2010 FIBA World Championship, Maric eventually also putting up his hand for selection. Matt Nielsen gave Brown another returning Olympian when he joined Andersen, Maric and Baynes as his "bigs".

Patty Mills, Brad Newley and Joe Ingles were returning tyros from the Beijing Games with guaranteed futures, fellow Olympians Mark Worthington and David Barlow adding to Brown's experienced crew. Damian Martin, Adam Gibson and Steve Markovic fought their way into the team absolutely on merit. And Brown never wavered from the team's goal. A medal.

On a joyous day for basketball fans across Australia, and Indigenous ones in particular, the late trail-blazer Michael Ahmatt was inducted into the Australian Basketball Hall of Fame in August 2010. Almost in conjunction with Ahmatt's long overdue recognition as the sport's historic first Indigenous Olympian in 1964, Patty Mills spent a day in Ahmatt's home state, courtesy of its NBL club, Adelaide 36ers.

"I took him around town and out to the Crows training," 36ers chief executive officer of the time, Ben Fitzsimons said. "Patty is a huge (Adelaide) Crows (AFL) fan so that was great, and then we came back to the stadium at Findon and he met with a group of about a half a dozen Indigenous kids organised by Pauly Vandenbergh to meet him. I believe Pauly was working for Port Adelaide's AFL club running its Indigenous programme at the time."

The upshot was Mills purchased a block of seats to all of the Adelaide 36ers' home games across the 2010–11 NBL season. Designated as the "Patty Mills seats", they acted as a reward for Indigenous youth who stayed in school. An Indigenous player of some note himself, Vandenbergh, who was walking the Kokoda Trail with a group of Indigenous youth at the time, determined the lucky recipients. "Patty and the 36ers are hoping this programme will introduce some new talent to basketball as well as instil a sense of achievement for all the recipients," Fitzsimons said then.

Vandenbergh, who cracked the Canberra Cannons' NBL line-up in 2001, had known Mills for years. "Our mums are cousins so we're family," he said. "When I was at the Cannons, I spent a lot of time at their house. He was about 11 or 12 and we spent a lot of time together." David Patrick also was on the Cannons' roster during Vandenbergh's time at the club. "When this (opportunity to sponsor a row of seats for Indigenous youth) came up, Patty was all over it," Vandenbergh said. "It was that first step for him. It's where he started to understand and recognise how important he was to the Indigenous community and the positive impact he could make." And he has never relented since.

Australia's preparation for Turkey included competing in the Boris Stankovic Continental Cup in Liuzhou, China. The Boomers were defending Cup-holders and opened the tournament against China. Trailing 62-63 into the final seconds, Patty Mills drove to the basket and dished a perfect pass to David Andersen who completed the play for the winning 64-63 score-line. Mills stood out with 13 points, Nielsen 12.

By beating Slovenia 77-63 with Mills and Adam Gibson leading the scoring on 15 apiece, missing the Cup final now was almost an impossibility. Mills led all scorers with 16 points as Australia guaranteed it would meet Slovenia again in the Cup decider by holding off Iran 69-60. In the final, this time it was the Slovenians prevailing 71-60, Joe Ingles and David Andersen tallying 14 points each.

Despite Coach Brown's exhortations to the contrary, most pundits did not truly believe Australia would be in the running for a medal in Turkey. Instead, another finish in the fifth-to-eighth region seemed a more realistic probability. For many, those bronze medal playoff appearances at the Seoul, Atlanta and Sydney Olympics seemed over-achievements for a country of 20 million people whose finest male athletes usually first were lured to AFL football or rugby league through the NRL. Those watershed fourth place finishes between 1988–2000 also occurred in an era Australian basketball was experiencing a huge rise in popularity.

Since those 2000 Games however, Australia had slipped markedly. That fact made the Boomers' 72-69 win over Brazil in their final FIBA World Championship warm-up tournament in Lyon, France a massively timely boost. It was the "new culture kids" who led the way, Patty Mills with 15 points, three assists and three rebounds, Joe Ingles 14 points, veterans Matt Nielsen and David Andersen 10 each.

"I thought the last five minutes we played excellent team defence and we needed to against a team with three NBA players," Brown said, Brazil boasting Anderson Varejao (Cleveland Cavaliers), Leandro Barbosa (Phoenix Suns) and Tiago Splitter (San Antonio Spurs). "Our entire team deserves credit." For the Boomers, now ranked 11th in the world by FIBA, the credit and confidence grew as Matt Nielsen scored a match-winning basket for a thrilling 67-66 victory over host nation France. Once again though, Patty Mills was the star of the game, with 18 points, four assists, two steals and two rebounds.

Smashing Ivory Coast 80-59 gave the Boomers a 3-0 sweep of the tournament and, combined with their 3-1 record at the Boris Stankovic Continental Cup — including a 1-1 split with Slovenia — left great scope for optimism for what might unfold in Turkey. And optimism was certainly preferable to hope or blind faith. The seedings for the group phase in Kayseri, Turkey, implied FIBA expected the Boomers to finish fourth which would mean advancing but facing the No.1 team from Group B — which would be the USA — in a knock-out crossover final. Confident it could beat Angola and Jordan, Australia needed at least one more scalp to avoid the American crossover, and increasingly, Germany looked the candidate. The Germans expected NBA star Dirk Nowitzki to lead their charge but he had withdrawn from competing. It set the door ajar for the Boomers, Argentina at full strength and Serbia both looking outside Australia's reach.

Reality struck with an almighty thud then when Jordan had four frantic shots at pinching victory before Australia held on for dear life to win their World Championship opener 76-75. The Boomers trailed for the majority of the contest against the world's 38thranked nation and it was only David Andersen's successful free throws with 13 seconds left which rescued them from an ignominious start. Down by 11 during the third quarter and still 69-75 with 82 seconds left, it was a miraculous escape. Patty Mills, who endured a rare off night going 4-of-10 from the floor with no trademark three-pointers, came through when it mattered, completing a three-point play.

Matt Neilsen scored a big basket, Joe Ingles drew a critical charging offensive foul and Andersen stuck the winning free throws. Aleks Maric, who was the last player to commit to the green-and-gold, finished with 23 points at 71 per cent, plus nine rebounds while Andersen was a monster for 22 points at 70 per cent, a team-high 2-of-3 three-pointers, nine boards and a team-best four assists. Patty Mills with 10 points was the only other Boomer in double-figures.

Argentina always was going to be a challenge but after their opening night scare, the Aussies came out with all guns blazing, jumping to a 10-3 buffer and leading right up to the game's final 6 minutes 30 seconds. Ahead by as many as 10 in the third quarter, the Boomers had a window to put the game further out of reach but instead gave up a 6-0 outburst by the Argentines. The world's No.1 ranked nation hit the front with 6:30 left and built that lead out to six behind the stellar play of forward Luis Scola. He finished with 31 points, none bigger than his two free throws with 8.8 seconds left to give Argentina a 74-70 break.

Mills missed a tough three-point attempt but Ingles rebounded it and thrust in a magical mid-air flipper, Australia within two with 3.7

seconds to go. Relentless defensive pressure on Argentina's inbounds pass saw the South Americans throw the ball out of court, giving Australia a final possession at 3.5 seconds left. The Boomers went to Adam Gibson for the match-winning three. At that point he was 1-of-5 for the game. Unfortunately for the Boomers, he finished 1-of-6. "We're very disappointed to lose that game," Brown said, Australia lacking poise at key moments. Ingles led the Aussies with 22 points at 60 per cent, Mills with 21 including four threes, and five assists.

Having experienced two near misses, one in their favour, one against, there was no real cause for high optimism in the Boomers' camp going into their key fixture against Germany. The Germans upset Serbia 82-81 in a double-overtime thriller and, similarly to Australia, lost a nail-biter to Argentina 74-78. Australia's hopes of advancement and a chance to progress to the medal round clearly hung on this result and every follower of the team knew it. It was the absolute personification of a "must win" scenario.

That established, no one quite expected the ferocity of the Boomers' assault. Australia not only beat Germany, it blitzed it 78-43 in one of its most dramatic and emphatic wins at a world series. "I can't say how proud I am of our guys," captain Matt Nielsen said. He had good reason to feel pleased. After Germany scored the match's opening basket, Australia marched all over it 12-2. If the Germans were in any way flat, Australia was the steamroller. It claimed the rebounding edge 40-30, forced 17 turnovers and contested virtually every shot, rotating and hustling defensively like madmen.

Earlier in the build-up, coach Brett Brown said he hoped the Boomers' offence would catch up to its defence in terms of efficiency and this was the match in which it did. And how. Australia shot the ball at 52 per cent and kept Germany shooting at an abysmal 26 per cent. "We spent a lot of time watching Germany in the lead up to this tournament and paid attention to their two games before we played them," Brown said. "We were fearful of this game."

It never showed. The Aussies poured everything into one superb 40-minute effort, Patty Mills leading the onslaught with 16 points and his tournament-best seven assists. His shot selection (he delivered at 60 per cent and stroked 4-of-5 three-pointers) and decision-making were on point, and centre Aleks Maric, who went pointless against Argentina, scored 15. "I thought they played exceptionally well," German coach Dirk Bauermann said. "They defended us extremely well and moved the ball around and shot extremely well. They played an outstanding game."

The Aussies now needing to beat Angola to avoid a fourth-placed finish and potential crossover elimination game against the USA, the pressure eased appreciably ahead of their match against Serbia. Unfortunately for the Boomers, Serbia was not in a charitable mood, winning every quarter en route to a comfortable 94-79 victory. Brad Newley's 13 points at 56 per cent led Australia, Mills with 12 and six assists, Nielsen and Maric scoring 10 points apiece. But it was a listless performance and carried over into the vital final intragroup fixture against Angola.

At an early time-out, Brown finally unloaded on his lethargic charges, reigniting the passion required to steer them through to the playoff rounds after a poor start. "Three-ball, three-ball, lay-up — are you freaking kidding me?" he bellowed at his men as Angola threatened to race away with the result, still leading 18-15 at the first break. That and a further feisty assessment did the trick as the Boomers, missing centre David Andersen with a stomach bug, ran up an 18-3 response in a 24-11 second period which underpinned the 76-55 victory. A 21-9 third quarter saw the Boomers at their finest, guaranteeing a third-place group finish behind Serbia and Argentina, setting up a KO crossover against Group B's second placegetter, Slovenia. Mills scored 11 points and was the only player in the game to reach double figures, Brown clearing his bench and every player scoring.

Having already split two games against Slovenia during their build-up at the Boris Stankovic Continental Cup in China, there was great cause for optimism that by producing a high-quality game, the Boomers would advance to the quarterfinal stage and be within a further win of the medal rounds. Any such dreams disappeared in a nightmarish start in which Slovenia raced to a 12-0 lead.

That pushed the Boomers into a game-long chase which was in no way assisted by its 31 per cent (in)accuracy from the floor. Held to a meagre eight-point first quarter, Slovenia was doubling that at the break before the Boomers managed an almost equally miserable 13 points in the second period. And again, Slovenia scored double that to have an unassailable 42-21 halftime cushion. Winning the third and fourth quarters, Slovenia's ultimate 87-58 rout was Australia's worst-ever international loss to any country other than the powerhouse USA or USSR teams. To say the 2010 FIBA World Championship ended in disappointment would be a huge understatement but it *did* create a new rivalry and a wound it would take just over a decade to heal.

The 2010–11 NBA season was just around the corner, Brown now casting his eyes toward the 2012 London Olympic Games and hopeful Andrew Bogut, David Andersen and Patty Mills would see enough on-court action to lead Australia's rejuvenated medal charge. "I'm particularly interested to see how Andrew responds to last year's season-ending injury," Brown said, his fingers crossed Bogut again would find the form which saw him fulfilling his No.1 draft status at Milwaukee. "He is the Boomers' crown jewel. In order for us to achieve something special going forward, we need him. The world is too talented otherwise. If he retains his health, I believe he will come back with the same second team all-NBA form he did last season when he was arguably the NBA's best true centre."

Back as an assistant coach at the San Antonio Spurs, Brown was excited Andersen was traded by Houston Rockets to Toronto Raptors and seeing plenty of preseason action. However his concerns for Mills' future were evident. "Patrick's situation at the moment (at Portland Trail Blazers) is a mystery to me," he said. "He has played few, if any, quality minutes in Portland's preseason and I'm not sure what their intent is. Life in the NBA as a young player is often times erratic and being a part of a few teams along a player's NBA journey is not uncommon."

Life in the NBA as a young player is often times erratic, as Patty Mills discovered in his sophomore season at the Trail Blazers. His season highlight was a career-best 23-point game against Golden State Warriors, Mills playing in 64 games for averages of 5.5 points and 1.7 assists in 12.2 minutes. He also suited for two Blazers' playoff games and scored in double figures 10 times. But the future appeared hazy at best. The NBA was heading for a lockout, the fourth in National Basketball Association history. Team owners instituted the work stoppage upon expiration of the 2005 collective bargaining agreement. The 161-day lockout began on July 1, 2011 and ended on December 8, 2011 and while it was going, players could not enter their franchise's training facility.

In limbo like so many others, for Mills it meant a chance to come home to Australia, no shortage of NBL clubs willing to open their doors for him. The Adelaide 36ers, coached at the time by Mills' former mentor at the Australian Institute of Sport, Marty Clarke — the man who also was key in his relocation to Saint Mary's College — felt they were right in the running to secure his services. Signing Mills, of course, came with the risk of losing him back to the NBA whenever the lockout concluded.

But the upside in signing him, for however long, meant ticket sales would be positively impacted, as would the credibility of any club he joined. Clarke said Mills had a $1.2 million (Australian) contract pending for a return to Portland prior to the lockout and also felt the playmaking star's agent would likely push him toward the bigger dollars of Europe. "Patty has gone back to Houston to work out and there's no doubt he wants to play somewhere (during the lockout) and he does love Australia," Clarke said. "Pat is Pat — he's always bubbly about wanting to do something in Australia.

"We have spoken with him but he'll get offers from Europe and if you're paying an agent big bucks, you're going to listen. Essentially, he needs to play. He doesn't want to sit on benches." Patty averaged 11.1 minutes per game across 74 outings with the Blazers across two seasons. He was ready to make a far bigger contribution. "If Pat decides he wants to play in Australia and Adelaide, it would be a great thing for basketball," Clarke said. "The danger is you bring a guy in and lose him in December or when the lockout is over." With Brett Brown holding a Boomers training camp at the Gold Coast in late July and Mills in attendance, it gave Clarke, as a national team assistant, a further chance to push the 36ers' cause.

At the July camp, which was organised ahead of an Oceania Series in September against New Zealand to qualify for the 2012 London Olympics, Mills declared his interest in competing for an NBL club while the NBA lockout continued. "The most important thing for me is to find somewhere to play," he said. "Definitely NBL teams have reached out. I am looking at that but also teams in Europe and other options. Right now there is no rush in making a decision. It will come over the next couple of months. Portland have offered me a qualifying contract which is the same position I have been in the last couple of years. When the lockout finishes, I will head back to Portland and see how things go."

Adelaide, the Illawarra Hawks (then running as the Wollongong Hawks) and Cairns Taipans all had cap space to comfortably accommodate him and looked the front-runners. Mills had strong Adelaide connections, watched many Hawks games as a youngster and was hugely popular in Cairns with its keen Indigenous population. All three destinations seemed viable. "I'm definitely not pushing aside coming back to the NBL," Mills reiterated. "It's definitely an option… but so is Europe."

Shifting focus to New Zealand and a prior "test" event in London to introduce some of the Olympic venues was relevant for Brown as Australia was now ranked 10th in the world by FIBA and the Tall Blacks of NZ 12th. "Their performance in Turkey (at the World Championship) more than confirmed they are extremely dangerous," Brown said. "They're a team that's very well coached, they're a team that's been together for several years, they're a team where a majority of their players play on an annual basis with their own domestic team in the NBL with the Breakers.

"They have tremendous chemistry as a result. In such an important series, where there is no second place, you either win and go to the Olympic Games or you lose and stay home." It was a succinct summary of what his Boomers faced in the best-of-three showdown with Australia's trans-Tasman rival. It made the London test event even more important as preparation, matches scheduled against China, France, Croatia, Great Britain and Serbia. The Boomers would open the venue with the first game of the London International Invitational at Olympic Park's Basketball Arena against China.

"It's a test event for London security as well as the basketball security," Brown said, Australia additionally scheduled to play two matches against Spain in Spain before the Oceania Series. "It's a reminder to our players what the end-game and our purpose really is," Brown said of the tour. "To visit the actual court and site where we hope to be next year is a motivational aspect that is really something special." The 14 players in Brown's touring party were led by Patty Mills, with David Barlow, Joe Ingles, Brad Newley, Matt Nielsen, Aron Baynes, Daniel Kickert,

AJ Ogilvy, Aleks Maric, Matthew Dellavedova, Peter Crawford, Adam Gibson, Damian Martin and Mark Worthington. Eleven of the players would be a part of Australia's 12-man team for the Olympics in London.

CHAPTER THREE
A TIME FOR TIGERS

Mills made a stronger impression at Portland in his second NBA season than his modest statistical numbers suggested. He became a regular part of the team rotation, often the first or second player off the bench, and could feel he belonged at this level. When injuries struck the Trail Blazers during the season, his minutes skyrocketed, in contrast to his injury-afflicted 2009–10 campaign. And off the court, he was feeling at home.

"This year, for whatever reason, the guys on the team responded and connected on another level," he told Fox Sports' Jeremy Hartcher. "And from what I've heard that happens very rarely in the NBA. You know once you take care of everything off the court, and everyone enjoys everyone else's company, you just make things better on the court. I was having so much fun, we were all hanging out, all having fun together. I think that was the moment. I really like being here (in Portland) now."

As the world's most elite and richest basketball competition, the NBA can boil down to very much a dog-eat-dog world. That's why it can be a joyful rarity when a group truly bonds and become friends. It happened for Luc Longley at Chicago Bulls and for Andrew Bogut at Golden State Warriors. "I think now we're not (just) teammates, we're more than teammates," Mills enthused. "We're actually friends — and that's how we see ourselves off the court. It's something that we've actually talked about, between us."

With the lockout looming though, that wasn't going to count for much. Coming off a one-year deal earning just short of $US1 million for the 2010–11 season, Mills and his NBA colleagues had the recent example of the NFL, where players worked out in public gyms for off-season training, their team facilities off limits.

Patty Mills knew he needed more than regular access to dumbbells and treadmills, and Australia's NBL was calling. "I definitely wouldn't rule it out. Obviously you'd need to look broadly — at all my options. Whether it is Australia, Europe… what I can say? During this lockout, I will need to play basketball, wherever that may be. There's a whole lot of factors that will come into play. But the most important thing for me is I will need to play — keep that game fitness up during the lockout."

Australia concluded a strong performance at the London Olympics test event with a dramatic 91-90 overtime win over host Great Britain. The Brits, minnows on the international basketball scene, clearly were energised by the fact they were automatic Olympic qualifiers as the Games host country, and keen not to just be fodder for recognised power nations. Brad Newley led the Boomers with 23 points, Joe Ingles backing up his dominant performance against Serbia to drop 16 points. Fill-in point guard Adam Gibson scored 13, Brown choosing to rest Patty Mills and Matthew Dellavedova.

The game against Great Britain hanging in the balance, Brown was pleased his Boomers found a way to win, saying it was just what they needed ahead of the Oceania Series with New Zealand. Australia completed the tournament with a 4-1 win-loss record, beating China 71-43, Croatia 78-66 and Serbia 78-69, its one loss a 67-71 setback to France. "I think we have been getting progressively better," Brown said. "I think the win (over GB) probably just shows that we were able to find a way to get a win. We sat out our two point guards.

"Like everybody else at this stage of the tournament, they're a little bit beaten up and a little bit tired, so we ended up sitting Patty Mills and Matty Dellavedova. Adam Gibson came in and I thought he did a great job. Joe Ingles had two good games in a row, and as a group, we needed everybody." The Aussies continued on to Spain for two games against FIBA's No.2 ranked national team, believing playing in front of hostile crowds also would steel the nerves for the coming best-of-three showdown with New Zealand's Tall Blacks.

Back in Australia and the news —the biggest news story in Australian basketball at the time — finally broke that Patty Mills had indeed decided to play in his home country's NBL competition rather than see out the NBA lockout competing in Europe. But the shockwave was created by his decision to wear the red-and-gold of the Melbourne Tigers, a club barely mentioned in previous despatches as a likely destination during his stint in Australia.

"Seamus McPeake was the club's owner at the time and he was a very astute operator," said Andrew Gaze, the basketball player most associated with Melbourne Tigers. Gaze played 22 NBL seasons for the Tigers from 1984–2005, winning the league's MVP award a record seven times and its scoring title 14 times. He guided the Tigers to NBL championships in 1993 and 1997 and clocked 612 games for the club. "Seamus put conditions into the contract which were extremely generous regarding Patty coming-and-going in relation to the NBA lockout, which suited him. It was very good of Seamus because you have to remember at that time, it was not as if Patty had established himself as an NBA player yet. He was definitely in demand, but no-where near the way he would be if he came home now."

Nonetheless, it still was the biggest recruiting coup in league history when Mills, 23, and with 74 NBA games at Portland under his belt, signed on for the 2011–12 NBL season. Renegotiating the contract of two players on the Tigers' roster, Melbourne also needed to free up space in a points system the NBL used to assess playing personnel. Teams were permitted

70 points in the system, with star imports and Boomers valued at the maximum 10 points. The Tigers had used 66 of the 70 points available for a team's roster but by placing off-guard Daryl Corletto onto their "inactive" list and thereby removing his six-point value, Melbourne had the 10 available points necessary to secure Mills.

The move caused something of a minor controversy but was actually very shrewd work by McPeake, Mills sure to draw huge crowds wherever Melbourne played. "Patty Mills is an NBA player in the prime of his career and one of Australia's best basketballers," Basketball Australia's chief executive officer Larry Sengstock declared. "For him to turn his back on much larger contracts in Europe in order to play here in Australia is an amazing vote of confidence in the NBL Championship. This is one of the most significant signings in NBL history."

For Adelaide 36ers coach Marty Clarke, it was not an entirely unexpected setback. "Patty is arguably our best player and certainly in the top echelon of players," Clarke said. "We can't know how long Patty will be here (in the NBL), so we should make the most of it." Despite knowing Mills would act as a major drawcard, Melbourne had no plans to shift its games from "The Cage", the State Netball and Hockey Centre, which had a spectator capacity of 3,500. The Tigers' small home venue was another reason many discounted the club as a destination for the playmaking superstar. They under-estimated McPeake.

"I was good friends with Patty's agent at the time," McPeake said, the Tigers' owner unconcerned at the prospect of losing him back to the NBA prematurely. "No, we would never have held him up. And he was such a super bloke, right from the get-go. Patty was so easy-going, so obliging and he certainly brought the crowds. He was especially good with kids and always gave them his time." McPeake's coup did not come without cost. Fans and family of Daryl Corletto harassed and harangued him over the decision to put the Tigers club stalwart on the inactive list but given the same option today, McPeake would not hesitate. "Patty was very good for us."

Mills said his final decision was a stressful one. "I'm very excited about joining Melbourne and playing back home in the NBL for a period during the lockout," he said. "The 36ers were always in the mix, especially with Marty Clarke the drawcard because he has been a big part of my development since the AIS. It wasn't an easy decision at all. It was a long and stressful process and I've done a lot of thinking." Signing with the Tigers ended his stress, allowing him to focus on the bigger immediate issue — the Oceania Championship against New Zealand which opened with Game One at his new home-court address, "The Cage".

Australia stole the early initiative in the quest for a position at the 2012 London Olympics in a fiery opening match against New Zealand for the Oceania Championship, winning 91-78 in Melbourne. The match simmered from tip-off, eventually leading to two fights and the ejection of aggressive Tall Blacks guard Mark Dickel. The game descended into a melee with the match evenly poised midway through the third quarter, Dickel in the middle of it. Another stoush between Australian forward Mark Worthington and his naturalised New Zealand counterpart Casey Frank erupted soon afterwards before more final quarter fireworks which led to Dickel's expulsion.

Dickel launched at Boomers rookie Matthew Dellavedova, prompting Aussie captain Matt Nielsen to step in, pinning Dickel to the court before all players became involved, resulting in a flurry of technical fouls. But as the heat went up in the kitchen, the Boomers started cooking, channelling anger into energy for a late six-minute third-quarter rampage which decided the contest. Worthington thrived on the drama, adding 13 points and providing much of the third quarter spark.

But it was Patty Mills' team-high 20 points which hammered in the coffin nails and gave Australia the 1-0 start it coveted. Joe Ingles and Brad Newley also were major contributors, drawing praise from coach Brett Brown. "These (two) guys have come back understanding to co-exist you're going to have to defend," Brown said. "Stuff like that's going to happen," he added, referring to the fiery incidents of the second half. "In our guys there's no back-down and in their guys there's no back-down. You draw a line in the sand. I don't feel we crossed that line. There were no punches thrown."

To clinch Game Two and with it a 2-0 sweep and tickets to London, the Boomers required a massive final quarter to post an 81-64 win in Brisbane. Trailing by two points at the end of the third, the result hanging in the balance, Australia dug deep in every facet of the game — rebounding, scoring, defending — to see off the stubborn Tall Blacks. The Boomers were at their best, containing New Zealand to 10 last quarter points, most of which came after Australia's withering 23-3 start, Brad Newley leading the scoring with 12 points, Patty Mills nine. An attendance of 4,070 also excited NBL boffins looking to revive the Bullets club in Brisbane.

With Game Three now a "dead rubber" in Sydney, the disconsolate Tall Blacks could not match the Aussie enthusiasm after halftime as the Boomers held them to 27 second-half points while piling on 47 in a 92-68 rout. Centre Aleks Maric led the charge with 27 points on 11-of-13 shooting, David Barlow scoring 17, Patty Mills 14, Aron Baynes 12 and Joe Ingles 10, Australia's floor percentage 54 to New Zealand's 35. The Boomers were going to the London Olympic Games and Patty Mills would be playing at home in Australia. Life could not have looked much brighter.

Yet earlier in 2011, when Queensland was being devastated by floods, it was not Patty Mills the basketball player who stepped forward. It was Patty Mills the philanthropist raising $40,000 for flood relief, designing and creating T-shirts alongside non-profit organisation Wears My Shirt. In 2012, inspired by the involvement of one of his Indigenous idols, Olympic gold medal sprinter Cathy Freeman, he too became an ambassador for Cottage by the Sea. He continued selling T-shirts to raise funds for the charity which cares for disadvantaged Australian children and families in need.

"It's important for me to use my stature to help charities out as much as I can," he said. "I know that once I finish playing basketball, and I don't have the same media attention behind me, I won't be able to help out as much. I need to do as much as I can now."

It is extraordinary how much Patrick Sammy James Mills loves Australia, but just how little grassroots "Australia" cared for him as a young Indigenous boy growing to manhood in the national capital of Canberra. For all intents and purposes, it was no less traumatising than any other "multi-cultural" Australian city or town. To say Patty at times was traumatised would be under-stating it, punched in the stomach by the class bully on his first day of school, a wide-eyed and happy five-year-old suddenly in a startling foreign new world of hurt. "I've been called black… everything under the sun," he told the San Antonio Spurs website. "As well as abo, darky, blackie, petrol sniffer, nigger, monkey, chimp. But for whatever reason, the worst one of the lot for me was being called a black c---. Unfortunately it was a constant for me and I just had to get used to it."

When someone throws a baseball at your heart, there are two ways to react. Haul on your baseball bat and hit that ball back as hard as possible at the pitcher, or catch it in a soft glove and gently roll it back. While large sections of white Australia understandably and rightly are ashamed of the attitudes of the past, borne of ignorance, insensitivity and intolerance perhaps more so than the generationally perpetuated irrational hatred found across the United States, it is no less brutal, hurtful or hateful to a young innocent's soul. Polite to a fault, Patty Mills preferred catching the ball in his glove and sending it back with love, kindness and education.

Australians like to think of themselves as custodians of sportsmanship, drawn to and extolling the virtues of humble champions more than braggarts or the entitled boors rapidly taking over the sports world. Australia sees itself as the Land of the Fair Go, but racism is rarely too far from the surface.

It was less than thirty years ago one of the most richly-talented Australian Rules footballers, the mercurial marvel who is Aboriginal superstar Nicky Winmar, served notice on white Australia he no longer would tolerate the relentless racial vilification to which he routinely was being subjected. Playing brilliantly for St Kilda against Collingwood at the latter's Victoria Park stronghold, he endured enough of being racially pilloried and symbolically raised his jersey, defiantly pointing to his skin and declaring: "I'm black and I'm proud to be black."

The moment in 1993 was captured and preserved forever by Melbourne newspaper photographer Wayne Ludbey, Winmar's gesture sending a powerful message to the nation that enough was enough. Racist-based abuse in Australian sport was no longer going to be ignored or tolerated. His action changed football for the better and in 2019 Winmar was honoured with a 2.75m statue at Optus Oval in Perth, recreating the seminal moment. The statue is much closer to where Winmar, a proud Noongar man, hails from.

How much did Australia learn from that episode? Not nearly enough. Adam Goodes — whose mother was another from the Stolen Generation — played in two AFL premiership sides with Sydney Swans and also twice won the Brownlow Medal as the sport's fairest and most brilliant player. Yet he still was hounded out of the sport by the relentless booing and jeering of opposition "fans". That followed an incident, sadly once more against Collingwood, where a young spectator racially vilified him and he pointed her out to AFL security staff.

Mills considered Goodes' measured response a model for any Indigenous athlete. "The press conference he held was absolutely perfect," Mills says. "He used the incident as an example of how racism is still out there and everyone can learn from what happened. Now he's the face of anti-racism." He was, but the constant weekly sideline derision drove him into retirement in 2015, a year after being feted as Australian of the Year.

In a supposed "less enlightened time" Aboriginal high jumper Percy Hobson was told to keep quiet about his Indigenous background before he won the gold medal at the 1962 Commonwealth Games in Perth. A decade later when Frank Reys became the first Aboriginal jockey to win the Melbourne Cup in 1973, to accommodate his acceptance in horse-racing, he accentuated his father's Filipino heritage. As recently as 2021, racial vilification and abuse continued to provide evidence of football's ugly underbelly but, in fairness, the sport merely was reflecting Australian society.

This is the world Patty Mills inherited, but embitter him? No. It strengthened his resolve to teach, educate and share his culture. His mother Yvonne was a shining example of love, tenderness and understanding. "I'm very proud of my mother," he said in an interview while playing for San Antonio. "Just the way you see her helping others is very warming."

Yvonne Mills' story inevitably shaped her son and enforced his belief nothing is impossible, not even reaching the heights of the NBA. And helping Indigenous people across Australia, first as an inspiration and also in more tangible ways, became his passion. His ancestors were the original inhabitants of the continent but Indigenous peoples now comprise only 3.3 per cent of Australia's population. This ancient civilisation passes along its culture, traditions and knowledge from one generation to the next via language, dance, storytelling, performance, protection of sacred sites and through the wisdom of the Elders. Understanding and embracing the land, spirituality and the relationship with their community are very much essential in the social and emotional wellbeing of Indigenous Australians. There are more than 150 different Indigenous languages being spoken across Australia.

But not only is their health poorer, income lower and life expectancy shorter, they are less educated and remain daily confronted by discrimination. In the official Government census, Aboriginal people and Torres Strait Islanders were not counted until 1971, seven years after Michael Ahmatt was a Boomer at the Tokyo Olympics. Patty Mills' regular exposure to an Indigenous community in Canberra, where his parents were working to improve conditions for Indigenous Australians, initially came within the Shadows Basketball Club his parents started. He was among non-Indigenous children daily at school.

Yvonne Mills' inner strength long has been a bedrock of inspiration for Patty. "I'm still learning how important and special my family really is," he says. Growing up in an era of maltreatment, indignity and degradation, it is difficult to conceive Yvonne picturing a life where her son would be playing as a professional basketballer right across the USA. The Stolen Generation is what her early life was all about.

"Young Aboriginal kids were taken from their family and put into what they called a missionary that was run by the Catholic church, along with the Australian Government," Patty says. "They were put into the missionary to learn what they called the 'white ways' of growing up. For example, they weren't allowed to talk in their native tongue. They weren't allowed to act in a native way. They were forced to grow up in another way from who they are. And they were separated from their family basically their whole life."

Lied to that her mother didn't want her, the truth — which Yvonne only would uncover in the 1990s — was her mother heartbreakingly begged the Government to return her daughter. Courtesy of a Government inquiry into the separation of Aboriginal children, Yvonne and her siblings found Gladys Haynes's desperate pleading letters to authorities: "Please give me my children back" and "A promise is a promise." Finally from the records, the siblings ascertained the truth of what really happened to her, how she fought to get her children back and how authorities continued to move the goalposts.

"Get a house." Then it needed a particular number of rooms. Her colour and "dark appearance" were referenced. Road-blocks continued to appear. But eventually Yvonne was reunited with her siblings and mother, becoming a leading advocate for Indigenous Australians. Founding the Shadows club with husband Benny, it was a safe haven for Indigenous youth in the national capital. Playing in tournaments around Australia, the team encountered the occasional racist taunt, but Benny and Yvonne insulated Patty and his teammates from the worst of it. "My main focus was to empower them," Benny says, "so that anything they'd face they could manage." And from the Shadows emerged Patty Mills, the brightest and greatest shining light of all.

Patty Mills' NBL debut with Melbourne Tigers in the NBL against Sydney Kings on October 7, 2011, was a 28-point tour de force with 6-of-11 three-pointers in an 82-76 victory. Welcome to the NBL. He followed it with consecutive 19-point games against Perth Wildcats and New Zealand Breakers, then back-to-back 20-pointers in wins over Illawarra Hawks and Sydney Kings. He produced his first 10-assist game in a comfortable win over Cairns Taipans before pairing 16 points and 10 assists in a road loss to Townsville Crocodiles.

The Chinese Basketball Association, becoming notorious worldwide for its rich player contracts, actively was watching developments with quality basketball players set back by the NBA's prolonged lockout. Meanwhile, Mills was leading Melbourne Tigers to victory over Perth Wildcats and preparing for that long-anticipated trip to Adelaide and the match against his former AIS mentor Marty Clarke. The match would be his last in the NBL, the CBA's Xinjiang Flying Tigers offering him a million-dollar contract to relocate to Urumqi in Xinjiang, China.

"We were always prepared to release Patty," Melbourne Tigers owner Seamus McPeake said without hesitation. "And we did release him to a $1million offer from China." Mills had one last game to play though, the irony it was against the Adelaide 36ers at a sold out 7,800-capacity Clipsal Powerhouse in suburban Beverley. Mills scored his NBL career-high of 32 points at a wicked 55 per cent but the 36ers and Marty Clarke had the last laugh, winning 95-89.

Mills' agent Bruce Kaider told AAP that Mills "absolutely" retained the long-term goal of returning to the NBA. "There were no guarantees in Portland. He would've had to go back there and fight for a spot and he may not have even been in Portland," Kaider said. "He probably wouldn't have played the minutes he will in China. Certainly leading into London 2012, I think it's important for Patty and the Australian men's programme that Patty is actually playing minutes and working on and developing his game."

Kaider was confident Mills would again fall under the notice of NBA scouts if he maintained his excellent form through to the Olympics in July. "Beijing was his coming out Olympics where people got to see him and what he could do for the first time really at an international event at that level," Kaider said. "I think London is going to be the evolution of Patty, where he's developed, how he can lead his team and how he can progress the Boomers beyond where they've been in the past."

"Without putting too much pressure on Patty, London is going to be a really important milestone for the next five years of his career." And so it proved.

Less than a week after facing Adelaide though, Mills was an instant star in the CBA for his new team of Tigers. His first game against Ningbo Rockets yielded a 28-point, eight-assist return, Patty shooting at 72 per cent in the 111-92 win. He next led Xinjiang Flying Tigers to a 96-84 win over Jiangsu Dragons before a 32-point outburst in a loss to Beijing Ducks. He upped his scoring intake to a 42-point season-high in a rout of Tianjin Pioneers, then averaged 22.7 points in wins over Qingdao Eagles, Shandong and Guangzhou Long Lions.

In road losses to Shanghai Sharks and Zhejiang Lions, he scored 22 and 39 points respectively, home wins over Jilin Northeast Tigers and Liaoning Leopards bringing him returns of 26 and 31 points. On December 23, 2011, an injured Patty played his last game in the CBA, a loss to Guangdong Southern Tigers. Feeling his hamstring, he sought a couple of weeks' rest to have it return to normal, a request Xinjiang flatly refused. MRI scans revealed Mills suffered a hamstring tear — a three to six week injury — but the club wanted him back on court in seven-to-10 days. In 12 games with Xinjiang, Mills averaged 26.5 points per outing and was without question the Flying Tigers' best overall player following the departure of the NBA's No.1 draft pick in 2000, Kenyon Martin.

Like Mills, Martin was playing in China due to the NBA lockout. He was released by the club on December 24 and five weeks later signed with the Los Angeles Clippers. The 206cm forward averaged 13.9 points as Mills' teammate at Xinjiang. Sacking coach Bob Donewald three weeks earlier, Xinjiang then cut Mills, claiming he was "faking" his injury. This, despite the MRI evidence. What the club's decision meant though was that Patty, who did not have any NBA "out" clause, had to remain idle until the CBA season finished in late March. On the plus side, it meant he had time to rehab and heal his injured leg.

Unamused by Xinjiang's accusation he was faking the injury, Mills tweeted in response: "Okay ... Firstly, hammy is doing well and is on track to be back in full swing by next Saturday. That will be 3 wks. I had both MRIs sent to my doctor in Aus. It was made clear from the start to EVERYONE that it was a torn hamstring and would take 3-6 weeks. So why the team and doctors over here are saying its not torn, only swelling and (I) should be playing totally defeats me. So basically everything in the Chinese media is totally inaccurate and false. I've been honest and professional throughout #towel".

The lockout over, Mills' NBA future no longer appeared to be in Portland anymore. Talks began with the San Antonio Spurs where Boomers coach Brett Brown was an assistant coach to Gregg Popovich and in March 2012, not that long after the lockout ended, he signed with the club. "That first year, he was a little bit of a wild card," Popovich said. "He'd make turnovers at critical times. We needed to inject him with a little more point guard savvy rather than that two-guard 'I'm gonna let it fly' mentality."

His fun, infectious personality to the fore, Mills had no trouble quickly converting teammates into fans. He turned towel-waving into a performance art to the extent his range of signature moves became the talk of San Antonio. On the Spurs' team charter, he hooked up his guitar to the P.A. system, serenading the team with songs such as Sam Cooke's *Cupid*. On the court though, he was far from a major contributor, even though he now was playing alongside and learning from French superstar point guard Tony Parker. Back in 2008, Oregon Ducks college coach Ernie Kent favourably compared the young Mills to Parker, already an established NBA pro at San Antonio.

On April 26, 2012, Mills had his first NBA career double-double and set career highs with 34 points and 12 assists in a 107–101 win over the

Golden State Warriors. It was the most points scored by an Australian in the NBA, topping Andrew Bogut's 32 points for Milwaukee Bucks two years earlier. The Spurs could see his potential.

⁓

A touring national squad from Greece was part of Australia's on-court preparation for the London Olympic Games, matches Basketball Australia marketed as the "Farewell Series". But "Greece" wasn't the word at Melbourne's Hisense Arena as the Boomers won the first game 87-60. "Boomers" was the word and most specifically, Patty Mills and Aleks Maric, who provided a potent outside-inside punch the Greek B-team never handled.

Mills had 21 points, connecting on 5-of-7 three-pointers, Maric with 17 points at 70 per cent. Aron Baynes also stepped up with 16 points on 6-of-7 shooting, Matthew Dellavedova dishing nine assists and Joe Ingles eight, while providing coach Brett Brown with an additional playmaking option. Australia connected on 8-of-13 threes before the game lost some last quarter sparkle as the Boomers' wealth of experience and size overwhelmed the young visiting team. As a team confidence-booster, it was a perfect hit-out.

Australia made it 2-0 in the three-match series with a comprehensive 91-51 hammering at Victoria's State Basketball Centre at Knox. The Boomers so completely outclassed the visitors, they had time to put on a show, featuring athletic dunks by Aron Baynes and Brad Newley. Joe Ingles started the match full of energy and although Matt Nielsen scored the night's opening basket, Ingles scored the next 10 points in a withering solo run. A reverse, a fast break (and bonus free throw) sent Greece into a time-out, but back on court Ingles drained a three-pointer, then finished a running hoop from a Patty Mills feed. Greece mustered its opening basket at 5:22, Mills immediately more than cancelling it with a triple in a 15-2 lead.

Greece's B-team — its A-team was in Venezuela competing in a pre-Olympic tournament hoping to qualify through one of the three available slots on offer for London — looked like overwhelmed young men in the series opener. But in this second match, they were mere boys among men, Mark Worthington coming off the bench to provide further rocket fuel. A touch pass to Matthew Dellavedova, a jumpshot and a three by "Wortho" ensured a whopping 25-9 lead at the first break.

The Australian Olympic team for London had only one surprise selection, 32-year-old Townsville Crocodiles sharpshooter Peter Crawford. Matt Nielsen, David Andersen, Mark Worthington, Aleks Maric and David Barlow were back to reinforce the Boomers' culture. But the "new breed" to keep moving Australia toward that medal podium comprised Brad Newley, Joe Ingles, Matthew Dellavedova, Adam Gibson, Aron Baynes and emerging leader Patty Mills.

At their final training camp on the Gold Coast, Mills predicted the Boomers' run of medal "outs" was about to end, even though he knew the absence through injury of Andrew Bogut meant more pressure would fall on his shoulders. "My role has definitely changed (since the Beijing Olympics)," he said. "I have more of a leadership role now, but it's a challenge I feel very comfortable with.

"I'm going out there to lead the boys from the front." And that is precisely what Patrick Sammy James Mills did.

CHAPTER FOUR
THE TOWER OF LONDON

Lauren Jackson is Australia's greatest ever basketball player. That's not to say Australia's greatest *female* basketball player but greatest player, with no gender caveat or bias. Basketball is, after all, played by both genders and while the list of internationally successful Aussie male players is legion, none has ever come close to being revered as the greatest player in the world. Certainly discussion among basketball fans is divided over whether our all-time best men's player is Andrew Gaze, or Luc Longley, Andrew Bogut, David Andersen, or Patty Mills — and it remains a rich debate. But at no point in any of their stellar careers was any one of them in the conversation about "greatest player *in the world*".

That's a conversation reserved for names such as Michael Jordan, Kareem Abdul-Jabbar, Wilt Chamberlain, Kobe Bryant, Larry Bird, Magic Johnson, LeBron James, with a non-American player barely in sight. Lauren Jackson is among the first names mentioned when asked who the greatest female player of all time might be. She held the mantle as the world's #1 for a decade, dominating Australia's WNBL, then the US pro WNBA, along with competitions in Europe and Asia. The tip of the iceberg of her career was three Most Valuable Player awards in the WNBA — the women's NBA equivalent — and two championships. She also was its scoring champion three times and named to the WNBA's 10th Anniversary Team, then its 15th, 20th and 25th Anniversary Teams. Her #15 singlet was retired by the Seattle Storm WNBA club.

While those keen still to stipulate she achieved these heights as a woman — and those are just a snapshot portion of her accolades in the world's top competition and do not include her four Olympics, captaincy of the Australian team which won the gold medal at the 2006 FIBA

World Championship, or her library list of successes in every competition in which she competed — so as to in some way diminish them, one clear reality remains. Lauren Jackson for a major portion of her career was universally recognised as the best basketball player in the world. No Australian male has achieved that… yet.

When it was revealed Jackson would be Australia's flag-bearer at the London Olympic Games, it marked the second time a basketballer was awarded this rare honour. The first, and very significantly given the Games were being held in Australia, was Andrew Gaze, who carried the flag with immense and evident pride at the 2000 Sydney Olympics. In London, Lauren led Australia out into the Olympic Stadium, her beaming smile reflecting the joy and anticipation of the team, and with good reason. Her Australian team, the Opals, were expected to bring home a medal while, as always, there were high hopes Patty Mills and Co could lead the Boomers onto the podium for that historic first time.

Losing their opening game 71-75 to Brazil then was a setback, though not the catastrophe it was made out to be at home in Australia. It unquestionably hurt the campaign because the format was the now familiar one, with six teams battling each other to finish in the pool's top four. The No.1 ranked team then would play a knock-out quarterfinal against the rival group's fourth-ranked team, and vice-versa. The team finishing second played the rival group's third-placed finisher, and vice-versa. Top seeded USA was in the rival group. To qualify for the quarterfinals, the Boomers had to finish in the top four but needed to avoid fourth place. Fourth would mean facing the USA in a KO quarterfinal. Sudden death, literally, in tournament terms.

No-one wanted that so in a tough group featuring Brazil, Spain, Russia, China and Great Britain, Australia really was seeking a top-*three* finish. That made losing to Brazil far from the ideal start as Australia also had lost two lead-up exhibition games to a Spanish team featuring NBA stars such as brothers Pau and Marc Gasol, Serge Ibaka, Rudy Fernandez and Jose Calderon. Spain was the Games' No.2 seed, meaning a likely loss as it beat the Boomers twice in warm-up matches. Historically, Australia had a poor record in the opening round of Olympic competition.

At Sydney 2000, disaster loomed largely when Steve Nash inspired Canada to an opening night win over the Boomers, and their record then slipped to 0-2 after going under to No.2 seed Yugoslavia next. They made it to the bronze medal game however, so even the prospect of 0-2 in London should not have been that daunting. Australia simply had to beat China, Great Britain and Russia, which would put it third in the group behind Spain and Brazil.

And the loss to Brazil still was a very encouraging performance, despite the ultimate result. The Boomers led at the first break, trailed at halftime and at the last break, then raced home strongly to just come up short. Patty Mills led the way with a game-high 18 points, seven rebounds and four assists, Joe Ingles with 15 points, David Andersen 14 and Aron Baynes 10. "We have to play fearless basketball," Brown opined as the Boomers prepared to face Spain, a comfortable 97-81 winner over China.

True to his word, Brown's Boomers came out fearlessly, throwing the Spaniards onto the back-foot, leading 19-14 after the first quarter. Spain took stock during that first break, brothers Pau (at 214cm) and Marc Gasol (216cm) owning the keyway while Rudy Fernandez was pinpoint from the outside, stroking 4-of-5 three-pointers. Spain's 23-13 second quarter put it ahead 37-32 by halftime but its 26-10 third period put this well out of reach. Australia fought it out, losing 70-82, Brad Newley and Joe Ingles with 12 points apiece and Patty Mills 11.

As expected, Australia now had to beat China, Great Britain and Russia to avoid a crossover quarterfinal with the USA. The American outfit was led by Kobe Bryant, LeBron James and Kevin Durant, with Chris Paul, Carmelo Anthony, James Harden, Andre Iguodala, Kevin

Love, Anthony Davis and Russell Westbrook among those also in uniform. No one wanted to face them at any knock-out stage.

The start against China hardly was what the Boomers hoped, trailing 21-22 at the first break, nerves arguably a factor. Their 28-11 second period was more like what Aussie fans were expecting, before China again fought back with a 19-12 third. But there would be no upset in London in this one, Mills with 20 points, guiding Australia safely home 81-61. The Boomers' best defensive efforts were on show, containing China to a paltry nine last-quarter points. Joe Ingles also again had an eye-catching performance with 13 points and seven assists, David Andersen on 17 points. Matthew Dellavedova was now also becoming significant, his lobs for Aron Baynes' dunks off a regulation pick-and-roll basketball play a regular match highlight.

Brown was not surprised Mills' scoring was going up a level. "People wouldn't believe what he did with me in San Antonio for three months prior to coming to Australia and starting again," he said. "We shot a lot together and more than I have with any other player, and I have been lucky to be around the great ones over my years. He's earnt the right to take the shots." Beating Great Britain next should have been a formality but when the host nation took Spain to a 79-78 decision, it was apparent any letdown in intensity had the potential to be costly.

In Australia, the prospect of beating Great Britain seemed a fait accompli but Brown was acutely aware of the pitfalls and almost reverential about the host nation's star at the NBA's Chicago Bulls, Luol Deng. "He is a very skilled player for his size and we are going to have to figure out as a team defensive things for him because he's very hard to guard individually," the coach said. "I think great Britain has more weapons. We will go back to the war room and watch our tape.

"We love it. We will go back there with a thousand coffees and dig in. They are the host nation. I experienced that when we hosted the Olympics in 2000 and right off the bat, there was an advantage. They are a physical team, they get after it defensively and they scare us. We understand the importance of this game, as they do."

If GB truly scared Australia, its first quarter must have been very disturbing, the hosts ahead 25-18 at the first break. Their second term was almost as efficient, a 21-18 success for a 46-36 halftime lead that had the crowd in full voice and sensing an upset. It was even worse in the third quarter when Great Britain was nursing a 15-point lead. And that was when Patty Mills decided it was time to take over.

Mills singlehandedly rescued the Boomers with a whopping 39-point game-busting outburst that had tongues wagging across the stadium. It was the most points by an Australian player since Eddie Palubinskas in 1976 dropped 48 points on Mexico in overtime, but by no means any less significant. Mills' 39 points came on 14-of-22 shooting or 64 per cent, his three-point accuracy even better, 5-of-7 triples amassed at 71 per cent. He was 6-of-6 from the free throw line, weaving and cleaving through Great Britain's increasingly brittle defence.

Australia turned around the third quarter 30-14, still saving the best for last, its 40-15 final period for a resounding 106-75 rout its greatest single-quarter score in an Olympic fixture. The Boomers connected on 13-of-24 three-pointers, but the manner in which Mills changed the complexion of this contest had to be witnessed to be believed. "He captured the emotion of what is needed to excel at the Olympics," Brown said. "But they all play with great spirit. I think in the culture of the programme and Australian sport, there is an inherent toughness amongst the group that I've inherited."

Russia loomed on the horizon, having stunned Spain and Brazil by beating both to head the group with an unblemished 4-0 record. The game was an epic, the Boomers shooting out of the blocks to take a 29-20 lead out of the first quarter, Russia bouncing back with a 25-17 second,

Australia ahead 46-45 at the main interval. The third again belonged to the Aussies 23-19 giving them a five-point lead going into the last quarter. But Russia would not be denied, pushing ahead of the fatiguing Boomers and leading 80-79 with 4.7 seconds left. Brett Brown took a time-out and drew up the play. Back on court and despite the heightened tensions, the Boomers looked calm and strangely assured.

Watching the play unfold was akin to staring at the Mona Lisa in the Louvre, a thing of beauty to be recalled forever. Joe Ingles played around with the ball for precisely the right amount of time, Matthew Dellavedova setting a great screen for Patty Mills to pop free near the top of the keyway. Ingles hit him with a picture-perfect pass, Mills caught it in rhythm and swished the three-pointer for a dramatic 82-80 win on the siren. It was a joyous moment for Australian basketball, captivating, entrancing and euphoric, all at the same time. Mills had missed his previous three three-point attempts but the coach knew — "cometh the moment, cometh the man".

Mills never would miss sinking the match-winner. "For 20–30 minutes at the end of practices, we went through last-second plays," Mills explained. "The one Brett drew up was one we had practiced and knew." That explained the composure and confidence Brown's charges showed when they exited his final time-out to run the game-clinching play. Nonetheless, executing it to perfection was still a joy to behold.

Mills first inbounded the ball to Ingles who posted his man out from the block and held the ball just long enough. Dellavedova set the screen, Mills popped out wide open at the top of the key, Ingles hit the pass, Mills hit the three. As simple as one, two, three — Mills, Ingles, Dellavedova. Mills had 13 points, Ingles 20 and three assists, Dellavedova 10 points and seven assists. Ingles rammed home seven of his 20 points in a 60-second assault, sticking a three, stripping the ball cleanly for an aggressive drive to the hoop, then dropping in a delicious floater through a crowd. At this time, Australia had only two NBA players — Patty Mills and Andrew Bogut. Clearly, more were on their way, the Boomers' future in safe hands.

The Olympic tournament, however, was not. Despite the win and the Boomers finishing on a 3-2 win-loss record, Russia and Brazil both unexpectedly finishing on 4-1 marks meant Spain also finished on 3-2. And Spain won its head-to-head match with Australia, which is how win-loss record ties are broken. The Boomers, yet again had finished fourth. The USA awaited in the quarterfinal.

Commentating for television at the Olympics, Aussie basketball icon Andrew Gaze arguably had the best take on what to expect next against the Americans. "If we play them 100 times, maybe we win once," he said. "Have you seen *Dumb and Dumber*? 'So you are saying there's a chance?'… It's like that."

Playing against these same players regularly in the NBA, the Americans held no great mystique or psychological advantage over Mills. "This is what basketball is all about, playing against the best," he said. "It's going to be awesome."

No false bravado was attached to those words as Australia did, in fact, produce an awesome performance which drew great praise from USA coach Mike Krzyzewski and superstar Kobe Bryant. The Boomers trailed 21-28 after one, but after a competitive second 21-28 quarter, still looked "gone", down 42-56 at halftime. But incredibly, and driven by Patty Mills' game-high 26 points and Joe Ingles' 19, eight rebounds and six assists, the Boomers drew within three points during a torrid third quarter. Just when the Americans expected to put the cue in the rack, Australia made them furiously have to chalk up instead.

And it was Bryant, with six three-pointers in the second half, who led the way back to a 119-86 USA win in which the score was anything but reflective of the contest. "They played very well and Patty Mills continues to get better and better," Bryant said. "Every time I see him, he continues to improve. They just came ready to compete and showed up ready to perform."

Krzyzewski was no less taken with the Aussie grit and effort. "They play so hard and so well together," he said. "I love the way they expressed themselves, and it's great to see at the Olympics how much their players love their team and love their country." Second-seeded Spain knocked out France in its quarterfinal, then took out Russia in the semi to set up the much-anticipated and hyped gold medal showdown with the USA, which comfortably handled Argentina in its semi. The gold medal game was a tight one before the USA claimed it 107-100, Russia beating Argentina for bronze.

Having beaten Russia, it was cold comfort for the Boomers to see their group victim on the podium while the Aussies again would be returning empty-handed from another promising Olympic campaign. They did have one further compensation though. Patty Mills led the Games' scoring, averaging 21.2 points per game. He joined Eddie Palubinskas (1976), Ian Davies (1980) and Andrew Gaze (2000) as Australians to lead an Olympic Games in that key statistical category. In second place was Patty's future Brooklyn Nets NBA teammate Kevin Durant (USA) on 19.5 points per game, with long-time San Antonio Spurs teammate Manu Ginóbili (Argentina) third on 19.4.

Joe Ingles, still playing for Barcelona in the Euroleague, was the Boomers' other stand-out performer in London. Ingles' 15 points per game made him Australia's second leading scorer, his 51 per cent accuracy the best on the Boomers and eighth amid all competitors at the Games. His 4.2 assists were behind only Matthew Dellavedova's team best 4.6, and his 5.0 rebounds second to David Andersen's 6.0.

"He's long, left-handed, multi-faceted at guard or small forward, he's stepped up in defence to take personal pride in guarding people and you've seen his competitive spirit," Brown said. "He's on the up." Within two years, Ingles would become a regular contributor on the Utah Jazz's

NBA roster. All things considered, for Mills, Ingles, Dellavedova and Aron Baynes, the London Olympics were career watershed moments.

Brown, however, decided that the ongoing Boomers' commitment was no longer one he could sustain on top of an 82-game regular season schedule as a San Antonio Spurs assistant coach. The perennially powerful Spurs regularly also went deep into the NBA playoffs. While Basketball Australia preferred its national coaches to complete two Olympic cycles, unlike his predecessors, Brown had an NBA commitment and it was hugely demanding.

Had he wanted to continue on to Rio in 2016, there is little doubt BA would have accommodated him. But his difficult decision to leave the role also meant he could spend the American summers with his family. For him, it was a no-brainer. For BA, the federation was back at the drawing-board.

At home in Australia during the off-season ahead of the 2012–13 NBA season at San Antonio Spurs, Patty Mills fulfilled another burning ambition — singing one of his favourite songs with his favourite choir, the Adelaide Crows AFL footy team. After watching the Crows dismantle Melbourne Demons by 69 points at the Melbourne Cricket Ground and wearing his Crows supporter jersey and tri-colour scarf, he was thrilled to sing the club song in the change-rooms with the team afterwards.

"Oh yeah. One of the highlights of my night," Mills tweeted after joining in with considerable gusto, flanked by one of his Twitter mates, forward Kurt Tippett, and Aboriginal utility Graham Johncock. Another of the Crows' Indigenous players, Jared Petrenko, was stunned and delighted the burgeoning NBA guard was in the AFL team's midst.

"I'm pretty happy about it," he said of Patty's singalong. "There's a lot of photos all over Twitter and Facebook with him there. I was pretty starstruck for a bit." Petrenko had plenty of mates in that regard, although Mills was his customary fun, approachable, genial self. The Crows finished the minor premiership in second place. "I'm spewing because I leave the country just before the finals," Mills said, his avid support of the Crows starting at an early age through time spent in the South Australian regional town of Ceduna.

His mother Yvonne was born in South Australia to Gladys Haynes, a member of the Ynunga Aboriginal tribe who grew up at Koonibba Mission, a Lutheran home for Aboriginal children on Eyre Peninsula, 800km west of Adelaide and 40km northwest of Ceduna. That was where Gladys learnt to cook, clean and sew. At the age of 12, Gladys was sent to work as a domestic for a white family, after being granted an "exemption certificate". She needed it for permission to live among white people. Otherwise it would not have been possible under the Aboriginal Protection Act.

Patty spent some of his early life in Ceduna with his mother's side of the family. "The whole family went for the Crows and I was brought up in that environment," he said. "I remember the 1997–98 (AFL) grand finals vividly because we had blue, red and yellow decorations up around the house."

Back on July 8, 2010, LeBron James, the NBA's reigning Most Valuable Player, announced in a much-derided television special called *The Decision*, that he was leaving his beloved Cleveland Cavaliers. Now a free agent, his line about "taking my talents to South Beach" became a punchline for critics and comedians alike. But by joining superstar friends Dwyane Wade and Chris Bosh at Miami Heat, he most definitely shifted the balance of power in the league. Initially at least, the attitude of the All Star trio appeared to smack of arrogance and outside of Miami, they subsequently were treated as villains by media and fans alike.

Their talent, however, was undeniable and they won the Eastern Conference to set up a best-of-seven NBA championship showdown with the Western Conference's Dallas Mavericks. Again, Wade and James did themselves no favours in the court of public opinion by mocking Dallas' German-born superstar Dirk Nowitzki when he was taken ill during the Finals. Consequently when Nowitzki led Dallas to the championship in six games after turning around a 1-2 series deficit and was named Finals MVP, there was little sympathy for Miami.

Clearly, the Heat had some thinking to do about how they wanted the world to perceive them. Did they wish to continue being seen as entitled, smug, rich brats or dedicated professional athletes at the peak of their powers? For the 2011–12 season, they wisely chose the latter, LeBron James leading the way across the lockout-afflicted season.

He won the league's MVP award and drove the Heat back to the Eastern Conference Championship. Coming out of the West was a young team dripping with potential, Kevin Durant, Russell Westbrook and Serge Ibaka leading the way, James Harden off the bench in an Oklahoma City Thunder that boasted a huge upside. But it wasn't ready yet for "King" James and Co, who won the championship in five games. When Patty Mills returned to the San Antonio Spurs for the 2012–13 NBA season, the Miami Heat were defending champions and the team with a target on its chest.

Coach Gregg Popovich once again helped assemble an eclectic and multi-talented Spurs roster, 208cm power forward/centre Aron Baynes leaving Slovenia to join Mills in January as the second Australian on the squad. San Antonio also suited Frenchmen Tony Parker, Boris Diaw and Nando de Colo, Argentinian superstar Manu Ginóbili, Canadian guard Cory Joseph and 211cm Brazilian centre Tiago Splitter. Its American content was headed by 211cm Tim Duncan, originally from the Virgin Islands, emerging star Kawhi Leonard, shooter Danny Green, big forward Matt Bonner, 15-year veteran Tracy McGrady secured in April, Gary Neal and DeJuan Blair.

The Spurs system under Popovich was to build their teams, Patty Mills not the first Australian recruited into the programme. Andrew Gaze was part of the roster which won the NBA Championship in 1999, alongside future club legends such as David Robinson, Sean Elliott, Steve Kerr, Avery Johnson and a young Tim Duncan.

With 12 returning members of the Spurs' 2011–12 squad, which went 50-16 over the lockout-reduced season and took Oklahoma City Thunder to six games for the Western Conference championship, the Spurs again were expected to go deep into the playoffs. Nicknamed "the Big Fundamental" and revered as arguably the greatest power forward in NBA history, Spurs captain Tim Duncan still was the team's centrepiece, even though he would turn 37 during the season.

San Antonio's own "big three" – Duncan, Tony Parker and Manu Ginóbili – were the lynchpins as the Spurs posted a solid 58-24 regular season win-loss record, second in the Western Conference to Oklahoma City Thunder's 60-22. Parker with 20.3 points and 7.6 assists a game led the Spurs in both categories and fellow starter Duncan averaged 17.8 points and a team best 9.9 rebounds and 2.7 blocks. Ginóbili came off the bench all season, Leonard a regular starter averaging 11.9 points and a Spurs' high 1.7 steals. Long-range shooter and defender Danny Green started in all 80 regular season games he played.

Patty delivered 5.1 points and 1.1 assists, seeing only an average of 11.3 minutes of action in 58 games. In San Antonio's 21 playoff games, he only saw action in nine and merely for an average of 3.4 minutes. That was despite the Spurs sweeping the Los Angeles Lakers 4-0 in the first round – late Aussie signing Aron Baynes inserted into the starting five for injured centre Tiago Splitter in Game Four and getting the better of Dwight Howard – then knocking out Golden State Warriors 4-2 in the semi finals and sweeping the Memphis Grizzlies in the Western Conference Finals. That set up the best-of-seven Championship Series against LeBron James and the "reformed" Miami Heat who clinched the Eastern Conference in seven games over Indiana Pacers and would enjoy home court advantage against the Spurs.

Having turned back their opponents far sooner, the Spurs had to wait nine days for Miami to get through the East and hold up its end of the bargain. "The break is a great thing because all the guys can work on whatever niggles they have and come back fully ready for who we match up against," Baynes said during the wait. "It's only a positive thing. Our 'big three' have a lot of experience in the post-season and know what we need to do to stay in shape. They guide the younger guys with what we have to do."

The Finals format saw Miami at home for the first two games, the next three in San Antonio, and the final two, if required, back in Miami. Despite his minimal minutes, Mills still attracted the positive attention of former New York Knicks NBA coach and ESPN television analyst Jeff Van Gundy. "You know what I love? Patty Mills," Van Gundy declared during the Grizzlies series as he honed in on Mills' supportive value as a teammate. "I'm telling you, if I ever coach again, this is the type of guy you need to keep the energy up through a long NBA season."

Kevin Garnett, Paul Pierce and Ray Allen may have been the original "big three" of the era, leading Boston Celtics to a championship, but now all the talk was about LeBron James, Dwyane Wade and Chris Bosh at Miami. Yet the trio few spoke about — San Antonio's Tim Duncan, Tony Parker and Manu Ginóbili — already had three championships under their belts together, Duncan additionally with a fourth. Now they were just three wins from a fourth together after Parker stroked a stunning banker jumpshot with 5.2 seconds left to clinch Game One of the NBA Finals 92-88 in Miami.

The Spurs' trio entered Game One against the Heat at American Airlines Arena with 98 playoff wins as a collective, second most by a trio in NBA history behind Magic Johnson, Kareem Abdul-Jabbar and Michael Cooper, who won 110 together with the Los Angeles Lakers. It was 99-and-counting after Parker hit 10 of his 21 points in the fourth quarter, Danny Green stuck a big three and Duncan nailed clutch free throws. Dribbling around on the Spurs' last offence, Parker fumbled the ball, fell down, gathered himself, turned and launched a five-metre bank shot a millisecond before the shot-clock expired.

Officials looked at the video from various angles and determined the ball left his fingertips just before the lights started flashing. That was when the lights went out for Miami. On a side note, Tim Duncan joined A.C. Green and John Salley as the only players in NBA history to make Finals appearances in three decades. That was the calibre of teammate with whom Patty Mills was rubbing shoulders at San Antonio.

As the Heat trudged off American Airlines Arena in the wake of their Game One home loss, they looked tired, uncertain and perhaps, lacking in a bit of self-belief. San Antonio would not disintegrate as Indiana did in the Eastern Conference Final and the Spurs had weathered Miami's best shots... and still won. There had to be some level of doubt but Miami erased it in no uncertain terms, tying the series 1-1 with its 103-84 Game Two home victory. Self-belief was restored as Miami went on a withering 33-5 tear with Mario Chalmers — of all people — leading the charge. Patty Mills finished a late lay-up to become the first Aussie to score in an NBA Championship series since Luc Longley for Chicago Bulls in 1998.

No one could foresee what awaited in San Antonio as the ball was tossed up to start Game Three. For sure, Spurs fans expected a win and maybe even suspected or hoped for a double-digit success. But a 113-77 rout with the third highest winning margin in Finals history? Who even believed San Antonio had the firepower to contemplate such a thing? And the Spurs dished that out with Tony Parker sitting off with a hamstring injury from part way through the third quarter!

"We got what we deserved," Heat coach Erik Spoelstra said. "Every shot they wanted to get, they got. We did not disrupt them."

Star shooter Danny Green, who scored 27 points for the Spurs — including 22 in the second half — was almost as stunning as "Jeri Ryan, Star Trek space babe" with his own "7-of-9" from beyond the three-point arc. Then there was Gary Neal burying a playoff career-high 24 points while Kawhi Leonard finished with 14 points, 12 rebounds and four steals, delighting an understandably raucous crowd of 18,581 at AT&T Center.

The Spurs enjoyed two monster second half runs — a 23-8 surge to start the third quarter and a 13-0 run to begin the fourth as they outscored Miami 63-33 in the second half. San Antonio also closed the first half exceptionally with Parker nailing an off-balance corner triple, Green blocking a shot by LeBron James and the ball swept forward for Neal to swish a three as the buzzer sounded. This was amazing stuff and San Antonio now also had history on its side. The Game Three winner in NBA Finals series that were split 1-1 had continued on to win the title 12 of the past 13 times.

Of course, Miami also had created some history of its own in the playoffs, never losing consecutive games and always bouncing back from a loss with a double-digit win. That was the case again in Game Four where the Heat turned up the heat 109-93 to level the series at 2-2. Game Five was the last in San Antonio, Australian fans glued to their TV sets disheartened to see Patty Mills join Aron Baynes behind the Spurs' bench in his street clothes for Game Four. Patty was ruled out for Games Four and Five after minor surgery to remove an abscess between the fourth and fifth toes of his right foot.

Fans at the sold-out AT&T Center in San Antonio were chanting "Man-u, Man-u" and Manu Ginóbili responded with a performance worth cheering about in Game Five. Before tip-off against the reigning NBA champion, a fan held up a "Manu Gino-believe" banner and 48 minutes later, there wasn't a disbeliever in the house. San Antonio won 114-104 to take a 3-2 lead and Ginóbili, restored to the starting line-up by coach Gregg Popovich for the first time since the previous year's playoffs, once again was holding up his end of the Spurs' "Big Three".

He started with a long-range bomb and by game's end delivered a season-best 24 points on 8-of-14 shooting, with 10 assists. Bear in mind, across the first four games of the Championship Series, it wasn't the Manu of old, but an old Manu, with a grand total of 30 points and 12 assists. But by the last break, the Argentinian magician had already paired 20 points with nine assists. And Danny Green, the feel-good story of this series, also delivered 24 points, sticking six threes en route to breaking the NBA Finals series mark for most three-pointers.

With 25 at this point, he broke Ray Allen's record of 22 at the Boston Celtics in 2008, Allen now shooting triples for Miami. Ginóbili became the first player this century to start in the NBA Finals after not starting all season. It was a Popovich masterstroke. But when it comes to master strokes, there are few better than Allen. The slick shooter Miami "stole" from the Celtics was the hero of the series for Miami when he saved the Heat from defeat in Game Six.

Ruled out again due to his injury, Patty Mills did not downplay the importance of Game Six. "This is the one," he said before tip-off. "I think if we want to win it (all), it has to be this one. We have to break out of the back-and-forth." San Antonio's wins in Games One, Three and Five were by an average of 16.7 points. Miami's wins in Games Two and Four were by 17.5 points. "Exactly," Patty said. "They have been big margins because it's a reflection of how small the margin for error is.

"With two such great teams, the slightest adjustment or wrong move? The other team will make you pay a heavy price. We really punished them on defensive transition (in Game Five) for example." Mills rushed to that game from hospital and his right foot was still in considerable discomfort. "I only just got out of the hospital but I went straight to the game," he said. "I wouldn't have missed it for anything."

In Game Six, it assuredly was Allen who saved the legacies of LeBron James and Dwyane Wade after Tim Duncan was an absolute monster for San Antonio with a 25-point first half of total mastery. But in the end, it was Allen who stepped back (travelled?) to make an amazing triple from the corner to force an overtime Miami had no reason to expect was even possible. And then it was Allen, recruited to provide exactly what he did in Game Six, making the clutch free throws that guaranteed a deciding Game Seven, Miami sneaking home 103-100.

Sadly for the Spurs, Duncan came up empty in the fourth quarter and overtime, ending a huge night with a heavy thud while still compiling 30 points on 13-of-21 shooting and 17 boards. "It's disappointing. I had some opportunities. We put ourselves in position to win the game. They made plays to take it from us," Duncan said. The Heat didn't just make plays to take Game Six, they made plays that set up Game Seven, bouncing back from the disappointment a big ask for the Spurs.

Tony Parker and Boris Diaw may have been the Frenchmen in the NBA Finals but it was LeBron James in Game Seven who was just "le magnifique", leading Miami to consecutive championships with its 95-88 victory in a decider for the ages. San Antonio chose to "pick its poison" and that was to give LBJ the J, rather than have him wreak havoc creating off the drive. The upshot saw King James go off for 37 points and 12 rebounds, cementing his legacy with the Finals MVP.

It was the Heat's first Finals Game Seven in the 25-year history of the franchise and a classic, every bit as good as the entire series as a whole, which was unforgettable. The teams appeared to virtually trade the lead on nearly every possession throughout the third quarter before the final period provided edge-of-the-seat drama until the final minute, the match tied 11 times, the lead changing hands seven.

Four-time NBA champion Tim Duncan went down battling in the first Finals series defeat of his illustrious career, finishing with 24 points and 12 rebounds. But he was a shattered man when he missed a layup at 88-90, then also a follow-up tip in. The 37-year-old superstar with the poker face slapped the floor in disgust at himself in what arguably was the sign this one might finally be over. He was right. "That's out of me just missing a bunny," Duncan said when asked about his rare show of emotion. "I got by Shane (Battier) and had a layup to tie the game. That's just frustration." This was a Finals loss which would burn in the bellies of every player on the Spurs' roster and every member of its coaching and support team.

It was 8.30 in the morning in Miami when Patty Mills heard his mobile phone beep, wondering who could be trying to get his attention so early. Mills was gearing up for his first trip to the best-of-seven Finals against the Miami Heat. "I heard the phone," he said, not realising the message was a tweet alerting him to the antics of his favourite AFL team, Adelaide Crows. Hindered by a lack of court-time had not retarded Mills' belief in what it takes to be a quality teammate, his towel-waving and enthusiastic sideline support endearing him across the league.

The Crows, led by their coach at the time, Brenton Sanderson, copied his array of towel-waving signature moves in a video designed to show the club's support on the eve of the championship series. "I saw the tweet about it, went to the video and I was crying and laughing in bed," Mills said.

"It got me pretty pumped up and ready to go — it was such great support from the Adelaide Crows boys. South Australia has given me awesome support with tweets and through Facebook but the Crows video? That was unreal. Patrick Dangerfield was the one though — he really got into it." Mills saw late-game action as the series wore on before his foot "blew up".

"It was weird," he told me. "I don't even know what happened. It was one of those freak things." Patty needed surgery to have an abscess cut from between the fourth and fifth toes of his right foot, effectively eliminating him from the rest of one of the NBA's greatest championship series.

Racing from hospital to ensure he did not miss Game Five in San Antonio, he made it to the sidelines for what would turn out to be the Spurs' last win of the series. "The atmosphere, the whole build-up to the playoffs and the championship has been phenomenal," Mills said, the little Aussie star now with a burgeoning cult following in the city of the Alamo. Some of that was because of his play, his personality and even his towel-waving. But there was more.

"Ever since I came to San Antonio, I've done a lot of community work, visiting schools and hospitals, stuff like that," Mills said. "I've tried to get into the environment and learn about Texas culture." Swing back to Miami where the Spurs needed a police escort to get to games, Heat fans giving them the thumbs down and booing from the footpaths. "It's all part of the atmosphere," Mills said. That atmosphere of Game Seven was very hot, Mills and Aron Baynes applauding their fallen Spurs teammates as they entered the locker-room post-game.

Mills now had his own future to consider. "I'm definitely coming home, probably in August," he said, Patty keen to play for Australia against New Zealand in front of his home Canberra fans in the Oceania Series. "But for me it's a very important (northern) summer, for a lot of reasons. I need to really grind and get down to work on my game in terms of being in the gym, getting a lot of shots up, eating well — all of it.

"I need to do everything I can to play in the NBA and be up there with the elite. Treatment, massages, whatever it takes to get into the best possible physical shape." Mills had a contract option with the Spurs for 2013-14 but Tony Parker remained one of the world's premier playmakers and San Antonio also had Gary Neal and Cory Joseph in the pecking order ahead of him.

"We don't train a lot in-season but I have gotten better as a player, having been taken under Tony Parker's wing," he said. "Watching how he goes about it and what he has to say has been very good for me." The elephant in the room though was had Mills, despite being in rarified air as the leading scorer at an Olympic Games, been devalued as a player because of his sideline enthusiasm and antics?

"The thing that matters to me is my teammates," the consummate team player said. "I do it for them, I do it for us and that's all that matters. I obviously love San Antonio but in the latter part of the season, I didn't get a lot of court-time. I still try to be a great teammate. Everyone wants to play but you have to make the most of it. I don't want to sulk. I do it (the towel-waving) for genuine reasons — not for publicity or anything."

Mills' team-first mentality drew rave reviews from coaches and analysts alike. But he definitively knew it was his game which would have to do the talking in 2013–14. "It is time to get away from basketball for a little while, see what my options are," he said. Sadly after the loss to Miami, visiting the White House to meet President Barack Obama with the NBA champion team no longer was an option, at least not this year. "I actually have had the pleasure of meeting Barack Obama at a dinner at Parliament House in Canberra when I was playing NBL with Melbourne Tigers," Mills said.

Meeting him again as part of the championship team would have been a huge buzz but now a break, then full-on commitment to being the best he could be was what lay immediately in store for the genuine Aussie champion. His lack of minutes through the playoffs was telling. "In the playoffs you have to trust a guy completely," Spurs coach Gregg Popovich said when asked about Mills' minutes. The ball most definitely was in Patty's court and he was ready to answer the challenge. In June, he exercised the option year on his contract to stay at San Antonio, the deal earning him $US1.1million ($A1.20million) in 2013–14.

"I absolutely love this place," Patty said. "The organisation is one of the best in sports worldwide and San Antonio is really laid back."

CHAPTER FIVE
THE SPUR FOR SAN ANTONIO

Basketball Australia found itself in a considerable dilemma when Brett Brown chose to focus on his family and steadily evolving NBA coaching career over a further Olympic cycle as Australia's national coach. Firstly it came as an unexpected surprise as a new culture was emerging under his watch. Secondly, there was no immediately obvious successor. In the end though, BA landed on its feet, suddenly finding itself with not one but two outstanding candidates for the role of Boomers' boss.

Rob "Bevo" Beveridge coached Perth Wildcats to the club's fifth NBL championship in 2010 and had the reins of the Australian men's team which won the gold medal at FIBA's 2003 Under-19 World Championship. That team included players such as tournament MVP Andrew Bogut, Brad Newley, Aleks Maric, Damian Martin and Steve Markovic, all of them among the current crop of Boomers players and aspirants.

Andrej "Drey" Lemanis coached New Zealand Breakers to three consecutive NBL championships, in 2011, 2012 and 2013. He also was Brown's lead assistant with the Boomers for his 2010 FIBA World Championship and 2012 Olympic Games campaigns. BA had an unspoken preference toward elevating assistants to the lead role in a smooth succession plan but this appointment was particularly challenging. Both men were outstanding candidates and success stories in their own right.

Though no one ever confirmed it, when Lemanis' Breakers faced Beveridge's Wildcats for the 2013 NBL championship in an encore of their 2012 grand finals showdown, BA delaying its Boomers coaching announcement until after the title was decided strongly indicated the two candidates likely were auditioning for the national coaching job.

Lemanis, who Brown also anointed as his preferred successor, finally was announced as Australia's eleventh national men's coach in May 2013.

Born the son of Latvian immigrant parents, growing up in the western suburbs of Melbourne, Lemanis' discovery of basketball was inevitable. Basketball in Latvia was and is huge. So when many Latvians fled the Communist regime post-World War II, their passion for hoops followed to their new homes. "Dad played basketball, which was a very popular sport in Latvia," Lemanis, 44, said. "In fact, dad's claim-to-fame is he played at Albert Park Stadium on its opening night."

When Lemanis' older brother took up the sport, he tagged along, fell in love with it and after a playing career which included an NBL stint, went into coaching. His NBL apprenticeship was alongside Ian Stacker, who in 1997 coached Australia to the gold medal at the FIBA 22 & Under World Championship. Just like his predecessor Brett Brown, one of Lemanis' first declarations was that his Boomers only had medal intentions.

Brown, meanwhile, interviewed and won the head coaching role of the NBA's Philadelphia 76ers, departing from San Antonio to take on a new and very daunting challenge. However the pain of losing the NBA Championship in such an epic seven-game series to Miami Heat had not greatly subsided. "When we got back to San Antonio and the dust had settled a bit, I think Pop (Spurs head coach Gregg Popovich) put it in some perspective though," Brown said.

"He said to the group, if that's the worst thing to ever happen to us, then we've lived pretty fortunate lives." Brown said that helped… a little. "There will still be that moment, and for the rest of our lives when, it doesn't matter if you're out driving, or going fishing or just daydreaming and we'll remember (losing the championship) and it will be 'damn' all over again," Brown said.

Lemanis' first appointment to his new Boomers staff was three-time NBA championship starting centre at Chicago Bulls, Luc Longley, as his lead assistant. "I didn't expect to be an assistant coach," said Longley, who had no previous coaching experience. "But then I didn't expect to be a divorcee, or a stepfather either."

Having been unable to leave the game on his own terms after injury prematurely ended it for him, Longley was estranged from the sport. But it was temporary. His love for it steadily lured him back into the fold. "I'm quite enthusiastic about the talent Australia has coming through, especially the big guys," Longley said.

Brown had utilised his services ahead of the London Olympics to mentor players such as Aron Baynes. "He talked me around," the triple-Olympian admitted. "If I can coach (Nathan) Jawai, have (Andrew) Bogut back into the fold, Baynes will be something, (Aleks) Maric is a fantastic player… it excites me. Basketball is something I know. At least I like to think so." Actually, Longley's basketball IQ was off the chart, his previous work as a Boomers consulting coach a huge asset for raw young talents, particularly Baynes. Many saw his appointment as a Lemanis master-stroke.

Despite missing the end of the NBA Championship series with his foot surgery, Patty Mills had every intention of suiting for Lemanis' Boomers in their Oceania Championship against regular trans-Tasman rival New Zealand. "That'll be right," he told me of his foot when we spoke as the Spurs prepared for the fateful Game Six against the Heat in Miami. "I've definitely put my hand up for it," he said of competing against the Tall Blacks.

"One of those games is in Canberra and I've never had a chance before to play for Australia in front of my home crowd," he said. The two-match Oceania Series, with the winner an automatic qualifier for the 2014 FIBA World Cup, was scheduled for Auckland and Canberra in August. With New Zealand's international prominence also in an upward growth phase, the Boomers team for this series was, out of necessity as much as anything else, one of the best for such a challenge.

It included regular selections Joe Ingles, Matthew Dellavedova, David Andersen, Adam Gibson and David Barlow, a quintet which, along with Patty, formed the backbone of the team. But Lemanis also cast an eye toward the imminent future by selecting Dante Exum, Ben Simmons, Ryan Broekhoff and Cam Bairstow who all would continue on into the NBA. A 203cm power forward, Anthony Petrie made his Oceania debut for the Boomers at 30, his performances in a warmup series against China clinching his selection as this team's "feel-good" story. Petrie was more than just a good story though, starting for the Boomers at power forward. Luke Nevill, a 218cm centre, rounded out Lemanis' dazzling dozen.

Basketball Australia, however, churned out minimal publicity or promotion for the Oceania Championship which caught Patty Mills' attention. His reaction was to use his social media influence, ostensibly via Twitter, to fire up fan interest. First he posed the question: "Just making sure but is everyone back home aware of the Boomers and Opals double header against New Zealand in Canberra coming up???"

Good question, it seemed, fan reactions revealing not as many were as aware as BA expected.

Mills answered his own query with the date — 18th of August — and the venue, AIS Arena, "The Palace". "Trying to pump this game up as much as we can so we can pack The Palace that night!" he tweeted, the match less than three weeks away. "This team is only together a few weeks out of the year. So when we do play, it's kind of special to all us. Would LOVE to get everyone along."

At this point, as one of his Twitter followers, I was reminded again just what a precious ambassador Patrick Mills remained for Australian basketball, regardless of where he was playing. But this, which included a photograph, really had me shaking my head in admiration: "It would be amazing if we could pack the arena out like the Canberra Cannons used to do in the 80s and 90s! I remember going to games at the AIS Arena as a kid and learning about Herb McEachin, Phil Smyth and Tad Dufelmeier and thinking to myself... I want to play in front of a crowd like this! Getting excited just tweeting all this!! Anyway hope we can get some support behind it."

Within days, BA announced the double-header between the Boomers-Tall Blacks and the Opals-Tall Ferns would be on live free-to-air TV. It may have been a coincidence but Patty, clearly recalling the sea of yellow T-shirts at many of the venues (Golden State Warriors, Indiana Pacers) during the NBA Finals, had another bold thought. "Oh just thought of an idea! What if we packed out the arena AND had a green or gold out. Everyone with free shirts and a sea of gold" he tweeted.

Question: What could have been better for the team, the TV product and the sport than a full house in Canberra? Answer: That full house of fans walking in to find a yellow T-shirt supporting the Opals/Boomers on every seat-back in the venue. Of course it didn't happen but Mills' talking point in itself acted as a super promotion.

The Oceania Championship opening in Auckland, Patty led Australia with 20 points, David Andersen with 12 and Matthew Dellavedova 11 as the Boomers took Game One 70-59. The Tall Blacks were shut down in the second half 38-20 and scored just two field goals in the last quarter, one of them by Tom Abercrombie at the buzzer as the Boomers turned their 32-39 halftime deficit into a runaway win.

Ben Simmons came in to steal the ball and throw down a two-handed dunk, then threw in an Abercrombie rejection for good measure, Dante Exum was solid and Ryan Broekhoff's three-pointer closed the first period with the Boomers ahead 21-18.

The game left New Zealand coach Nenad Vucinic a disappointed man. "The last quarter, we really dropped our performance," he said. "Whether there were valid excuses or not, it's for us to analyse before the second game." Corey Webster led the scoring for the home side with 14 points, captain Mika Vukona prominent with 11 points and eight rebounds.

"Right now, it's an 11-point game at halftime," Boomers coach Andrej Lemanis said. "It's going to be war right down to the end. I know that with those New Zealand guys."

If anyone did, of course, it had to be Lemanis. Despite BA's poor promotion, close to a sell-out rocked the Palace in Canberra for Game Two, a devastating 28-7 third period by the Boomers clinching the Oceania Championship 76-63. New Zealand simply was unable to sustain its intensity after halftime.

The win, paced by Patty Mills' 21 points, made it a 2-0 sweep, Australia now qualified for the 2014 FIBA World Cup. The match certainly had its share of niggle, with Tall Blacks new faces Reuben Te Rangi and Jack Salt both giving up unsportsmanlike fouls as the Boomers bolted away. The raucous and supportive crowd not only saw the present but also the future in the blistering third period.

Trailing 33-39 at halftime, the Boomers blasted the Tall Blacks with a 10-0 start to the second half. Mills started the rally with a steal — he finished with five — and lay-up. Joe Ingles (12 points, five assists) saved a ball, throwing it back to Mills trailing and he drained a three-pointer. Then Ingles drove and scored, adding a bonus free throw as the difference in class began to become apparent.

Australia forced a 24-second violation on the Kiwis' next forward foray before sweet passing from Mills to Ingles to Anthony Petrie saw him flip in a reverse basket. That made it 43-39 before Corey Webster broke New Zealand's drought but it made little difference as Mills stuck another triple. When Mills stole the ball from Everard Bartlett, frustrations boiled over and Te Rangi put him to the floor to cop the game's first unsportsmanlike.

Mills converted both resultant free throws, then swished a three on the additional possession for a 53-41 lead. Yes, he was thriving on genuinely playing "at home". Burgeoning young talent Cam Bairstow rejected a shot by BJ Anthony, then was monstered by Alex Pledger at the other end, sticking both free throws. Australia was on a 22-2 roll as coach Lemanis sent Dante Exum into the fray, his entrance marked by loud crowd appreciation. A free throw by Adam Gibson extended the run to 23-2 before David Andersen lobbed a ball for Exum to finish.

And another future star, Ryan Broekhoff closed the quarter with a three, Australia keeping New Zealand to 3-of-13 shooting for the period to lead 61-46, the Oceania Championship in the bag. The Boomers had closed the first quarter strongly with Ben Simmons throwing down a dunk before a terrific last defensive stand on New Zealand's final possession, Jarrod Kenny stripped of the ball.

The Aussies were trailing 30-36 when Matthew Dellavedova sank a three-pointer but Webster wiped that away as New Zealand took a 39-33 lead into the halftime interval. It was shades of the opening game in Auckland where the Tall Blacks led 39-32 at halftime. Again, they could not resist the Aussies after the main break.

Patty Mills knew his NBA career was at a turning point as the shadows of the 2012–13 season faded into the distance. It was time for some of *him* to fade into the distance and for the rest of him to return to San Antonio in the best shape of his life. No more commentary from excruciatingly blunt coach Gregg Popovich about "Fatty Patty". It was time to become who he could be on an NBA court.

Mills made himself over physically, adopting a variation of the paleo diet and in the process, halving his body fat to below 7 per cent. "He'd been a little bit of a chub," said Popovich, abundantly aware the extra kilos reduced Patty's ability to defend efficiently. "As soon as he came to camp, we noticed he was quicker, faster."

The positive impact was immediate, Patty the leading scorer in San Antonio's first practice game and again against Orlando Magic in another of the Spurs seven exhibitions. He then led an early point-scoring surge to help the Spurs to a 101-94 home win over the Memphis Grizzlies in their 2013–14 NBA season opener. Newly-promoted as the Spurs' back-up point guard to Tony Parker, Patty didn't miss a beat, adding 12 points in just nine minutes in the rematch of the previous season's Western Conference finalists.

Sporting his new toned body, when the 25-year-old Mills was subbed in, he provided an instant energy boost, draining three straight three-pointers and a free throw to give San Antonio a 37-22 lead with 6:48 left in the first half. Mills was one of six Spurs who finished with double figures, led by Kawhi Leonard and Boris Diaw on 14 points, Parker with 13. The merit of the win was heightened by the fact Tim Duncan left the game in the third quarter with a chest contusion after taking an inadvertent elbow and did not return for the rest of the game.

Not necessarily reborn as an NBA player but definitely regenerated, Patty Mills still did not lose focus on events away from the basketball court. At home in Australia, the Logan Thunder, the newest Women's National Basketball League club and one based near the Queensland capital of Brisbane, was close to falling over before the season tipped off. Unable to meet the financial commitment, the Thunder were perilously close to having the plug pulled until Basketball Australia mounted a rescue package. More than $10,000 was raised in six hours through donations at the Thunder's Facebook page as high-profile athletes including Patty, Andrew Bogut, Jenna O'Hea and Micaela Cox rallied to help save the club.

In Toronto, now it was Aron Baynes showing his worth, feted by Spurs teammates and coaching staff alike after scoring his NBA career-best 14 points on 7-of-9 shooting in a 116-103 win over the Raptors. He also snared six rebounds in his 20 minutes and added two plays to the game's highlights package. The first was a soaring power dunk, the second a leap to save a ball flying out of court, which Spurs teammate Marco Belinelli flicked on to Patty Mills for a three-point swish.

On December 20, Australian basketball experienced a memorable "first" when San Antonio promoted Patty Mills and Aron Baynes into its starting quintet against Andrew Bogut's Golden State Warriors. At the time, Australia had four NBA players, Matthew Dellavedova now a part of the Cleveland Cavaliers roster. The historic NBA first of three Australians starting the same game was facilitated by the Spurs being down injured playmaker Tony Parker (shin) and coach Gregg Popovich's decision to rest veterans Tim Duncan and Manu Ginóbili. Mills played 34 minutes and scored 20 points and had two assists and three steals as the Spurs won 104-102.

Baynes battled Bogut for the opening tip, the ball going straight into Mills' hands; the three Aussies were first to touch the ball. One of the match highlights for Australian observers occurred late in the first half when Patty stole the ball from Bogut and drained a three-pointer from the top of the arc. That play was an instant hit on Twitter, Mills' name trending worldwide during the halftime break before the Spurs went on to claim the road victory.

"It was an unbelievable feeling to start an NBA match alongside two other Australians," an elated Mills wrote. "I don't think any of us realised what was actually occurring until just before tip-off. I got told earlier in the day that I was starting and I knew Aron Baynes was going to as well.

"We walked out on court together and I saw Andrew Bogut out of the corner of my eye and went up to him to wish him luck and all of a sudden it started to sink in what was happening. There were three of us Aussies starting the match and it was really special to be involved in what was a first for Australian basketball."

And in another first, FIBA revealed its four groups for the 2014 World Cup — the global federation having upgraded its four-yearly World Championship to a World Cup — had Australia in a very "gettable" pool. Given the tournament's sudden similarity to the most-watched sporting event in the world, soccer's World Cup, writers across Australia were desperate to steal a regular cliché from that sport by claiming the Boomers drew "the group of death".

In fact, Group D was a very promising prospect for the Aussies, with its matches also being played at Gran Canaria in Spain. That was where Boomers regular Brad Newley was playing professionally, fans living on the Canary Islands therefore gravitating to Australia as their "home" team. The Boomers were capable of grabbing first, second or third in the group. Typically, all of those options were preferable to finishing fourth and the cross-draw with Pool C's No.1 team — which, barring the (very) unforeseen, would, as usual, be the USA. In truth, there was no "group of death" for FIBA's intrapool matches.

Group A (Granada), "The Group of Severe Back Aches": 1. Spain; 2. Serbia; 3. France; 4. Brazil; 5. Egypt; 6. Iran. Group B (Seville), "The Group of a Very Nasty Migraine": 1. Philippines; 2. Senegal; 3. Puerto Rico; 4. Argentina; 5. Greece; 6. Croatia. Group C (Bilbao), "The Group of a Large and Painful Hickey": 1. Dominican Republic; 2. Turkey; 3. USA; 4. Finland; 5. New Zealand; 6. Ukraine. Group D (Canary Islands), "The Group of Promise": 1. Slovenia; 2. Lithuania; 3. Angola; 4. Korea; 5. Mexico; 6. Australia.

Slovenia and Lithuania would be challenging, but a top-three finish definitely was on the cards for Lemanis coaching at his first major international competition. "Every team that qualifies for a world championship is going to be tough in its own way," he said. "It's an interesting mix of teams there. We've simply got to come out and play well against the teams we are drawn against and give ourselves a chance of advancing. I've got great confidence in our group and I'm looking forward to going down to Gran Canaria. Hopefully we can get some support down there and have a great tournament."

San Antonio continued to flourish across the 2013–14 regular season, Patty Mills enjoying an NBA hot streak, pouring in a season and game high 32 points in the Spurs' come-from-behind win over Charlotte in February. The Spurs entered the final quarter trailing by a point before Mills went on a shooting spree, racking up 18 of his team's 30 final-quarter points to set up the victory. With starter Tony Parker continuing to play through injury, Mills had to be more assertive, scoring 71 points in less than 70 minutes on court in San Antonio's three previous games.

Against Charlotte, he connected on 10-of-13 field goal attempts, including 4-of-5 from three-point range and sank 8-of-9 free throws. He also dished four assists, snared seven rebounds and stole the ball twice, rescuing the Spurs on a night their starters struggled to find any shooting rhythm. "It was nothing different than any other game," a humble Mills said. "Just a couple more shots fell in for me, which was fortunate. They are the shots I usually take. I had no idea how many shots I had hit or missed. I was in the moment. Take the shot, if it missed, get back (on defence)".

On April 11, Patty scored 26 points as San Antonio tamed the Dallas Mavericks 109-100, the Spurs closing in on the NBA's best record. Tony Parker missed his second straight game with a back sprain but San Antonio notched its 61st win to sit atop the Western Conference standings. With the 2012–13 season the "one that got away", the Spurs' 2013–14 season of redemption indeed saw them finish on a 62-20 win-loss mark, not only the best record in the West but the best record in the NBA.

The Miami Heat finished on 54-28 behind Indiana Pacers' 56-26 in the Eastern Conference, ironically losing both their first game of the regular season and their last to Brett Brown's Philadelphia 76ers. Corralling the Mavericks late in the season was not the same challenge as in the first round of the Western Conference playoffs. Following a 90-85 Game One win, the Spurs found the series tied after a 113-92 Mavericks stampede. And suddenly the "season of redemption" was in serious jeopardy when they went down 108-109 in Game Three.

Patty enjoyed his first double-digit return of the playoffs when he contributed 10 points in a 93-89 Game Four win which tied the Spurs back at 2-2. A 109-103 Game Five success restored order, San Antonio now only needing one more win to advance. Dallas again had other ideas, its 113-111 Game Six upset now forcing this series to go the best-of-seven distance. Tony Parker's 32-point haul in the decider ensured San Antonio advanced, winning 119-96.

Having experienced a close shave against the Mavs, San Antonio left no doubts in Game One of the Conference semi finals against Portland, whacking the Trail Blazers 116-92, six Spurs led by Parker's 33 points, scoring in double figures, Patty one of them, with 10. Seven enjoyed double figures in the Spurs' equally emphatic 114-97 Game Two blitz and the series became mostly academic after San Antonio shook Game Three 118-103.

Portland took some measure of pleasure avoiding a 4-0 sweep by claiming Game Four 103-92 but the Blazers only truly delayed the inevitable. Danny Green and Kawhi Leonard had 22 points apiece and Mills 18 as the Spurs stormed into the Western Conference Final against Oklahoma City Thunder with a decisive 104-82 elimination Game Five, the series done 4-1. Tony Parker exited in the second quarter, Mills' 18 points further complemented by three steals, three rebounds and two assists in 26 minutes.

As much as anything, Patty's determination at the defensive end led to his increased role within the team. His harassment and aggressive defensive persona from the moment the ball was inbounded resulted in 79 steals, including 11 in 12 postseason games. His emergence also allowed Parker to relax on the bench and even mimic his understudy. Parker leapt from the bench for some serious towel-waving when Mills hit a big shot late in an earlier win over Portland. "No, he didn't, no he didn't," a delighted Mills exclaimed when told. "I wish I had seen that. I need to see some footage."

∽

OKC still boasted Kevin Durant, Russell Westbrook, New Zealand centre Steven Adams and multiple LA Lakers NBA champion Derek Fisher on its roster but copped a 122-105 welt in the series opener. There was no sign of any let up either in Game Two, San Antonio monstering the Thunder 112-77 for a 2-0 lead. Additionally working against OKC was the absence of centre Serge Ibaka through injury for the first games.

His return in Game Three turned the tables on San Antonio and brought the NBA's Western Conference Championship back to life with the Thunder winning 106-97 at home to cut the Spurs' series lead back to 2-1. Missing the first two Spurs' blowouts, Ibaka was big with 15 points on 6-of-7 shooting, seven boards and four blocks in 30 minutes.

OKC also looked considerably better when Kiwi centre Steven Adams was on the floor instead of overpaid centaur Kendrick Perkins. Adams had seven points, nine boards and four blocks in 28 intense-effort minutes off the bench. He even made Tim Duncan change shots which is something Perkins could never do. At any time Adams was on the floor and Perkins was not, OKC looked a more formidable opponent. That's without even mentioning the mind-blowing three-point shootout Russell Westbrook had with Manu Ginóbili to close the first half. That sort of skill and audacity is what makes the NBA riveting and compulsive viewing.

Westbrook did not slow down in Game Four either, leading all scorers with 40 points, Kevin Durant on 31 as Oklahoma City turned the

Western Conference Final into a real series, tying it at 2-2 with a 105-92 victory. No-one scored more than 14 points for the Spurs who now, unmistakably, were staring down the barrel.

Game Five then was a statement match for the Spurs, the chance to reassert their dominance which they did, convincingly winning 117-89, six players scoring in double figures and Patty Mills next with nine points, swishing three three-point baskets. OKC did not go without a fight in Game Six though, ultimately held off 112-107 as the Spurs clinched the Western Conference Final 4-2. This classic had to go to overtime, Boris Diaw the surprise performer with 26 points to pace the Spurs. Waiting on the other half of the draw were the Miami Heat, successful in claiming the Eastern Conference Championship with a 4-2 erasure of the Indiana Pacers.

San Antonio versus Miami was the championship rematch everyone was hankering to see. Gregg Popovich had done an incredible coaching job yet again to take his Spurs to the Western Conference Championship, keeping their appointment with the reigning champs for the NBA Championship. Even overlooking the fact he masterfully managed his troops to beat Oklahoma City Thunder to clinch Game Six after losing superstar Tony Parker for the second half (and overtime), it is difficult to describe how motivational he had been.

The Spurs blew the 2012–13 Championship Series and the aftermath of that disappointment had the potential to be devastating. Game Six, the Spurs up 3-2 and ahead by five with 30 seconds to play. Yet Miami comes back and its preseason investment in Ray Allen pays off when he swishes that step-back three — the shot of the year — to tie the game at its death. Miami then wins in overtime for 3-3 and escapes with a gripping Game Seven win for back-to-back titles, LeBron James Finals MVP again.

The psychological devastation that could have wrought on a lesser group truly was inestimable. Only one NBA team ever recovered after leading 3-2 in a seven-game Championship Series which it then lost, to play off again for the title a year later. Most were too devastated to recover. The Detroit Pistons lost in seven games at The Forum in Los Angeles after leading the Lakers 3-2 in 1988 but successfully regrouped to win it all in 1989.

But the potential for lamenting what might have been and wallowing in self-pity, if not self-admonishment, was huge and easily could have derailed the Spurs this time around. As Philadelphia 76ers coach and Spurs assistant from that 2012–13 campaign Brett Brown reiterated, the defeat preyed on everyone in the San Antonio organisation. "You think you're over it but then at some random moment, like you're stopped at some traffic lights or something, and your mind wanders and there it is again," he said. "The pain of losing it and how it unfolded."

Well aware of that, knowing he had an ageing team, knowing the window was closing for Tim Duncan, Manu Ginóbili and Parker, Popovich not only motivated and challenged his men, but the Spurs finished with the best record to now not only be back in the ultimate series but favoured by home-court advantage. It proved huge the previous year for Miami but now provided an amazing back story to further spur San Antonio.

CHAPTER SIX
FOREVER THE CHAMPION

"Does anybody know what today is?" The man asking the question was San Antonio Spurs head coach Gregg Popovich. The men being asked were the members of his team roster, sitting together in the video room, expecting to learn their assignments and adjustments for the playoff series to come. It was June 3, 2014, two days before the start of the best-of-seven NBA Final against the Miami Heat and it was Patty Mills swallowing deeply. "It wasn't just any practice or meeting. It was to prepare for the NBA Finals and the Miami Heat. We're all geared up, and that's the first thing he says," Mills told *Sports Illustrated* in a 2015 interview.

It was "Mabo Day", the unforgettable day of June 3 in 1992 when Australia's High Court ruled six to one in favour of Eddie Koiki Mabo and secured the validity of "native title" into Australian law. Eddie Mabo did not live to see his historic fight finally succeed against the injustice of denying his right to inherit land passed down through generations of his family. Sadly, he died five months earlier at 55. And though Eddie Mabo may not exactly have been Australia's equivalent of America's Martin Luther King, his quest for Indigenous equality was no less significant. Eddie Mabo also happened to be Patty Mills' great uncle on his father Benny's side.

Patty was speechless, dumbfounded as a portrait of his great uncle appeared on the screen and Popovich prepared to enlighten his team. Aron Baynes, the only other Aussie in the Spurs video room and who grew up in Mareeba, a small town in Far North Queensland, informed his peers: "It's Mabo Day," Mills still dealing with the surprise, a little overcome. "You could see that he was pretty moved by it all," Popovich said, the coach the lead architect in creating an inclusive team culture.

"Nine of our 15 (players) are from elsewhere, and I'm always looking for ways to make them part of the story." His theory was that his players having a deep awareness of each other's off-the-court stories helped bond them on the hardwood. "It builds camaraderie and helps them grow as people, and all that carries over," Popovich says. "They feel connected and engaged and do better work."

Argentinian swingman Manu Ginóbili saw *Rabbit-Proof Fence* — a movie about three Aboriginal girls brutally torn from their mother — on Mills' advice and Patty had shown his teammates video of himself doing island dances, explaining the choreographed narratives of island life and legends. "I started doing traditional dancing around the same time that I could walk, so I've been doing it for a long time and thoroughly enjoy it," he told Spurs Stories.

"Dancing for me was a very strong — along with songs and music, traditional songs and music — was a very strong gateway I guess, into my culture. My parents have inspired me through many different ways. The most specific has got to be how important culture and background is to me. And then, as I've gone on and understood more, I've understood my identity more. Our identity. The family's identity. And that's (en)abled me to grow to understand how I can then teach others about it."

Gregg Popovich bringing up Mabo Day definitely was a shock for Patty and straight out of left-field. The Indigenous land rights activist had a captivating story, banished to the mainland from Murray Island in Torres Strait as a 16-year-old after a romantic liaison Elders refused to sanction. Eddie Mabo worked on the wharves, railroads and cane fields before founding the Black Community School in Townsville. It taught and passed on the traditions of the Torres Strait to students of islander descent, with a focus on traditional music and dance.

The Black Community School sustained itself for 12 years as a vital centre for the Torres Strait community in Townsville, and at its peak in the late 1970s, had an enrolment of 45 students. In 1975, Mabo's achievements as an educator were recognised when he was asked to join the National Aboriginal Education Committee, an advisory body to the Commonwealth Education Department. It is where he met Yvonne Haynes, who one day would marry his nephew Benny Mills. Yvonne's commitment to the Indigenous cause was born of her own story, best represented by the multiple award-winning 2002 movie *Rabbit-Proof Fence*. Hence Patty's recommendation to teammate Manu Ginóbili to see it.

Befriending two university professors at James Cook University where he was working as a gardener, they brought to Eddie Mabo's attention the fact the state considered his father's plot on Murray Island as "Crown land". Incensed, Mabo learnt as much as he could about pertinent Australian law and at a land rights conference in Townsville in 1981, was joined by attorneys and activists anxious to mount a test case.

Benny Mills, Eddie Mabo's nephew on his mother's side, was in the room exhorting and encouraging his uncle as the legal team discussed the process and ways ahead. After all, it was Eddie's land by birthright, even if the state refused to acknowledge it. Mabo's legal team introducing "Malo's Law" was a master-stroke. It was the law by which people in the eastern Torres Strait lived.

Malo's Law states: "For thousands of years we have owned the land and Malo who was the Meriam centre of it made sure that members of the society were given land. They are our laws. We have Malo ra Gelar. It says that Malo keeps to his own place; Malo does not trespass in another man's property. Malo keeps his hands to himself. He does not touch what is not his. He does not permit his feet to carry him towards other men's property. His hands are not grasping. He holds them back. He does not wander from his path. He walks on tip-toe, silent and careful, leaving no signs to tell that this is the way he took." The god Malo came to Murray Island in the form of an octopus. The island's eight clans worked together through Malo's guidance.

Eddie Mabo was lead plaintiff in the legal challenge to the doctrine of "terra nullius", which broadly means land that is legally deemed unoccupied or uninhabited, prior to European settlement. That settlement began in 1788. It took a decade, but when the High Court ruled in Mabo's favour, "native title" was part of Australian law. The pre-existing legal regime "made the Indigenous inhabitants intruders in their own homes," one justice wrote in the landmark decision.

"We talk a lot about what we want to do after our careers are over," Patty's French teammate Boris Diaw said. "With Patty, it always comes back to his heritage. One thing he wants to do is help make Mabo Day a national holiday in Australia."

Whether Popovich invoking Patty's ancestry played any role in how well he competed in the NBA Final is cause for conjecture and possibly adds a mythical component to the Mills story, if not Popovich's. Suffice to say, Patty's contribution was hugely significant. Game One on June 5 was a 110-95 message San Antonio fired right across Miami's bow, letting the Heat know there would be no missed opportunities this time around. Yet then, lo and behold in Game Two, the Spurs missed their opportunity.

Seconds away from a 2-0 series lead, one of the Heat's alleged "Big Three", Chris Bosh, caught the ball in the corner and unleashed a three-point attempt. (He also dished a crucial feed.) Suddenly, Miami had stolen a 98-96 victory. The stunned crowd at the AT&T Center was in shock. The Spurs? More annoyed than anything else. That was not supposed to happen.

In Miami for Game Three, San Antonio showed no ill effects of its home reversal and, in tennis terms, having "lost serve" in Game Two, convincingly broke back 111-92 for a 2-1 series lead. Kawhi Leonard led the Spurs with 29 points, raising his game to another level. But next, a super-charged San Antonio seized the series by the scruff of the neck in Game Four, putting its Australian duo of Patty Mills and Aron Baynes within one win of joining Luc Longley and Andrew Gaze as NBA Champions by seizing a 3-1 lead in Miami.

The Spurs' second consecutive rout of the Heat in Miami – this time 107-86 – after dropping Game Two at home on that Chris Bosh triple, meant they now had the luxury of two chances to close it out at home, either in Game Five or Game Seven. (Not to mention Game Six as well, albeit in Miami.) In gambling parlance, the Spurs now were playing with the house money.

Patty, who had one of the series' great plays in Game Three when he recovered from trying to over-sell a LeBron James charge by hitting the floor, jumping up when the ball bounced loose and hurling himself after it to tip it forward for Manu Ginóbili to dunk on the breakaway, was great again in Game Four. In just 16 minutes of important action, he hit 5-of-8 from the floor, 4-of-6 dialling long distance, for 14 points. Kawhi Leonard had 20 and Tony Parker 19, with Patty's tally next in the team-oriented Spurs offence.

Mills also had a rebound and a couple of assists, James leading the Heat with 28 points and eight boards but the momentum now completely with the Spurs. The other two of the Heat's big three — Bosh and Dwyane Wade — had 22 points between them on a combined 8-of-24 shooting. Baynes also hit the court, with enough time to make another basket, just as he did to close Game Three.

While the Aussies still had a lot to do to win their first NBA championship rings, they now stood on the threshold of joining their Boomers assistant-coach Longley as Championship winners. Longley won three as a starter on the great Chicago Bulls threepeat. And Gaze also won a ring with San Antonio, though he was not in the active line-up during the Finals Series.

Forever the Champion

IN seven minutes of Game Five of the NBA Final, Patty Mills did more good for basketball, the Indigenous population and Australia than is even immediately quantifiable. The tenacious little guard with the heart of (green and) gold came back into the contest for San Antonio with 7:01 left in the third quarter and proceeded to turn the heat up on Miami. A baseline drive and reverse against a stranded LeBron James, drawing a charging foul from Ray Allen and four three-point swishes as he hit 5-of-5 shots for the quarter, made what was left of a contest into a resounding belting by the best basketball team on the planet.

It left the Spurs with one final period to complete their redemption after the previous year's seven-game heartbreak in Miami and they did it in a style every coach and player should be using as the blueprint for how to play this sport. The 104-87 devastation of the franchise whose star once promised "not one, not two… OK, maybe two" championships, made San Antonio's fifth NBA crown its finest fit, its tireless warhorse Tim Duncan admitting the win "even made last year OK".

Because not only did the Spurs win the best-of-seven Final 4-1 but the four wins were by 15, 19, 21 and 17 — conclusive proof of the ancient adage a champion team always will beat a team of champions. And thoroughly. Miami's solitary win was that lucky escape in Game Two. The Heat was never in the series again.

Spurs forward Kawhi Leonard winning Finals series MVP was a no-brainer, Miami's "big three" reduced to just King James (31 points, 10 rebounds, five assists, two blocks) as his cohorts Bosh and Dwyane Wade turned Miami's "MIA" abbreviation instead into Missing-In-Action. At just 22, Leonard became the youngest Finals MVP since Duncan in 1999 and the fourth youngest behind LA Lakers legend Earvin "Magic" Johnson, who twice won it while younger.

Gregg Popovich, the best coach in the NBA, said he did not call any plays for Leonard but he expected that would change. Not substantially though, the Spurs winning because, in Popovich's words, they didn't let the ball "stick", unselfishly and confidently moving it around to find the open man. Manu Ginóbili belied his days were numbered after an indifferent Finals in 2012–13 with a withering performance of artistry, including a sweet driving dunk in his 19 points as San Antonio spurned Miami's early heat with a second quarter fightback.

Leonard led with 22 points and 10 boards. After going 0-of-10, Tony Parker finished with 16 points, going 7-of-8 the rest of the way. Duncan was superb, his sheer ecstatic delight at Ginóbili's dunk revealing rare emotion from the 38-year-old. Boris Diaw had a game-high six assists with his nine boards and then there was Patty, making fans around Australia roar with pride and leap from their lounge-room chairs, joining the 18,000-plus celebrating in Texas and across the state.

And the world.

There were a lot of people shedding tears of joy and pride as Mills turned on the single-best NBA Finals quarter by an Australian, with all due respect to the great trail-blazing Luc Longley. Mills had commentators talking about his Torres Strait Islander father and Aboriginal mother, giving background on the landmark Mabo Day decision, talking about his uncle, Olympian Danny Morseu. When he heard about it later, Patty said: "I think for those people back home who watched it, whether Indigenous or not, being Australian and hearing it for themselves was special, and that was what I got a kick out of.

"It's Australian history and we are proud of it — to educate people not just in Australia but overseas was the next level. To use pro basketball to help educate people on our culture is something I've always tried to do — so to have it come off like that was special."

Mills became the poster child for all the values that people try to teach their kids — to believe in yourself and follow your dreams; that hard work and perseverance will pay off. On the sport's grandest stage, Patty Mills stood far taller than his 181cm and anyone who calls himself or herself an Australian stood tall with him. It wouldn't be for the last time, either.

He was outstanding as the Spurs reserves outscored the Heat's bench 22-2 in the first half, then 41-6 to the end of the third quarter when the game — and the Championship — had been wrested. Midway through the third quarter as the Spurs huddled in a time-out, Manu Ginóbili could sense the Heat were melting. Now was the figurative time to stamp the foot on their throats.

Mills confirmed just that in an interview with *The Age*'s Roy Ward. "There was a time out midway through the third quarter and it felt like there was an opportunity for us to take the game and Manu (Ginóbili) had sensed the same thing," he said. "As soon as he sat down he started screaming at everyone, picture him screaming in an exaggerated way — 'this is our moment, it's right now, it's right now, we need to do this, it's right now' — I will never forget that moment.

"I know I came into the game after that time-out or soon after and we managed to make the most of that opportunity. We managed to get some stops and make the most of them on the scoreboard."

Mills shot 14 of his 17 points in the frenetic run as San Antonio broke all Miami resistance, taking a 19-point lead into the last break. "He's a special guy," Popovich said of Patty after the game. "His energy has been important to us all year long. He's a real significant reason why we got to the Finals."

Patty wasn't alone in carrying the flag for Australia, Aron Baynes getting on late and converting two free throws — the NBL also able to take a measured bow. Patty chose to play in the league at Melbourne Tigers during the NBA's lockout season and Baynes was a member of the Cairns Taipans Academy. In one fell swoop, they doubled the number of Australians with NBA Championship rings as they joined Longley and Gaze.

For years the uninitiated and supposed "knowledgeable" pundits and basketball aficionados regularly mused how boring San Antonio was to watch. There was little love for the "unspectacular" Tim Duncan — as if his nickname of The Big Fundamental was some sort of negative — or the fact there were no spectacular superstars to get the highlight reels pumping. These philistines, brought up on a mind-numbing diet of NBA Action-type shows and spoon-fed on streetball and dunk comps, really were shown how gloriously basketball's *team* game can be played.

NBA star, ex-Golden State Warriors coach and ESPN commentator Mark Jackson described San Antonio's ball movement and team play as "a thing of beauty". Anyone who truly understands basketball knows exactly what he meant. In a self-absorbed age of me-me-me, it was refreshingly joyous. This was and forever will remain a true championship team. "You represent your family, mum and dad, your school and your culture," Mills says. "Now that I get a chance on the big stage, it's even more important to remember where I came from."

As Mills told Roy Ward, the emotional Spurs' celebrations were something of a blur, especially after the devastation of the previous season's seven-game defeat. "We were a lot closer than a couple of shots last year — it was just one rebound," he said. "(That loss) was on everyone's faces in the way they carried themselves all year — everyone's determination and passion was evident. We were focused on taking our opportunities and not leaving it to one shot or one rebound or one free-throw miss."

The post-game locker-room champagne fiesta and celebration was one thing. But when the team gathered together the next day, the reality of their achievement sank in. "When just us players and coaches were in the one, small room, it started to make sense then," Mills said, still processing the major role he played in the ultimate success. "No, no, never did I think I would do that — that will be the hardest part of this process," he said. "To understand the impact I had on the game and being involved in those moments is just so special that there is going to be a stage when I will need to sit down by myself and reflect on it.

"You just try to live in the moment (on court) and make the most of small opportunities. As Coach Popovich says, you either make shots or you don't — then you live with the results. But I was lucky enough those shots were hitting on the day. A couple of close friends have said to me I was 1-of-4 or 1-of-5 shooting going into halftime and I didn't even know that.

"I had no clue, but the feeling I had felt like I had already made a few shots. I think that is the mentality you have as a shooter — if it misses you go on to the next one and that is the feeling I had going into the second half."

Popovich, who was born to a Serbian father and a Croatian mother, took great personal pleasure in not only combining his eclectic mix of US and foreign players, but learning and sharing information about his players' lives and backgrounds. His attitude was a staunch "park your ego at the door". He coached players who, as he often has said, "have gotten over themselves".

Patty's trek from seldom-used sub to major contributor was, he felt, because of the role Popovich forged for him. "I came to an understanding very early on (in San Antonio) that you have to remember who you are as a player," Mills said. "I'm not a Steve Nash or a Magic Johnson who is going to come out and throw 15 assists and do all these crazy passes. That is not me and it's not my game.

"I understand my game better and what I do well, what I do is shoot the ball and find ways to score and that was the feedback from the coaches to me — remember who you are and let the ball fly." Mills' third season in San Antonio yielded 10.2 points, 2.1 rebounds and 1.8 assists in 18.9 minutes, his career-high to that point. He doubled his points from 5.1 in 2012–13 and his minutes went up from 11.3 a game as he meshed his strong shooting with pressure defence.

"I think it's a combination of being given a role from the coaching staff, one, and then two, understanding that role and sticking to it," Mills said. "You don't do more than that, just meet that expectation. Everyone understood that and we learnt that if everyone did that and had faith in each other, we could progress rapidly together. Everyone understood that from day one and carried it throughout the year."

Covering himself in the Torres Strait Island flag in honour of his family, and handing Aron Baynes the Australian flag, Mills was the personification of unbridled joy. His parents Benny and Yvonne, Danny Morseu and Mills' then girlfriend — now wife — Alyssa Levesque all were part of the crowd and celebration in San Antonio.

"That is how it was, you have all these emotions and feelings — you are looking here and looking there and just trying to work out how to react to such an unbelievable achievement," Patty said. "My mum and dad and uncle were in the crowd, so was my girlfriend who has been such a big part of this journey for me and then my US friends, who have become family, were there as well.

"So I was trying to locate them on the court and then to see how many fans were still in the stands celebrating — it was a blur."

Mills' Boomers running mate, Joe Ingles could not have been more delighted Patty "stole the spotlight", capturing nationwide and even international attention for his outstanding exploits in that series clinching Game Five win. "Just the circumstances of the game, the series, what Patty did in taking that game, he really broke it open," Ingles said. "It wasn't only Patty — Manu Ginóbili was great — but what Patty did was pretty special and he deserves all the limelight and I'm happy for him to have it. I was rapt for him."

In any other year, Adelaide-born Ingles, 26, would have been feted across the Australian basketball community for his own outstanding international season, sweeping the triple-crown of the Israeli Cup, the Euroleague

Championship and the Israeli Championship with Maccabi Tel Aviv. The Euroleague rates behind only the NBA in international prestige.

"I said it in my first interview in Israel that I thought we had a team which could win everything," Ingles said, his words prophetic and anything but false bravado. "After my time at Barca (Barcelona), I just thought that situation at Maccabi would be ideal. I wanted to go somewhere and play and be a big part of it."

Maccabi and Ingles was a match made in heaven, initially at least. Coach David Blatt, who heavily recruited Ingles, cut into his court-time as the season wore on. But much like Patty Mills had in the NBA and showing the same true Aussie team spirit, when your club is achieving success, you play your role in that, however lean it may become. "We had a pretty special year and I didn't want my (lack of) court-time to become any sort of distraction," Ingles said.

"We (Ingles and Blatt) got along fine and during the last off-season, he was pushing me to join him at Maccabi. Maybe I should have taken the Memphis (NBA) deal but I don't regret going to Maccabi. It was a great year to be part of and a pretty special one with what we achieved."

The NBA's Memphis Grizzlies had offered Ingles a one-year guaranteed contract, with a team option for the second year. But Maccabi Tel Aviv was more attractive with the chance to be a contributor and also for the life experience. "I've never played NBA and I won't retire disappointed if I don't," he said at the time. "At the same time, if an opportunity comes, I'd love to do it." Opportunity, in fact, was waiting just around the corner for Ingles in the NBA, an opportunity he would seize with both hands, ultimately flourishing at the Utah Jazz.

Flourishing was the story of Patty Mills' 2013–14 NBA championship campaign. Having recognised his own shortcomings, he made the decision to step up in every way, then did it. Outrageously blunt Spurs coach Gregg Popovich put it this way: "He was a little fat ass. He had too much junk in the trunk. His decision making wasn't great, and he wasn't in great shape. He changed his entire body. He came back svelte and cut and understood you have to make better decisions, point-guard type decisions. He did all those things better and he earned it. He's been real important to us, obviously."

Understanding the sometimes-gruff public demeanour of his coach, Patty was unfazed by the comments, coming, as they did, on the back of the title win. "There is no way at all I would be able to play this long or strong for that amount of time last year," Mills said. "I think my fitness base has given me the ability to play stronger for longer periods of time. It's definitely helped for sure, I'm glad I did it." As for Pop's comment? "I took that as a compliment, if anything," he said. And he meant it.

It was almost time for Patty Mills to turn his attention to the next Boomers campaign, the FIBA World Cup in Spain, NBA free agency also on the radar. "Everyone is asking me about it but with the amount of hard work and energy that has gone into this year with the Spurs — you kind of don't want anything else to ruin this moment that we have worked so hard for — I'm going to enjoy it to the max," Mills said. "I haven't thought about anything after that but playing for Australia is very important to me and we will play when we come to Spain."

Aron Baynes was waiting to ascertain whether the Spurs would take up a team option to sign him for the next season, but intimated he definitely would play for the Boomers, regardless what state his contract was in. Mills initially intended to take a few weeks of rest in San Antonio, while soaking up the celebrations. "The Spurs won't be coming together again until September and with Australian commitments, I really only have about two weeks to rest," Mills said.

"I think I will be doing nothing at all and just resting here in San Antonio. I never thought this dream would become real but it has." It did have to *feel* surreal, becoming an NBA champion as someone barely six feet tall, with a grandfather who was a pearl diver in Torres Strait and a grandmother raised in a mission home out "in the bush". When Patty was two, the grandfather in question, Sam Mills, put up a basketball hoop outside his home on Thursday Island. It was expressly so Patty could practice his shooting during visits to the Strait. He was shooting the ball at the age of two, playing for Shadows in Canberra at four, and fearless throughout.

His plans to "soak up the celebrations" in San Antonio though were to be short-lived. Just how good and how courageous Patty was through that epic 2013–14 season became glaringly apparent, even beyond the analytics which showed he covered more distance per 48 minutes than any other player in the NBA. There was the nagging issue, however, of his persistent shoulder soreness.

Scans revealed he would need an off-season operation to repair the torn rotator cuff in his right shoulder — his shooting shoulder — and meant he would miss up to four months of the 2014–15 NBA season. He carried the injury through most of San Antonio's title-winning run and was about to embark on explorations of his newly-acquired free agency when he discovered the necessity for shoulder surgery.

"I haven't been through free-agency before. Having this injury changes everything again," Patty told the *Canberra Times*' Chris Dutton. "I have no idea how it works, but I'm guessing it will affect my next deal. But it's out of my hands. It is what it is. We've got to make the most of the situation and move on."

After his quality season and break-out performance in the championship series, Mills was poised to test his value on the NBA open market, a multi-million dollar deal likely and the New York Knicks among possible suitors. While there were now concerns what the future may hold, it remained difficult not to still be further impressed considering he was managing a wear-and-tear shoulder issue throughout.

"It was a shock," Mills said. "I didn't know it would be this bad. You think nothing can deflate you (after winning a championship). I had to find a way to process the injury news and what's going to happen. It's not until now that it's sinking in. It's going to be a brutal recovery process. I'll go straight into surgery, but I'm told the next four-to-six weeks I won't be able to do anything, and it will be brutal."

But the worst impact for Patty was that the injury, surgery, rehabilitation and recovery would rule him out of the 2014 FIBA World Cup where, yet again, confidence was high Australia could claim its maiden international medal at one of the "majors" — an Olympics or World Cup. It was devastating news.

"Missing the Boomers is the toughest of it all," he said "I have a tremendous amount of pride to play for Australia. This is a huge year for the team... It's an exciting time and I've told the boys I'm going to be involved in any way I can. I have all the faith in the world this team can go and get something done. It's just another hump in the road, some more adversity that I've got to deal with.

"I've dealt with things before, but not like this. It's going to be tough, but it's going to build my character and make me a stronger person. I'm going to come out of this more hungry and determined." Surgery though and potentially seven months on the sidelines definitely gutted the tenacious Aussie star.

No one following Australian basketball could have taken the news well but the man himself was shattered. Wearing the green-and-gold, representing Australia, representing Torres Strait Islanders, representing the Aboriginal community, representing Indigenous people — hell, representing *all* Australians on the world stage — his fondest passion. "I feel for Patty," Australian coach Andrej Lemanis said. "He loves representing his country and this would be devastating for him."

No sooner had the news broken, than Mills, not surprisingly a widely sought free agent after his performances in the NBA Finals, was retained by the champion San Antonio Spurs for a further three years and a reported $12 million. Progressing from a guy waving a towel to one waving a flag, Patty was a signing priority for the Spurs, even if his injury meant missing the first two months of the 2014–15 season.

The decision to commit $12 million to keep an injured free agent had everything to do with the respect Patty had from the coach, teammates and Spurs management alike, not to mention diving on all those loose balls with a battered shoulder. Popovich says, "It wasn't even a question. Obviously he can shoot the basketball and has a lot of energy. But he's beloved on this team for his enthusiasm, his kindness, his understated gravitas. As long as I'm here, he's going to be here. Unless we can't afford him."

Brett Brown, now head coach at the Philadelphia 76ers, watched the Spurs' season unfold from afar but still thoroughly enjoyed San Antonio reversing the championship result. "More from just a human standpoint, when you see the people navigate through that gut-wrenching loss (last year) and come out bigger and better," Brown said.

"To see those people react that way, my 12 NBA years were with them and it was a hell of a story. Patty Mills, you just see him and the thing that makes me most happy is we've shared in his journey. He waved a towel in Portland, had the injury, the experience (playing) in China. I helped him get to San Antonio ahead of the Boomers (Olympic campaign).

"Then he finds a way to grab a position, then comes back in such great shape. You see his growth as a teammate and then to a legitimate piece of a championship team. You see it from A-to-Z."

CHAPTER SEVEN
BALA LAZZA AND THE WORLD

Mills' injury was a massive blow for the Boomers who already had lost Andrew Bogut (rehabilitation from injury) and Aleks Maric from their 2014 FIBA World Cup medal assault. "Aleks just needs a break from the basketball treadmill and I understand that," Australian coach Andrej Lemanis said. "He needs a long period off."

The unforeseen absence of Mills, Australia's leading scorer, had the Boomers' new boss lamenting his star's bad luck, while adopting his customary philosophical viewpoint. As much as missing Mills was a tragedy for the Boomers, it opened the door for players such as Damian Martin and Adam Gibson, while accelerating the international rise of NBA #5 draft pick Dante Exum. Gathering himself from his own disappointment for Mills, Lemanis said it opened the possibilities for other players.

"There are opportunities that flow from it," he said. "Patty Mills was going to play 30-plus minutes per game and that void has to be filled somehow." Lemanis said there were ways to generate offence as a team to cover Mills' scoring prowess. "Dante is an interesting one," he said. "He will get his opportunities in the lead up and we'll see what he does with them."

Lemanis saw Exum more as a point guard than a shooter or combo guard, liking his work with the ball, decision-making and willingness to pass. "And I think he's a more effective scorer with the ball in his hands." Lemanis said Matthew Dellavedova and Mills would most likely have started together in Spain at the Worlds, sharing playmaking duties. "Delly played some two (off guard) with Kyrie Irving (at Cleveland Cavs) and we do run that way with him and Patty," Lemanis said, moving somewhat "back to the future" by revisiting a past when teams just had two guards, distinctions such as "point" or "shooting" largely irrelevant. "The game is drifting that way," Lemanis admitted. "But this will definitely accelerate Dante's development."

Melbourne Tigers' dual MVP Chris Goulding also now was a definite selection. "Chris is doing well in his NBA work-outs and will be playing in the (NBA) summer league so yes, he's very much in calculations and you can presume he will be in the squad," Lemanis said. Ultimately, he was in the team, along with regulars Joe Ingles, Aron Baynes, Matthew Dellavedova, Brad Newley and David Andersen, plus Adam Gibson, Ryan Broekhoff, Cam Bairstow, Brock Motum, Nate Jawai and Dante Exum. Jawai's dream of sharing the international stage with his fellow Indigenous star Patty Mills once again was dashed.

Arguably the most notable omission was Ben Simmons. The 18-year-old prodigy tweeted: "(I'm) really disappointed (I) didn't make the world's team, good luck to all the guys who did #grindtime" Simmons, son of Melbourne Tigers NBL import Dave, had committed to attend Louisiana State University where Eddie Palubinskas, Australia's first player to top score an Olympics, cut his college teeth.

It already was evident Simmons would become a marquee player down the line, but in not wishing to rush too many new, young faces in too soon, Lemanis may inadvertently have rocked the young man's desire to play for Australia. He had more than held his own among the men at the previous year's Oceania Series with the Boomers but now returned to Montverde Academy in Orlando to continue his high schooling.

"Ben just wasn't ready yet," Lemanis said. "He will be a good player and will certainly feature in Boomers campaigns in the future. But he has been competing against high school kids. He is not far away." He probably still isn't.

"The team has very good chemistry," Lemanis observed. There also had been a noticeable attitude shift from the hopeful and tentative days of medal dreaming to a more confident and forthright approach, even with Mills and Bogut missing.

Dual-Olympian and Euroleague champion Joe Ingles was outspoken about Australia's medal chance in Spain. "We're not afraid to say it's going to be hard and we're not afraid to say it's going to be our goal over there to get a medal," he reiterated. "We're not going to change our goals after a few injuries."

No NBA champion ever took the Larry O'Brien Trophy — the championship trophy — "to the people", a la Stanley Cup-style, prior to 2014. But these Spurs, a mix of foreign players and Americans, the ultimate example of "team", were a different bunch. Matt Bonner was first to seek permission to take the trophy "on the road" back to New Hampshire for the annual music festival. The word spread quickly through the San Antonio camp when he received the "all clear" to do it.

Manu Ginóbili jumped the queue, taking the trophy home to Argentina before it also spent time "touring" across five states of the US, and also Brazil, Canada, France and Italy. The Spurs designed the itinerary, the trophy visiting Australia and six cities in seven days, with interviews and an array of meet-and-greets for Patty Mills and Aron Baynes. The duo handled the events with typical candour, good humour and grace, Mills not even mildly discouraged by his right arm being in a sling, courtesy of his shoulder surgery. In Torres Strait language, "bala" means brother. With "Lazza" the Aussie slang for Larry, in this case as in the *Larry* O'Brien Trophy, Patty even christened their two-foot-tall, gold-plated treasure "Bala Lazza".

In Melbourne, the Trophy Tour almost suffered an unexpected mishap when Mills and Baynes danced around, video-bombing Fox Sports Australia reporter Julian de Stoop. Reporting on a live television cross from outside the Lexus Centre, headquarters of the AFL's Collingwood Football Club, de Stoop did not realise it was Mills and Baynes simply playing around, even though they mentioned the trophy during their brief shenanigans.

As they carried Bala Lazza behind him, laughing and exuberant, he pushed Mills in the chest, fortunately not near his injured arm, and commented: "Get off boys, off... There's always some idiots out down here." Back in the studio, they could not let that pass, informing an acutely embarrassed de Stoop that he had "palmed off none other than Patty Mills, with the trophy".

"Yeah, highly embarrassed about that now. I'll have to apologise to him down the track," de Stoop admitted. "I had no idea it was him. I just thought it was another couple of Collingwood nuffies doing their thing." Later de Stoop explained: "One of the hardest things about reporting live is your surrounding environment. Anything can happen. Rowdy fans, background noise, planes roaring overhead — it's all part of the business. I thought Mills and Baynes were a couple of Collingwood punters. Oops. I guess the NBA championship trophy — which has been beamed around the world countless times over the years —should've given it away, but my mind was fixed on reporting the latest news on Nick Maxwell, Dane Swan and the Pies.

"I can honestly say that this is the first time I've been punked by a bloke with a newly-minted three-year, $12 million NBA contract. And I'm pretty confident in saying that I've never previously been photobombed with a major US sporting trophy."

In Sydney, there was no such drama — or mischievous mayhem — as Bala Lazza was posed beside international landmarks the Opera House and the Harbour Bridge. And in Canberra, about a thousand fans lined up for autographs and selfies, the line filing around a city block. When the Trophy Tour reached the Thursday Island ferry wharf, the Spurs' delegation was given a traditional welcome. Met by Mills family members and Elders, the dance troupe from Murray Island featured one of Patty's aunts and Eddie's descendants, Betty Mabo.

They danced again into the twilight and on through an evening feast, a traditional dance around Bala Lazza which Mills and his family members could not resist joining. "I wanted to jump in from the get-go," Patty said. "But I was in the sling, and if there was video, I didn't know what Pop would say. Then I thought: 'You know, I'll deal with Pop back in San Antonio'." Who knew what Pop also may have said if he saw the incident with de Stoop outside the Lexus Centre? He most likely would have laughed, as did most people who saw it.

Bala Lazza had further duties to perform before Patty left the island. Gently he put the trophy between his grandparents' tombstones in Greenhill Cemetery. He also placed it in his grandfather's favourite chair on the balcony of Sam Mills' old home. There is a much-loved family photograph of a 10-year-old Patrick shooting the ball at the basket his grandfather erected. The hoop long since removed, Patty posed Bala Lazza for a photograph, signifying his journey's early beginnings and what unprecedented success it now had attained.

The Boomers were not intentionally trying to hammer the point but yes, they were going to Spain in pursuit of a World Cup medal. Fifth place remained Australia's best return from a World Championship and starting point guard Matthew Dellavedova — a London Olympian in 2012 — was excited about what lay in store at the first major international campaign for coach Andrej Lemanis.

"It's a pretty balanced team," said the impressive young guard who joined Andrew Bogut, Patty Mills and Aron Baynes in the NBA for the fateful 2013–14 season. "Defensively we'll get after it and offensively, well, without Patty we will have to find the points in other ways. Obviously it's really disappointing for Patty he can't play.

"You know how much it means to him playing for the Boomers, especially after the season he's had. No one person will replace his scoring. There will be a lot of ball movement."

An NBA season with the Cleveland Cavaliers alongside Melbourne-born point guard Kyrie Irving changed Dellavedova's life and it would evolve even further in the next season with LeBron James returning from Miami Heat as a teammate. In the meantime, it was great to be home among his Australian contemporaries. "I think I forgot how much fun it is to train and play with the (Boomers) boys," he said. "It's been even better than I remember — how focused everyone is on doing what's best for the group."

The stated goal of a podium finish kept the team's aspirations very keenly focused, which only made for positive, tough and highly-competitive sessions. Everyone was pushing each other to be the best they could be. "Overall we're a pretty young team but there's some very experienced players too, (such as) David Andersen, Joe Ingles, Brad Newley," Dellavedova said.

"It's a good mix with some great inside targets for us." Australian basketball fans who watched the London Olympics, knew to expect more of that undeniably spectacular Dellavedova-Baynes "pick-and-roll for the dunk" action. "It's fun combining with Baynesy," Dellavedova said. "He sets such good screens you have to reward him on the roll."

At the London Games after Australia thrillingly upset Russia on Mills' siren-beating three-pointer, David Blatt, coach of the Russian Federation, had some kind words for Dellavedova. "He came up after and said: 'Good game' — he remembered Baynesy and I running the pick-and-roll."

Interesting how the universe deals its cards. Blatt, who then coached Maccabi Tel Aviv to the Euroleague Championship with dual-Olympian Joe Ingles in his line-up, now was the new head coach at the Cleveland

Cavaliers. "He coached us at Summer League," Dellavedova said, the Maryborough junior excited by the prospect of playing and training with LeBron James, at the time the world's best player.

"In the NBA, anything can happen," Dellavedova said. "I've already had five-six teammates traded. (My goal is) to keep getting better every day and do whatever the team needs to help us win. That's what I did last year and it worked well. This season is about trying to consolidate."

Clearly Dellavedova wanted to stay in Cleveland, Australian NBA fans salivating at the prospect of the Cavs and the champion Spurs going head-to-head for a Championship, meaning Delly and Patty — two of St Mary's College's all-time greats — going head-to-head as well. "That would be great," Delly agreed. The only thing better than trail-blazing Aussie Luc Longley winning an NBA Championship was two Aussie teammates winning one.

Utah Jazz soon also would boast a pair of Aussies, with Dante Exum taken at #5 in the NBA Draft and Joe Ingles getting a call-up as the season was about to start. Brock Motum also forced his way into the Jazz's camp with his performances at Summer League in Las Vegas but was unable to snare a roster spot. Exum was the one all eyes were on and, before he was beset with injuries, the youngster handled the additional pressure with genuine aplomb.

"Dante will contribute (in Spain) and has a really, really bright future," Dellavedova said. "He did well at (Boomers) camp and showed why he was taken so high in the draft." Dellavedova believed that after Summer League, Exum's steppingstone into the NBA via the World Cup would prepare him well, playing against men and "international big bodies".

"It's a big step up for him but having I think 10 practice games, then the World Cup leading into the NBA will be a big help," Dellavedova said. "It's an 82-game schedule and the key thing is to take care of your body. The number of games, plus the travel, can take its toll."

That said, it had to be mentally difficult for players to always bring their A-game when, for example, it might randomly be Game #47 or #63 on the schedule. "In the situation I was in? Every night you're fighting for your NBA career so it was pretty easy to get up for every game," Dellavedova said. "There's a lot of people who'd kill to have your job so motivation wasn't an issue for me."

Seeing his family in the stands at a Cavs game, knowing how much his parents and sisters contributed to get him where he was, Dellavedova never would take it for granted. But being based in the USA had its downside. "Apart from family and friends, I think I miss the footy and the banter that goes with it," the dyed-in-the-wool Collingwood fan said. He lost a bet to Boomers teammate and Hawthorn fan Ingles when his beloved Magpies went down to the Hawks, and also heard it from Mills, the Crows' ambassador, when Adelaide lowered Collingwood's colours. It comes with the tribal nature of football following.

Mills' pending absence from the Boomers meant more responsibility for Dellavedova in Spain. "I will have to take on more of a leadership role," he said.

Heading to the FIBA World Cup without Patty Mills in tow still was an unusual experience for the core group of Boomers who knew him as one of the team's leading culture drivers. Their opening round 80-90 loss to Slovenia in Gran Canaria was a reminder of the harsh realities of international play. Baynes led the Aussies with 21 points at 62 per cent and seven rebounds, Goran Dragic with the identical numbers for Slovenia. David Andersen was next for the Boomers with 14 points, Brad Newley 13, Joe Ingles 12.

Hardly an auspicious start, the Boomers bounced back by trouncing Korea 89-55, in their second match of intragroup play. They assuredly still looked like a work-in-progress but there was a distinct advance from their opening night jitters. Joe Ingles played a complete game — which was not bad considering he only saw less than half a game of court-time — Aron Baynes stayed a constant with a 13-point, 10-rebound double-double, and Matthew Dellavedova resembled the player Australia now needed him to be. Ryan Broekhoff and Brock Motum also were value-for-minutes played.

Broekhoff saw some action during Australia's nine-match European build-up to the Worlds and was so consistently good, forced his way into the starting line-up in Gran Canaria. Dellavedova, Ingles, Andersen and Baynes had their spots locked away, but Broekhoff, working his way from the team's 12th man to first five was the shock and spoke volumes about him.

"With any team, it's who plays best together," Lemanis said. "He's certainly done well for where he was when we selected the team. He's certainly made the most of his opportunities." As in most international tournaments, the key for the Aussies was to stay away from a crossover match-up against the USA. Winning Group D or coming third made it possible for the Boomers to avoid the USA until beyond the quarterfinal stage. Finishing second or fourth meant potential disaster.

Fourth now would mean a round-of-16 crossover against the Group C winner, which would be the USA. Second potentially meant running into the Americans in the quarterfinals. Against Lithuania, Joe Ingles led an amazing onslaught which saw the Boomers ahead 30-20 after one, then holding the Baltic champs to an eight-point second period to lead 47-28 at halftime.

Naturally Lithuania rallied but to little avail, Australia winning 82-75, Ingles scoring 18 points at 64 per cent, with four assists. Baynes had 14 points with eight rebounds, Dellavedova 13 points and Brad Newley 10. "We forced them into 22 turnovers and that obviously ignited some of our offence for us," Lemanis said.

Mexico fell 62-70 as Aron Baynes scored 21 points, Brad Newley 12 and

Ryan Broekhoff 10. The win meant Australia would advance from the group stage, where it finished now of greater interest. A loss to minnow Angola meant a third-place conclusion — and no chance of seeing the USA before the semi finals. It did not guarantee it, but made it likely, with the loser of the Lithuania-Slovenia game facing that American prospect.

When Australia did lose to Angola, Slovenian media was outraged, accusing Lemanis of throwing the game. And that was despite the fact Slovenia only had to beat Lithuania to claim first place in the group. "Nobody likes losing," Lemanis said of Australia's 83-91 defeat to the African nation. "That doesn't guarantee us third spot. We have no control over that (Slovenia-Lithuania) game. We always, as Australians, compete the right way."

Chris Goulding had an international career-high 22 points, including six three-pointers and Lemanis afforded extra time for Dante Exum, Brock Motum, Cam Bairstow and Nate Jawai who responded with points returns of 12, 13, 11 and 10 respectively. The coach's decision to rest Joe Ingles and Aron Baynes, while only giving Dellavedova and Andersen four minutes each, raised the fury of the Slovenians and even ultimately the ire of FIBA.

And it only became a more heated debate when Slovenia lost to Lithuania 64-67, only scoring two points in the final quarter. As a result, Lithuania finished first in Group D, Slovenia second, Australia third and Mexico fourth. It gave Australia a round-of-16 knock-out match against Group C's second placegetter, Turkey. An enraged Goran Dragic, Slovenia's NBA star, took to Twitter, posting: "Basketball is a beautiful sport, there is no room for fixing the game like today Australia vs Angola! @FIBA should do something about that!"

Typically, Europe-centric FIBA reacted to the accusation by its star, launching a sudden investigation into Australia allegedly "tanking" against Angola. "The on-court behaviour displayed by Australia in that game generated huge disappointment by basketball fans and experts," FIBA said in a statement. "It is widely suspected that Australia lost that game in order to avoid having to face the reigning world champions USA until the semi-finals. Basketball Australia has an opportunity to state its case before FIBA decides whether and to what extent disciplinary sanctions shall be imposed."

BA cooperated fully and nothing came of the "investigation". Not until the Rio Olympics anyway, where it widely was suspected FIBA took its own subtle revenge with a couple of late calls in the Boomers' bronze medal game against Spain. Suffice to say Australian basketball greats such as Andrew Gaze, Andrew Bogut and Phil Smyth lined up to admonish FIBA for tainting the nation's international reputation when all Slovenia had to do to avoid an eventual confrontation with the US was beat Lithuania.

Much of the debate was moot though when Australia, arguably distracted by the sudden furore, lost its round-of-16 game to Turkey 64-65. It was not really until the final few minutes of that critical game that Patty Mills' absence from the Boomers was starkly evident and pronounced. The difference between the world #7 ranked Turks and Australia was brutal. The Boomers led 64-59 with the final, fateful 62 seconds to go and Turkey needed a hero. Emir Preldzic stepped up not once, but twice nailing miraculous three-pointers to steal the win.

In between them, Australia had a 24-second shot-clock violation trying to find a player to take the right shot. When Preldzic dribbled down the clock ahead of his second super shot, his confidence was so high, he could have been in the heavens sitting on God's lap. That still gave the Boomers five seconds, but even after Lemanis drew up a play, they flubbed it. Twice in the last minute, Australia did not get a shot off.

Credit was due to Turkey's defence to some extent — while also lamenting the Aussies aborting nine of 19 free throws — but Mills would have taken or created shots in that excruciating environment. Throughout the intragroup stage, the Boomers found ways to win, Aron Baynes exceptional at times and Joe Ingles starring. Ryan Broekhoff was the revelation of the World Cup with his stellar outside shooting and less acknowledged but equally significant defensive work.

Preldzic hardly sniffed the ball when Broekhoff defended him through the first half. Australia had Turkey on the ropes, ahead 48-36 with 5:56 left in the third quarter, the Turks with a bench technical foul on top of an unsportsmanlike foul. But the Boomers added just two free throws for the rest of the quarter, again unable to deliver the killer blow or, more accurately perhaps, without Mills, the man whose very DNA made him the one to deliver it. Baynes led the way with 15 points, Dellavedova with 13 and Ingles 10. And, once again, Australia came up short.

Had Patty Mills not required shoulder surgery, he not only would have been the first player selected for the World Cup campaign but would have guaranteed the Boomers made it at least to the quarterfinal stage, where Turkey then was eliminated by Lithuania. Through the group phase, the Boomers found a way without him. But when the offence broke down against Turkey, his absence was the difference between medalling or merely meddling.

Slovenia brushed past Dominican Republic in the round-of-16 but was crushed 119-76 by the USA in their quarterfinal. The Americans belted Serbia 129-92 for the gold and France beat Lithuania 95-93 for the bronze. Not for the last time, the Boomers came home empty-handed.

CHAPTER EIGHT
PUTTING THE BOOTS INTO WELLINGTON

Finding the magic again was a definite challenge for the Spurs in their 2014–15 NBA title-defence. Patty Mills was missing when the season tipped off and starters Tony Parker, Finals MVP Kawhi Leonard and Brazilian centre Tiago Splitter, all suffered significant injury issues costing them games. Consequently, finding that rhythm and confidence of the championship run was easier said than done. "I want the ball to move like it did last year in the playoffs, and I haven't seen that yet," coach Gregg Popovich said. "We've had guys who've been out coming back, pressing a little bit and wanting it too much, instead of trusting each other and the system."

Popovich was speaking before a game against Sacramento Kings, the Spurs' first home match after their annual three-week exile accommodating the rodeo coming to San Antonio. Down by a point after a quarter, they were ahead by double figures at halftime and wound up winning by 27.

There were flashes of the slick ball rotation and touch passing which sent Miami packing the previous year, and Patty Mills was his usual cool self in his familiar role as Parker's backup. "He's just beginning," Popovich said, "to feel his oats again." But it remained a struggle for the Spurs, Danny Green and Boris Diaw the only real constants, both managing to play in 81 of the 82 regular season games, Tim Duncan 77, Aron Baynes and Manu Ginóbili both 70.

After six months out with the shoulder surgery, Patty suited for 51 matches, Tiago Splitter 52 as San Antonio finished strongly, winning 11 consecutive games in its final 12 to take its win-loss record to 55-27, its

16th straight regular season with 50 or more wins. That was good enough for sixth in the Western Conference and a best-of-seven first round final against the Los Angeles Clippers of Chris Paul, Blake Griffin, DeAndre Jordan and Co.

Dropping Game One 92-107 in Los Angeles was no huge surprise. San Antonio winning Game Two on the road, and in overtime 111-107 after scores were deadlocked 94-94 at the end of regulation, well *that* may have shocked some. It didn't shock any fans of Patty Mills who sank the two key free throws with eight seconds left in regulation that sent the game to its five-minute extension. Tim Duncan led the Spurs with 28 points and 11 rebounds, Kawhi Leonard scoring 23 and Patty adding 18 points — including 6-of-6 free throws — in 19 efficient minutes.

A comprehensive 100-73 win in San Antonio gave the Spurs a 2-1 series lead as they looked every inch the defending champion. The Clippers trailed 16-25 after the first quarter and suffered another meltdown when the Spurs went 24-11 in the third. It was Chris Paul's turn to ignite his team in Game Four, the playmaker leading the Clippers with 34 points and seven assists as they escaped from San Antonio with the series back on level terms at 2-2. Six Spurs, including Patty Mills with 14, scored in double figures, led by Kawhi Leonard's 26. But even the Spurs' faithful couldn't inspire their team across the finish line.

Tim Duncan had his big boy boots on as San Antonio went into Game Five in Los Angeles, the veteran stomping on the Clippers with a 21-point, 11-rebound double-double. Scores tied going into the final term, the Spurs again found their championship form to win 111-107, Patty with 13 points. It meant the champs were heading home ahead 3-2 and with a chance to close out the series and move on to the Western Conference semi final.

The Clippers forgot to read the script though and despite San Antonio's Italian star Marco Belinelli going off for a playoff career-high of 23 points, Los Angeles won 102-96 to tie the series at 3-3, sending it home to Staples Center for the deciding seventh game. Elsewhere in the West, Andrew Bogut and the Golden State Warriors were advancing toward the Conference final.

It actually turned into something of a crying shame that one of the most memorable seven-game first round NBA playoffs in the league's storied history should come down to — literally — the last second. Chris Paul was magnificent for the Los Angeles Clippers as they clinched Game Seven at home 111-109, eliminating the champion San Antonio Spurs. It was a minor tragedy such a hard-fought, classily-played, epic series, consigned to a first round when it would have made a better Western Conference Final — Golden State Warriors' march onward notwithstanding — ultimately was marred with 1.0 seconds left as the Spurs prepared to run their potential match-and-series-saving play.

On court from the time-out, they started the play but a score-table siren stopped it dead. A mistake? Deliberate? Anxiousness? Calculated? Assume whatever you wish. But what that score-table error did was expose the Spurs' play to the Clippers. It was no coincidence Matt Barnes suddenly knew he could cheat so far off sharp-shooting Marco Belinelli on the wing that he would bat away the lob pass intended for Kawhi Leonard in the middle of the key, preserving LA's victory.

But if the Spurs left with a sour taste in their mouths, they were far too classy to show much of that in the post-game. Asked whether seeing the play before the restart influenced its outcome, San Antonio coach Gregg Popovich deadpanned: "Absolutely." He did not dwell on it though, preferring instead to congratulate the Clippers organisation for the way their team had evolved and seeming genuinely happy for them, albeit sad his own team was out.

Los Angeles coach Glen "Doc" Rivers echoed those sentiments and could not have been more effusive in his praise for the class and dignity of the Spurs and their coach, describing him as "the best coach to me, ever, or one of the top ones." Describing it as a "series for the ages", Rivers said it was all basketball. "There wasn't any crap, I don't know if there was a flagrant foul in the entire series. I'm a better person because I went through this series."

There were amazing moments throughout Game Seven, Manu Ginóbili drawing a backcourt shooting foul on Austin Rivers in the final seconds of the third quarter. To describe that as "a rarity" would be to completely undersell it. He made two of his three free throws for a 78-76 lead, then Chris Paul, hamstrung by a first quarter hamstring injury, nailed a monster three-pointer to close the third.

There still were huge shots to come from Clippers JJ Redick, Jamal Crawford and Barnes, and also from Tony Parker and the venerable 39-year-old Tim Duncan, whose 27 points and 11 boards were his sixth double-double in the seven-game series. LA's Blake Griffin produced his second triple-double of the series with 24 points, 13 rebounds and 10 assists but it was Paul, with 18 of his 27 points in the second half, including four big three-pointers, who would not let Los Angeles lose.

Could Patty have been given more time harassing Chris Paul, as he did way back at the Beijing Olympics? It was certainly a reasonable question. Parker had 20 points but was 10-of-21 from the floor. In the end, it didn't matter. It was what it was. And what it was would be remembered as one of the epic first round series of all time.

Sadly for the Clippers, the "curse" of eliminating San Antonio when the Spurs were defending champs, continued for Los Angeles, knocked out in the Conference semi final. That saw them join Phoenix Suns (2000), Los Angeles Lakers (2004), Dallas Mavericks (2006) and LA Lakers (2008) as teams which KO'd the Spurs but could not go on to win a championship.

Even though Patty and Aron Baynes now were out of the playoffs,

Australian interest did not wane because the nation still had two competitors in the NBA Final. Andrew Bogut was starting centre on the eventual Western Conference champion Golden State Warriors, while Matthew Dellavedova had worked his way into a key role with the eventual Eastern Conference champion Cleveland Cavaliers.

Dellavedova took Aussie NBA fans on a deja-vu journey with a game reminiscent of Patty Mills' performance for San Antonio in the Finals close-out game. Although Cleveland's 94-73 road win over Chicago to clinch their Eastern Conference semi final 4-2 did not win a Championship, it was up there in terms of courage and stepping up to the challenge. For starters, Delly copped it from the Bulls crowd when he entered the game, fans unforgiving for his role in "Leg-lock-gate," an incident which led to the expulsion of Chicago forward Taj Gibson in Game Five.

The first thing Dellavedova did in the face of his sudden notoriety as "Dirty Delly" — a media misnomer if ever there was one — was lob a ball for a Tristan Thompson dunk. Nice start, but it was small potatoes. Battling both ankle and back issues, LeBron James (15 points, 11 assists, nine rebounds) was playing hurt, and Kyrie Irving went out of the match early in the second quarter with a knee injury when scores were tied 35-35. Additionally factoring in the twin injury-forced absences of Kevin Love and Anderson Varejao, and it was going to take something special for the Cavs to close this out.

But Dellavedova came up huge. He not only played wicked, committed defence on Derrick Rose, but unleashed a team-high 19 points on 7-of-11 shooting. Dellavedova pointing acknowledgement to King James for a sweet assist in his scoring tally was a sight to savour. The hard-nosed guard had only top scored once before for the Cavs in 149 games. But, like Patty, he answered the call big-time.

"He's the toughest guy on the team," James said. "I know he's tough as nails and the one thing about Delly is he never makes one mistake. I'm so happy for him and proud of his performance in the absence of Kyrie." Aussie NBA fans were lapping it up. Once the Cavs and Warriors qualified for the Finals, it meant either Dellavedova or Bogut — winning defensive awards on a Warriors' team more notable for the exceptional range and shooting of Steph Curry and Klay Thompson — would give Australia another NBA champion to join Mills, Baynes, Longley and Gaze.

Rod Laver Arena in Melbourne was confirmed in May as the first leg of the Oceania Championship for qualification to the 2016 Rio Olympic Games. Australia's Boomers would host New Zealand's Tall Blacks and the Australian Opals would host the New Zealand Tall Ferns in the women for what promised to be a monumental double-header. Tickets quickly went on sale for the August 15 event at which the Boomers looked very likely to suit their strongest-ever team outside of a World Cup or Olympic Games. New Zealand responded by predicting Oklahoma City Thunder centre Steven Adams would anchor the Tall Blacks.

Promoters already were rubbing their hands together in glee, the second legs of the Oceania Championship slated for Tauranga, New Zealand for the women, and the capital Wellington for the men. There was every likelihood the Boomers would feature Patty Mills, Aron Baynes, Andrew Bogut and Matthew Dellavedova, along with Utah Jazz duo Dante Exum and Joe Ingles. Never forgetting his roots, Ingles was back "home" at Morphett Vale Stadium, supporting his junior club Southern Tigers.

And across from South Australia in Victoria, Exum was attending a Big V match in the state league. "A lot of people (in the US) want to take Instagrams and that sort of thing but even coming back, I went to a Big V game and people were asking for autographs," Exum said, surprised by his newfound notoriety. Ingles was experiencing the same degree of love from fans in Adelaide.

Fresh off their rookie seasons with the Utah Jazz, Ingles initially appeared to be signed by the Jazz as a "caretaker" for Exum, but quickly established his worth as a quality player with a high basketball IQ. Exum's star was on the ascendant. Drafted at #5, it in itself was an extraordinary achievement rivalling even Andrew Bogut's historic 2005 milestone as the first Australian taken at No. 1 by the NBA. Bogut was a recognised star at University of Utah... and 213cm. Exum was an unknown quantity — even dubbed the "international man of mystery" by US scribes — who was coming out of high school in Australia, and junior basketball.

Consequently the angular 198cm Exum was subjected to relentless scrutiny by American critics, his initial struggles documented with almost a degree of told-you-so joy. "I didn't pay any attention to what people were saying or writing," Exum said, the confidence of his coach, teammates and the Jazz organisation far more compelling. "I expected it (the NBA) to be hard and I thought I adjusted. I'm lucky to be with Utah because everyone's a good guy.

"I could have been at a team where players were going in and out, getting big (name) players and that sort of environment. But, and Joe and I talked about this a lot, we came into a young group where we could grow as a team. The core is young and we can create relationships." That wasn't always the NBA way. Even though Exum was a rookie, he understood the Jazz situation was one in which he could thrive.

"My rookie season was actually pretty good," he said, neither he nor Ingles subjected to too many of the rituals that come with being a débutante. "It was funny because a lot of the guys talked about their rookie seasons and what (rituals) they had to do but because we were a fairly young group, we didn't have to do a lot of that."

Ingles joined the franchise as a 27-year-old "rookie" with vast Olympic and international experience, including a Euroleague title. "Coming in from Europe, he'd already been a professional and knew what was what," Exum said. "He was great because he'd already been through a lot."

Exum said after Australia finished the 2014 World Cup, the players made a commitment to each other. "It was driven by (coach) Andrej (Lemanis) but after our disappointing loss in Spain, everyone was like 'we need to make the commitment' for Rio," Exum said. Step One along that road to a medal at the Rio Olympics was having as many of the players as possible available for the two-game qualifying series against New Zealand in August.

And it would be Andrew Bogut, exemplifying Golden State's motto and credo of "strength in numbers" — who would come into the Boomers' team as its latest NBA champion. The Warriors clinched the franchise's first championship since 1975 with a 105-97 win over Cleveland in Game Six. In the process of claiming the series 4-2, it was Bogut and "sixth man" — and series MVP — Andre Iguodala who best exemplified the essence of their credo.

In becoming the fifth Aussie behind Luc Longley, Andrew Gaze, Patty Mills and Aron Baynes to win an NBA Championship, Bogut reinforced it was winning that mattered most with his team-first mentality and acceptance of being relegated from the starting five to the bench from Game Four onwards. "Whatever it takes," he said.

Similarly Iguodala, a starter for 10 years, accepted the role rookie coach Steve Kerr gave him at the start of the season to come off the bench and provide spark for the Warriors. When asked to step up and start from Game Four-to-Six, he was ready to go. All Star power forward David Lee also was prepared to accept a substantially reduced role in a team which proved selflessness was not the sole domain of the San Antonio Spurs — coincidentally where Kerr won his last two championships as a player for coach Gregg Popovich.

Bogut did not take long to shift his attention to the forthcoming Oceania Championship and the two-game challenge from New Zealand for Rio Olympics qualification. "It's very important that we win those two games," he said. "Brazil could possibly be my last Olympics so hopefully we can get there."

Getting there became somewhat compromised when Joe Ingles reluctantly withdrew from the Oceania Championship and Patty Mills was omitted from Andrej Lemanis' Boomers team. Mills was available for the two matches on August 15 and 18, but not for the team's preliminary warmup matches against Lithuania and Slovenia in Europe. He was having additional shoulder rehabilitation work, after surgery impacted his NBA campaign with San Antonio and also forced him out of Australia's previous World Cup team.

Ingles withdrew because he was getting married to Australian netball star Renae Hallinan. Since his selection for Australia seven years earlier, he always was one of the first with his hand up to wear the green-and-gold, which made his decision doubly difficult. "I take great pride in representing my country in international competition, and for that reason, this decision was very difficult for me," he said in a statement released by Basketball Australia.

"Everyone associated with the Boomers — the coaches, my teammates, and the support staff — have been integral in my development as a basketball player and as a person. I believe that a summer of rest is the best thing for my basketball career and will also ensure that I am in peak condition to fully dedicate myself to my team and country as we pursue a medal at the Rio Olympics."

The absence of Ingles and Mills had the potential to sting but in the court of public opinion, the decision to omit Mills received a resounding rebuttal. Lemanis had reason to feel good about his team, no doubt, considering he was starting with Andrew Bogut and Matthew

Dellavedova — fresh off their NBA Championship Series. He also rolled in Dante Exum, Cam Bairstow, Brock Motum, Ryan Broekhoff, Brad Newley, Nathan Jawai, David Andersen, Chris Goulding and NBL stalwarts Adam Gibson and Damian Martin.

It was none too shabby, but omitting Patty Mills when he was available had many shaking their heads in disbelief. Playing matches in Europe against Lithuania and Slovenia would sharpen the team for the two-game Oceania qualifier against the Tall Blacks but surely staying flexible for Mills was warranted? Lemanis sagely consulted his main players on what the Boomers' culture should mean, and fully committing to a programme — be it an Oceania or a World Cup — was a key element.

Availability for the Boomers' European tour matches were part of the programme ahead of facing the Tall Blacks for direct entry into the Rio Olympics and apparently, a non-negotiable. Mills bought in to that culture as much as anyone and understood that making exceptions weakened the culture's very foundation. The team being together for weeks to genuinely become a single-minded, well-oiled, fully-functioning unit comfortable with roles and rotations, was something for which it was worth striving.

That said, the prevailing mood hung on one simple fact: we were talking here about Patty Mills, perhaps the one player — maybe the *only* player — for whom the Boomers *could* make the exception. After all, he was the personification of the new culture and as fair dinkum a true blue Aussie as you could ever hope to find. A larrikin too, wearing the Opals bodysuit with teammate Mark Worthington while supporting the Aussie women in Beijing. Few Australian sportsmen, if any, had already captured the public's imagination and admiration as much as Patty Mills.

His list of achievements already was a figurative mile long, from leading all scorers at the London Olympics to being absolutely instrumental in San Antonio winning an NBA championship. Then he and Aron Baynes had brought the NBA Trophy home to show off around the country. Mills and basketball had become synonymous in Australia, much like Andrew Gaze and the sport similarly were entwined and mutually identified.

And it was not as if Mills was unavailable for the European component because he was playing golf or sipping pina coladas on a sunny beach. Not fully recovered from injury, he needed further work to ensure his shoulder again was at 100 per cent. He would be available by the time the two qualifying matches came around. The question being asked around Australia at the time was what might the USA do if a Kevin Durant or a LeBron James had to miss some warmup games but would be available for those that mattered? Would they be selected?

Did Andrej Lemanis have a rule for some but not for others? Clearly the answer there was no. But like Ingles, Mills had shown himself to be among the most dedicated and high-profile players Australia produced in the preceding decade. Always proud to wear the green-and-gold, he was no stranger to the Boomers.

He already had played with Bogut, Dellavedova, Newley, Jawai… virtually everyone on the current roster, and was essential to the very fabric which comprised this new culture. Conjecture persisted selectors could have chosen 11 players for the Euro tour and kept Patty's spot open, then brought him off the bench at Oceania to minimise any potential disruption. Or they could have taken 12 but told one player he would make way for Mills in Melbourne and Wellington.

"At the end of the day, you've got to make a decision in what you believe to be in the best interest of the team," Lemanis said. "Patty's obviously passionate for playing for Australia — he's a little bit disappointed but I think more so respectful of the need for us to develop as a team." What Lemanis was saying made sense, in-and-of-itself. But the fact Ingles was out, and Baynes withdrew to have surgery to clean up an ankle joint, the absence of a third key figure seemed to render the coach's argument moot, if not redundant.

While even-handed observers understood exactly why Lemanis and his selection team felt they could not include Mills this time, they misjudged how important he was to the sport's profile, if not the team. But then the unthinkable happened. During the Boomers' tour match against Slovenia, Dante Exum suffered a terrible injury, suffering an anterior cruciate ligament tear in his knee. It would mean 12 months off the court, not only sidelining him from his Utah Jazz NBA team, but also meaning he would miss the Rio Olympics if Australian qualified.

The Boomers immediately reached out to Patty Mills to fill the breach, that decision a no-brainer. Suddenly all the premises on which he was omitted were irrelevant. Mills lobbed back from the US on August 10, ahead of the Boomers going back into camp, getting back on the track the next day, timing which always suggested his return was imminent. He had Andrew Bogut's public endorsement and was the obvious man to bring in once Exum suffered his cruel injury.

Mills had accepted his initial omission with grace but when Exum went down and he received the SOS, he naturally answered the call. His addition to the team was the least disruptive, Mills already across the Boomers' systems. "Although Dante's injury is still fresh in our mind, we need to adapt quickly and move on as our focus now is on beating New Zealand," Lemanis said. "Patty is the best-placed player to come into the team quickly. He's an elite player, an NBA Champion and seasoned at international play. And importantly, knows the Boomers' system and style of play.

"If we were going to add a player to replace Dante, we needed someone who can help us beat New Zealand and that is Patty Mills." It always was. But not only did his inclusion now give Australian fans the man they wanted to see in live action, it also guaranteed a sell-out attendance for the double-header with the Opals-NZ at Rod Laver Arena.

"I'm excited," Patty said of returning to the Boomers' line-up. "I'm more than excited to be back with the boys. The situation isn't obviously ideal with Dante going down. But nonetheless this decision was about the boys and the teammates and what we've built, not only in the last few years with Drej (Lemanis), but what I've added to the culture since I came in, in 2006. I have full confidence in my shoulder and my conditioning. My experience is what's going to trump learning plays and Xs and Os."

No one was arguing… until: "Will Patty Mills' late inclusion upset the Boomers' chemistry?" Crafty New Zealand Tall Blacks coach Paul Henare posed the question as the mind games began ahead of the series opener. Before anyone could answer, Perth Wildcats captain Damian Martin withdrew from the Australian team, rehabilitation on his calf strain not sufficiently effective to have him at full fitness in time. Cairns Taipans shooter Cameron Gliddon, who, like Mills was not part of the European tour, was brought in almost through a backdoor to avoid controversy. There would be one other drawcard player missing from the series. New Zealand's NBA centre Steven Adams again would be absent when the Tall Blacks ran onto Rod Laver Arena.

A packed stadium of 15,062 spectators, an amazing attendance when the double-header was being shown live on free-to-air television across Australia on the Nine Network, raised the roof as the Boomers won 71-59 and the Opals also scored a 61-41 victory. The Boomers were made to look rusty and out-of-sync by a much smoother Tall Blacks unit which played seven warm-up games, had no major player disruptions and had everything to play for.

To get the Game Two cushion for the rematch in Wellington into double figures was a great effort against a very good team and it was fabulous to see Patty, Bogues and Delly — in particular — but also the super key David Andersen, live in action for Australia in Australia. Not surprisingly, Patty led Australia with 17 points and four assists, Andersen also with 17 and Dellavedova with 15 points, four assists.

In Andrew Bogut's own words from his post-game tweet: "Great win @ AussieBoomers! Need one more in NZ on Tuesday. Rod Laver Arena was rocking... Thank you Melbourne!!!" The supportive crowd noise definitely helped, as did having Mills in uniform. He showed he remained the heart of the Boomers.

Patty had those three-point goggles back on at Rod Laver Arena and the fans loved it. But for all that invaluable preparation he missed, how badly did the Boomers need him? And how valuable was that preparation when it came down to those hectic final few minutes? Andersen stood up to be counted — as always — and Matty Dellavedova played right to the siren. How important his final basket on that siren, to swell the margin to 12, was, remained to be seen.

But in a two-game series where the points differential would possibly be a factor, 12 was a better cushion than 11, better than 10, way better than three. Bogut wearing the green-and-gold also was a treat, as was the further steady emergence of Ryan Broekhoff as a force. Game One was not his best night but his battles with Tom Abercrombie were significant. These Boomers loved playing together and at home but no-one had any illusions about the battle and task awaiting in Wellington.

To be brutally honest though, the Boomers were super impressive in Game Two. It was tense in TSB Arena in Wellington as New Zealand's Tall Blacks warmed up, focused, intent, determined. As 4,015 filed in to fill the city-based venue, everyone knew what was at stake. But for the Tall Blacks, victory would be insufficient. It had to be victory by 13 points or more.

"Our mindset was never to defend a 12-point lead," Andrej Lemanis said, his game-plan and strategies rising to the challenge. The Boomers looked every bit as focused when they hit the hardwood, weathering another emotion-charged haka. They opened aggressively too, Dellavedova leading the way with seven points of their initial 11-4 buffer, the Tall Blacks unable to make their shots, delivering 5-of-16 for the period.

Their star in Game One, Corey Webster, managed four points on two tough shots, the second with a particularly high degree of difficulty as the 211cm David Andersen switched on to him, his long arms outstretched. New Zealand trimmed it to three at 10-13 before former Adelaide 36ers teammates Adam Gibson and Brock Motum conspired for four unanswered points. Ahead 21-14 at the first break, the Boomers had reasons to feel good, considering Andrew Bogut was hit with a phantom foul after 18 seconds of play and had a second when he and Mika Vukona bumped into each other in the open court at 6:34.

When he returned midway through the second quarter, New Zealand was fashioning the first of many runs at the Aussie lead which had moved to 26-18 after Dellavedova fed Andersen for a triple from the top of the key. Webster ignited the Tall Blacks with a sweet drive aided by a rock solid Vukona screen, before intercepting a pass meant for Chris Goulding. He pushed the ball up the hardwood, feeding Isaac Fotu for the running slam dunk, the crowd roaring its appreciation.

Fotu ran off seven straight points, following his slam with a three before swishing a fadeaway jumpshot. Dellavedova got the ball to a hesitant Bogut who scored anyway. His next bucket, a spin for a slam, was more strident. Patty Mills and Andersen extended the lead to double figures at 40-30 before Reuben Te Rangi iced a three to close the half. The Boomers were shooting at a wicked 53 per cent to 38 and enjoying a 20-13 boards edge. A 7-0 run to start the second half put the Boomers into a commanding position at 47-33, Bogut a colossus at both ends.

When he wasn't terrorising the defensive keyway, he was throwing down a dunk on Broekhoff's missed free throw, drawing appreciative applause from even begrudging local fans. The Tall Blacks dragged it back from a 14-point deficit to 40-49. But when Mika Vukona bricked two free throws, the Boomers swept forward and Mills stuck a triple which was a dagger. The Aussies twisted the knife with Mills' crosscourt pass for the first of two Brad Newley threes.

Aussie turnovers and a lack of composure contributed to an extraordinary 16-2 run which drew the deficit to 77-82. The Boomers then stepped it up again, Dellavedova's three a back-breaker before the benches were cleared. Talking back-breakers, the Boomers kept the parlous state of 213cm Bogut's tender back in-house and he showed little evidence of it troubling him in a powerhouse performance.

But he did it in pain. There were times less-informed basketball followers in Australia used social media to ponder Andrew Bogut's commitment to the Boomers' national programme. They questioned whether the NBA champion was injury-prone and whether he was genuine when saying he was passionate about wearing the green-and-gold. Those followers were huddled in a dank corner somewhere as Bogut turned in a Herculean performance and the Boomers stamped their passports to a 12th consecutive Olympics at Rio by beating New Zealand 89-79.

It wasn't that Bogut's numbers were so imposing, though 10 points, 10 rebounds and three blocks after early foul woes did stand up. Frankly, standing up was more than he could do 48 hours before the game as the Aussie camp fought to keep a lid on speculation he might not play in the FIBA Oceania Championship's vital second leg in Wellington.

"We really didn't know for sure," Boomers coach Andrej Lemanis said. "He has a tender back and he is a big man. Sitting in cramped aircraft tends to aggravate it. He was in so much pain, no-one would have been surprised if he'd said he couldn't play."

When Bogut missed an on-court session, speculation began. Few realised he simply would force himself to rise above his back pain and compete. Lemanis' game-plan had all the requisite adjustments from

Game One, including running New Zealand sharpshooter Webster ragged defensively to add tiring legs to his offence. "He couldn't rest at the defensive end," Lemanis said, his confidence in his players well justified, their commitment evident.

Dellavedova was the star of the show, attacking the Tall Blacks from the start, and also there at the end with the three-point dagger that finally deflated a late, belated but aggressively belligerent home team. In between the Golden State Warriors' big man and the Cleveland Cavaliers' little man, Australia had numerous key cameos, from consecutive threes by Brad Newley, to some David Andersen aggro, memorable Chris Goulding drives, Patty Mills' customary slickness, Cam Bairstow effort and some Nate Jawai power.

Somewhere in there too, Ryan Broekhoff again erased Tall Blacks swingman Thomas Abercrombie as a factor as the Boomers bounded in, seized the initiative and maintained it until their late hiccup.

"Andrew Bogut couldn't move 48 hours before the game," Boomers doctor Graham Lee said. "He was better on game day though, a combination of will power and desire. Now why would you make him angry? The Tall Blacks made him angry."

That was a huge mistake. Bogut didn't turn green (or gold), but his hulking presence in the key forced the Tall Blacks to consider other avenues. None were the road to victory. Dellavedova also sung the big man's praises, reiterating how inspirational it was that he was there among his teammates on the TSB Arena hardwood. Then Delly, like Mills and the rest of the most sought Aussies, hung back in the venue, signing autographs and posing for photographs with hundreds of excited young basketball fans.

Bogut didn't make it back out for that. He was on a massage table receiving treatment for a back on which he helped carry his country into another Olympic Games.

CHAPTER NINE
THE ROCK DOESN'T BREAK

It was at Saint Mary's College in Moraga where Patty Mills' growth into the man he would become received a further boost. "I appear African-American, so it's not until I start talking that people go, 'Hold on, there's something not right here.' But it's an awesome conversation starter," he recalled. "I open my mouth, they get curious, and I say, 'Got a few minutes? Have a seat.' There's a part of me that's very stereotypically Australian, with the lingo, or for lack of a better way of putting it, the way white Australians would speak. And then, oh that's not all I am…"

Patty met Alyssa Levesque while both were attending St Mary's. Born in Martinez, California, their romance was an amalgam of diverse cultural backgrounds and blossomed for a decade before they married in 2019. Graduating from the university with a bachelor's degree in business, Alyssa founded a swimwear company known as Strait Swim. She made no secret of the fact the swimwear line she designed was inspired by Patty's native Torres Strait Islands, describing the brand as a "chic, sophisticated swimwear line influenced by tradition".

"She really respects the Indigenous Aboriginal and Torres Strait culture, and I'm really proud of her," Mills said. The couple were inseparable, Alyssa joining Patty in his fight against social injustice and social advocacy.

For now, his focus shifted back to the Spurs and the 2015–16 NBA season which also would launch his Australian team into the full-on quest for a medal at the Rio Olympic Games. On February 2, he tied his season-high 22 points as San Antonio recorded its 26th straight home victory, making the Orlando Magic disappear 110-97. Patty checked into the contest with five minutes left in the opening quarter after Tony Parker had a second shot blocked.

He made an instant impact, draining a three-pointer with his first shot. The 27-year-old continued in the same vein, drilling 3-of-4 from behind the three-point arc and 9-of-13 shots overall. LaMarcus Aldridge, who Patty first teamed with at Portland Trail Blazers and now was on the Spurs roster, also thrived for 28 points.

A month later, Boomers coach Andrej Lemanis revealed a 26-man squad for the Rio Games, headlined by Patty Mills, Andrew Bogut, Aron Baynes, Matthew Dellavedova, Joe Ingles and Cam Bairstow, all of whom were playing in the NBA. Lemanis also named the injured Dante Exum and Ben Simmons, who was attending Louisiana State University but projected as a possible No.1 NBA draft selection. That always was likely to cloud his availability for the Olympic campaign.

Australia's legion of stars in Europe, led by Boomers regulars Brad Newley, David Andersen, Ryan Broekhoff, Aleks Maric and Brock Motum also were named, as was Kevin Lisch. A dual winner of the NBL's Most Valuable Player award and a championship winner in the league to boot, the American import was due to receive his Australian citizenship, making him eligible to wear his new country's colours.

The squad's NBL contingent included Chris Goulding, Nate Jawai, Damian Martin, Adam Gibson, Cam Gliddon, Angus Brandt, Todd Blanchfield, Clint Steindl, Mitch Creek, Lucas Walker, Daniel Kickert and Mitch Norton. "We have a fantastic core group and we have some exciting young talent," Lemanis declared. And everyone following basketball in Australia agreed wholeheartedly. This would be the Boomers' time to shine.

First though, there was the small matter of settling the 2015–16 NBA Championship. Aron Baynes no longer was with the Spurs, having signed with Detroit Pistons in the Eastern Conference. The Pistons finished as the eighth seeds into the Conference playoffs where they were swept 4-0 in the first round by Matthew Dellavedova and the top-seeded Cleveland Cavaliers.

The Rock Doesn't Break

Andrew Bogut's Golden State Warriors finished atop the Western Conference rankings with an unprecedented 73-9 win-loss record. In second place sat Patty Mills and the San Antonio Spurs, once again topping the 60-win mark with a 67-15 win-loss record, the best in franchise history. The Spurs also tied the NBA record of the 1985–86 Boston Celtics for most home wins in a season with 40 of a possible 41. Their only loss was to the defending NBA champion Golden State Warriors. Joe Ingles and his Utah Jazz finished out of the post-season, going 40-42 for ninth in the West.

Patty scored 15 points as San Antonio thrashed Memphis Grizzlies 106-74 in Game One of their first round series, then had 16 as the Spurs made it 2-0 in a 94-68 cruise. There was tougher resistance in Memphis but San Antonio still won the next two games relatively comfortably 96-87 and 116-95 to sweep the series 4-0.

LaMarcus Aldridge was on fire for 38 points as San Antonio smashed Oklahoma City Thunder 124-92 in Game One of their Western Conference semi final. It was a different story in Game Two, which finished amid controversy. Leading San Antonio 98-97 and taking an offensive sideball with heartbeats remaining, OKC escaped penalty for a blatant foul on Dion Waiters' inbounds pass when he shoved Spurs guard Manu Ginóbili to create room for his pass.

Ginóbili was entitled to be right up next to the sideline, harassing the inbound pass, provided he did not break the plane of the line, which he did not. For Waiters, outside the court, to aggressively shove him backwards should have resulted in a foul and a chance for the Spurs to steal a win. But none of the officiating panel flinched. "At times, it's frustrating," Aldridge said of the refereeing, the Spurs' big man again leading all scorers, this time with 41 points.

It took a 100-96 thriller in Game Three in Oklahoma City for the Spurs to take back the series lead 2-1, which the Thunder then struck down

111-97 in Game Four, Kevin Durant unstoppable for OKC with 41 points at 56 per cent. The series turned on Game Five when OKC won 95-91 in San Antonio. Sadly for the Spurs, another review of the officiating in their home loss showed two officiating errors that should have gone their way after Oklahoma City also won Game Two in San Antonio with the NBA later acknowledging five incorrect non-calls over the final stretch.

It was cold comfort. Back in Oklahoma City for Game Six, a 30-12 second period set OKC up for a 113-99 victory and a 4-2 series elimination of the Spurs. Tim Duncan, who led San Antonio to its first NBA title in 1999 and still is revered as the Spurs' greatest player, retired after 19 years in the league. Duncan led the Spurs to five championships and a playoff appearance in every season of his 19 years in the NBA, an extraordinary run of success.

OKC had found its best at the right end of the season and proved it by leading Golden State Warriors 3-1 for the Western Conference Championship. The Warriors dragged themselves out of that perilous hole to win the series in seven games. They were out of the blocks quickly in the NBA Finals, seizing a 2-0 buffer over the Eastern Conference champion Cleveland Cavaliers. Andrew Bogut set an early tone as Golden State dismantled Cleveland 110-77 in Game Two.

Bogut blocked four shots in the opening 7:15 of the game — as many as the Warriors blocked in all of Game One — with one of his rejects leading straight to a Steph Curry three-pointer. Cavs superstar LeBron James went scoreless in the first period for the first time in his Finals career.

Excited by what they were witnessing, the public relations experts at Basketball Australia let their emotions ahead of the Rio Olympics get the better of them. Expectations were at an unrealistic all-time high, Basketball Australia as guilty as anyone of fanning them when it started advertising its "farewell series" for the national team against the Pac-12 All Stars in the Rio lead-up, by describing their Boomers as: "arguably the greatest team Australian basketball has ever assembled". In doing so, it added pressure to a team that was not yet even selected, but also disrespected much of its own history. And labelling this Boomers team as our nation's "greatest ever" was fraught with peril, given they had not yet achieved anything.

Australia had contested the men's basketball section of the Olympics 13 times, assembling some fairly impressive teams, none of which medalled. And it had a quartet of players — Eddie Palubinskas, Ian Davies, Andrew Gaze and Patty Mills — who had led the Olympic Games in scoring.

BA's 1988 team, which went to Seoul and included three young bucks with extraordinary potential named Luc Longley, Mark Bradtke and Andrew Vlahov, was very solid. The trio joined a few of our all-time greatest players such as Phil Smyth, Andrew Gaze and Ray Borner and made it to the bronze medal playoff. In Atlanta in 1996, Gaze, Bradtke, Vlahov and Borner all were back, along with "the athlete" Sam Mackinnon, the monster John Dorge and the man who made "the shot"(against Croatia) — Tony Ronaldson. Those guys did pretty well too, making it to the bronze medal playoff.

Four years later in Sydney the Boomers again fielded a fairly decent side. After Gaze, there was Bradtke, Longley and Vlahov for one last time, Chris Anstey was there and so too Paul Rogers and a naturalised Ricky Grace. Once again the Aussies were back to the medal round, beaten for bronze by Lithuania.

David Andersen and Andrew Bogut debuted in 2004, with CJ Bruton, Matt Nielsen, Brett Maher back for his third Olympics, Jason Smith and Martin Cattalini back for their second. Start rolling in Anstey, Andersen, Bogut, Bruton, Neilsen, Glen Saville back for his second Games, and add Joe Ingles, Patty Mills, Brad Newley and Mark Worthington for Beijing and no-one would say those teams were in any way lacking.

In London, there was Patty and Joe, and Delly and Baynes, plus a holy host of others. So throwing the "greatest" tag at the potential Rio Olympic team was ill-advised, at least until it achieved something. "The proof will be in the pudding, if we do better than fourth or fifth," Boomers assistant coach Longley said, Australia's Olympic best still fourth, its FIBA World Cup best fifth. "It's as simple as that."

In the wake of Game Two of the NBA Finals, featuring Andrew Bogut's Warriors and Matthew Dellavedova's Cavaliers, it was easy to get carried away. Bogut won a ring the previous year with Golden State, Patty Mills and Aron Baynes held the Larry O'Brien Trophy 12 months earlier with San Antonio. Ingles was a recent Euroleague champion and playing NBA at Utah.

On paper, the team Australia was likely to assemble would boast some incredible talent and depth. It had a stated goal of coming home from Rio with a medal and it certainly needed to by the way Government funding was going to be distributed post-Games. Everyone supported that stated goal but at this point, it was just that — a pinnacle for which the Boomers would strive.

Basketball Australia's overt enthusiasm for the potential of its team probably was understandable to some degree. Midway through the NBA season, when the league took a break from regular season play for its annual All Star Game, the most likely selections on the Boomers team for Rio gathered for a holiday together in sunny San Diego.

Patty Mills initiated the idea and Andrew Bogut, Joe Ingles, Aron Baynes, Matthew Dellavedova, Cam Bairstow and Dante Exum took advantage of the free time to gather with their wives and girlfriends for an all Aussie catch-up in the Californian sunshine. The one topic they did *not* discuss was the Rio Olympics. But the camaraderie of this "magnificent seven" buoyed anyone following Australian basketball.

"It wasn't discussed in San Diego," Mills told AAP, saying the purpose of the vacation was to spend quality time away from the basketball court with his Olympic teammates. The entourage hired a house in San Diego, revelled in the sunshine, ate, drank, joked and relaxed, away from the rigours of the NBA season. It was more about enhancing team chemistry away from the sport than discussing strategies or revisiting the quest for that historic first ever Olympic medal.

"That was the purpose of the trip, not to really switch our minds on to anything but just hanging out together," Mills said. "It was just a relaxing weekend. We didn't plan too much other than a boat trip. Other than that, it was just go with the flow." All part of building a culture. After all, much of those medal conversations occurred after beating New Zealand in Wellington to qualify in the first place.

"We feel like we have the best chance Australia has ever had going into something like this, but the conversation is serious," he said. "We understand what's on the line and what's at stake and we are all on the same page together with that. We know what we have to get done."

On their San Diego sojourn, it never became too serious for Australia's NBA contingent, Joe Ingles the team joker. "He was great," Mills said. "Him and Dante definitely have a cool little bond there being in Utah together. He's definitely the big brother of the two, or the father almost, looking after Dante." Of the seven players, Exum was the only one in any doubt for Rio as he continued his rehabilitation from his torn ACL.

Chasing back-to-back NBA titles after their 73-9 season, Golden State reversed a 30-point loss to Cleveland in Game Three with a 108-97 road win that gave them a seemingly insurmountable 3-1 series lead. Unfortunately for the Warriors though, in Game Five they lost Andrew Bogut for the duration when he went down clutching his left knee during the third quarter. Cleveland kept the series alive, winning 112-97. At home next, it won 115-101, tying the championship 3-3.

Sensing history was within their grasp, the Cavaliers took Game Seven 93-89 to win the first championship for Cleveland in any pro sport for

52 years. LeBron James was, of course, magnificent but the victory also meant Matthew Dellavedova joined the growing ranks of Australian basketball players with an NBA Championship ring. At the 2016 NBA Draft, Ben Simmons was taken at No.1 by the Philadelphia 76ers, following in the shoes of Andrew Bogut more than a decade earlier.

Bogut's shoes though would take some filling, the deep bone bruising injury to his knee throwing into jeopardy his chances of playing for Australia in Rio. Dante Exum, still rehabilitating his knee, withdrew from Lemanis' Boomers squad to focus on returning to 100 per cent fitness and Simmons, on advice from the 76ers, also withdrew to focus on his game during the NBA off-season.

Lemanis reduced the squad to 16 men, retaining Bogut, but his bone-bruising of the left knee was a serious injury requiring rest. If he could be fit in time though, he was going to make the Boomers better, just by the mere cache of his undeniably compelling presence. "A team with Andrew Bogut, you would suggest, has got a better opportunity for success than a team without him," Lemanis said.

"But we need to keep in mind the whole preparation phase — does his skill level overcome the lack of preparation he's had with the team? It's not an easy question to answer. We need to work with the circumstances as they play out and see how late in the process it is, how confident he is on the knee, where the Golden State Warriors sit with all this and how the team performs without him."

Bogut told Lemanis he did not want to be the guy that "wrecks the chemistry" of the group. That was completely unimaginable. The Boomers played without him at the 2012 London Games and 2014 FIBA World Cup. His return for Australia against New Zealand in the qualifiers was profound. It was simply going to be a case of wait-and-see.

Bonding at Uluru as a group ahead of the Rio Olympic Games turned into an exercise in national inspiration for the Boomers. Australia's extended national men's squad found, or in some cases *rediscovered* their "Australiana" after a weekend in the Northern Territory before heading into a selection training camp in Melbourne. If there is any single place on the continent of Australia to realise a sense of awe and wonder, it is at Uluru in the nation's red centre. Naturally, it was Patty Mills who drove the idea to bring the Boomers to this place of spiritual inspiration.

The NBA Players Association and the Australian Basketballers Association both backed Mills' initiative. "It was about team bonding, with no staff members or anyone like that," London Olympian Adam Gibson said. "We refurbished a court up here for the local Mutitjulu community with new hoops, lines, and what a great location for a court."

Gibson said the sight of Uluru was awe-inspiring. "Without a doubt. Being able to see the Rock, you don't realise until you stand beneath it how imposing it is."

Dual-Olympian Brad Newley was one of the few Boomers already with some first-hand experience of Uluru. "We lived up in Alice (Springs) about 20 years ago," he said. "It's a special feeling. It has a real aura, so large, with the colours and the spirit of it." Newley said he believed the players would draw strength from the weekend visit to Australia's most iconic landmark.

"A rock is really solid and can't break," he said. "I'm sure we'll draw a lot from this when the going gets tough in a game."

ABA chief executive Jacob Holmes said Mills conceived the visit to the red centre. "It was Patty's idea and a great one to launch the Olympic campaign from Uluru," Holmes said. "The NBAPA and the ABA, plus Adam Quick whose management group has Patty and Joe (Ingles) got it all up and running, with the idea to let the players drive it." Only Andrew Bogut missed the trip, still racing the clock to have his knee rehabilitated in time for the Games.

"There was a desire for me before this (Rio) campaign started, to make sure everyone on our team understood why we play for Australia," Patty said. "I organised a trip to the centre of the country, to the heart of the country, to Uluru, so everyone could understand and feel that presence of the land and the country.

"It doesn't matter what background you have, whether it's Indigenous or not, you find whatever reason you have of why you're putting on these green-and-gold colours. And once you grab on to that, let's go and give this a crack."

But this was going to be more than just a crack at it. Bogut was the first to say it aloud and dual-Olympians Joe Ingles and Brad Newley reiterated it. The Boomers were not just chasing a medal in Rio, they were panning for gold. "We're going with the intention of winning gold," Newley said at a lunch speaking engagement in Adelaide, Ingles nodding his agreement. Bogut had declared going to Rio to simply target the dais was aiming too low.

"Our goal is to go in and win a gold medal because you don't want to go into an Olympics saying: 'Let's go finish fourth, let's go get a bronze'," Bogut said. Matthew Dellavedova was next to chant the same line, while confessing seeing Bogut go down in Game Five of the NBA Championship caused him some concern. His first thought when Bogut crashed to the floor, clearly in acute pain, wasn't for the NBA Championship but for their joint venture the following month in Brazil.

"It's a serious injury," Dellavedova said of Bogut's bone-bruising. "When he went down, my first thought was: 'Rio'.

"He is working on it and we all know how much it means to him. I know (coach) Andrej (Lemanis) will give him until the last possible moment to get it right. It looks doubtful but he is keen (to come). He showed that last year (in the Rio qualifier against New Zealand) when he hurt his back and had to fly in (to Wellington) later. His presence on the court just changes the whole dynamic."

The Olympics drawing ever closer, finally in July the 12-man team to pursue a medal in Rio — already labelled by Australia's host federation as "arguably the greatest Australian team ever assembled" — finally was announced. The team charged with the task of breaking the Olympic medal ceiling for the Boomers was Matthew Dellavedova, Patty Mills, Joe Ingles, Aron Baynes, Andrew Bogut, Kevin Lisch, Chris Goulding, Ryan Broekhoff, Brock Motum, David Andersen, Damian Martin, Cam Bairstow. (Added as a "13th" player in case Bogut's injury did not sufficiently respond in time was Aleks Maric.)

The shock omission was Brad Newley, 31 and the slashing 198cm swingman who was a fixture in the team from the moment he debuted in 2006 at the Commonwealth Games where Australia won gold. (Commonwealth Games gold, while still an accomplishment, is not viewed as relevant in international basketball circles as usually it only comes down to a battle between Australia, New Zealand and Canada.) But it was gold nonetheless and only three years after winning gold for Australia at the 2003 FIBA Under-19 World Championship alongside fellow Olympians Andrew Bogut, Aleks Maric and Damian Martin.

In 2006, Newley had continued on to the FIBA World Championship, his first of three, wrapped around Olympic selections to Beijing in 2008 and London in 2012. On the squad's bonding trip to Uluru, it was Newley who coined the team's catch phrase: "The Rock doesn't break and neither will we." Not having Newley coming off the Boomers' bench providing instant energy, a spark who knew his role and played it to perfection, was going to be odd.

His absence, and to a lesser extent the omission of another Boomers regular in Adam Gibson, were surprises. Such a good and well-balanced team though was not really cause for much criticism. "Telling Brad (he had missed selection) was absolutely my worst moment in coaching," Lemanis admitted. "His service to international basketball and to the Boomers — to be that coach to have to end that for him was an absolute shit day."

Breaking the bad news to Gibson also was no picnic. "That also was a very hard one for me personally," Lemanis said. "There's so much emotion involved. As you would expect though, they handled it as absolute professionals and wished us and the team well."

The only minor reservation with the selection of American-born Kevin Lisch, who naturalised in 2016, was how he would mesh into such a now well-established team culture. As a player and a person, there were zero doubts he was a great fit for the green-and-gold. Lisch and Damian Martin were Perth's NBL championship backcourt in 2010, the import winning the Larry Sengstock Medal as MVP of the Grand Final Series. He also won the league's MVP award in 2012 at the Wildcats and again in 2016 with Illawarra. As the league's reigning MVP, Lisch would have been among the first players considered for an Olympic berth, his addition obvious.

Australia was due to open its Games assault on August 6 against France, the French line-up including NBA players Nicholas Batum (Charlotte Hornets), Boris Diaw (Utah Jazz), Rudy Gobert (Utah Jazz), Joffrey Lauvergne (Denver Nuggets) and Tony Parker (San Antonio Spurs).

Serbia, anchored by Nikola Jokic (Denver Nuggets) was next on August 8, before the USA two nights later, a line-up featuring *only* NBA players including Kevin Durant, Kyrie Irving and Carmelo Anthony. Next followed China, then Venezuela on the 14th. Even the Venezuelans had an NBA player in Greivis Vasquez (Brooklyn Nets). There were not a lot of easy nights ahead, unlike the two-game "farewell series" in Melbourne against the Pac-12 All Stars.

Well, they were expected to be easybeats but no-one informed them they were supposed to be playing the Washington Generals to the Boomers' Harlem Globetrotters at Hisense Arena. Those pesky Pac-12 kids kept coming back and trying to make a game of it before Australia

— down Matthew Dellavedova (NBA insurance issues), Andrew Bogut (knee) and Chris Goulding (ankle, precautionary), then Ryan Broekhoff after just 10:12 of action with an ankle injury — saw them off 92-83.

This was the "new Boomers" first hit-out as the team for Rio so starting a little tentatively and lacking some sync was to be expected. The college kids just had a red-hot go and kept coming until the end which, after all, was what the Boomers needed, given no national team took up the invitation to play this Farewell Series. So while initially it was the Pac-12 announcing "Hello World", once the rhythm started to come, Australia's men were too physical and experienced.

They trailed by seven at one stage and led by 18 at another, dominating the middle stages of the contest and especially after halftime when a 10-0 run pushed the Boomers to 60-48 and on their way to out of reach. Aron Baynes was a keyway monolith, his new shaved head-mohawk haircut adding to his aura. Baynes went for a game-high 28 points and nine rebounds and also revealed far greater range than advertised. Australia's 52-34 rebound disparity also was a huge factor, Patty Mills supplementing a couple of sweet buckets for 15 points with dazzling assists, and David Andersen such a reliable asset. Kevin Lisch was a standout with his work rate at both ends of the floor and his smarts.

"Defensively we had some issues in the first half with their speed and ability to get to the rim," Lemanis said. "The guys came out and made some adjustments and offensively we had some nice execution. I don't want to get caught up in the negatives — we have only been together for a week and this group of 12 has only practiced together once."

He was right not to worry. The rust was gone, any untidiness from Game One polished up, and defensively the Boomers at times were exemplary as they sent the Pac-12 Conference All Stars home 93-63 losers in their second bout at Hisense Arena. Australia should have won handsomely, of course. But the manner in which they did it was considerably more impressive than their understandably tentative debut.

Their defensive pressure, halfcourt traps and fullcourt heat startled and inhibited the college kids who, initially at least, worked hard to prevent Aron Baynes again exerting his Game One influence. Baynes ultimately overwhelmed them again for 19 points on 9-of-13 shooting, and eight boards but the star of the show indisputably was Patty Mills.

The San Antonio Spurs playmaker delivered 29 points at 55 per cent, including 5-of-9 threes, and was on the end of some of Joe Ingles' most breath-taking assists. The Pac-12 All Stars kept it within single digits for most of the first half, before Australia pushed its lead to 40-28 at the break.

Mills took over for Australia in the third quarter, collecting eight of his 29 points in the third period alone. He extended the Boomers' lead to 53-36 with a four-point play midway through the third. Ingles had 11 assists, perhaps none better than his instinctive three-quarter-court pin-pointer for Mills to lay in. The Boomers were ready to board the plane to Rio.

Meanwhile Basketball Australia was alerted to the fact it probably should investigate the future eligibility of one of the Pac-12 All Stars, a 196cm Pac-12 swingman named Matisse Thybulle. The 19-year-old Thybulle, born in Scottsdale, Arizona, moved to Sydney, Australia with his family in 1998 when he was two. They lived there for seven years before settling in Sammamish, Washington in 2005.

"I remember the beaches by our house," Thybulle said. "I remember I thought it was so weird when we came to the US because the Santa Claus in Australia wore a speedo and rode a surfboard. And when I came here, he was all dressed up in cold weather. The seasons are opposite so our Christmas was basically in the summer.

"I have some childhood friends that are still over there that I've kept in touch with a little bit." Thybulle played quality minutes in both matches against the Boomers, not a soul yet guessing how big his contribution to Australian basketball would be in the not-too-distant future.

CHAPTER TEN
I GO TO RIO

Dream big, don't aim low. The Boomers were en route to Brazil, confident and full of self-belief, the team's only concern still over injured centre Andrew Bogut. "We'd want some clarity probably by August 1," Australian coach Andrej Lemanis said. "From a medical point of view, Andrew has to get past certain tests and get through three phases. For example, one leg has to be at 80 per cent of the other to get to Phase Two.

"But he has played with injuries before and he will know how much pain he can play with. He will know in his heart of hearts." The Boomers had complete faith Bogut would make the right call and that would be the one in Australia's best interests. Without him, they still looked a formidable team but not quite the same. Aron Baynes and Bogut together had the potential to be a terrifying partnership, for example. Aleks Maric would not be called upon for Bogut-type duties but still could grab a rebound and set a bone-jarring screen.

"Andrew has been great and absolutely diligent in his rehab," Lemanis said. "He is very keen to play and is giving himself every chance. He has good days and bad so we just don't know." The medal dream was far from out of the question, but it never took much for a campaign to unravel.

Australia beat Argentina in Argentina as part of its warm-up for Rio, then took a welt from Brazil and a smackdown from Lithuania. On August 1, the date Lemanis had said the Boomers would need a definitive answer into the prospects of Bogut anchoring the campaign, he was in uniform for an exhibition game against China. Bogut only played for a quarter but the growth in confidence within the team was huge. Unless he pulled up very sore — which he did not — the medal quest was afoot.

Australian basketball fans sat spellbound in front of their television sets and somewhat in disbelief as the Boomers opened their Rio Olympics account by soaring to a magnificent all-the-way 87-66 rout of France. Ranked #5 in the world by FIBA and a bronze medallist at the 2014 World Cup, France had no answer to the inside presence and dominance of Andrew Bogut (18 points at 90 per cent, five assists) and Aron Baynes (14 points, game-high eight rebounds), or Australia's teamwork and precision shooting.

The Boomers shot at 50 per cent and had 29 assists on their 35 baskets, in stark contrast to France's 12 on 24 makes. Bogut was a beast as Australia won its opening match at an Olympics for the first time since beating Korea by 23 in Atlanta to open its 1996 campaign. An omen perhaps? And France was at a very different level to Korea. Patty Mills led all scorers with 21 points (five assists) and Matthew Dellavedova had 10 assists as the Boomers received contributions across the board, coach Andrej Lemanis with the luxury of getting all 12 men into the contest.

Consecutive buckets by Baynes kick-started Australia to 4-0, Bogut made it 6-3 after Boris Diaw struck a three-pointer for France before Mills unloaded with two three-pointers in an exceptional eight-point personal run. Baynes' free throws bumped the lead to 16-7 and Australia was rolling, ahead 20-14 at the first break.

A 12-3 run to start the second kept the momentum going, Ryan Broekhoff aborting two free throws before coolly converting a triple from the top of the key for 30-17, David Andersen bumping it to 32-17. Throughout, fans were tempted to pinch themselves, waiting for the crash to come. Australia was leading 34-19 before it was "Parker Time" as France's NBA championship playmaker and Mills' mentor Tony Parker seized the game by the scruff of the neck.

Parker singlehandedly led the French resistance, steadily narrowing the margin as the Boomers struggled for a response. The dynamic guard unloaded 16 points for the period, dragging France back as Lemanis even copped a technical foul 7.9 seconds out from halftime. The Boomers' boss had cause for angst, especially with some of the calls which particularly hindered Joe Ingles. But Parker slotted the free throw and on the additional possession and with time ticking away, stuck a jumper to rip Australia's interval lead back to 36-33.

Dellavedova-to-Bogut for a basket, then Delly-to-Mills made it a fast start to the third quarter. Parker missed a three from the corner, busy flopping to try and draw a foul as Australia instead raced down the floor for Mills to nail a three-pointer in transition, the lead back out to 10. Dellavedova down the lane made it 48-36, before feeding an alley-oop pass to Bogut for 50-38.

Bogut put his body on the line to draw a charge from Diaw, then threw a wicked bounce pass to Mills cutting for a reverse layup. This was just joyous stuff to savour before Mickael Gelabale led a mini-revival to draw France back to 46-53.

Then, with 6:07 to play, Bogues took the ball from the outside, drove to the hoop and slammed down a dunk for 71-52 and France was not going to get back. Working on his rehab so hard and for so long just to ensure he could even take the court, Bogut now was having the time of his life.

Despite his foul woes, Ingles still had six assists, and finished with two delightful fast break plays as well, Australia closing on a justified high from an outstanding performance. What a start!

Anyone in any doubt Australia's Boomers had anything but medalling on their minds had a rude awakening when they wound up smashing Serbia 95-80. Matthew Dellavedova turned in arguably his greatest single game of elite basketball, burying 23 points on 7-of-8 shooting, including 3-of-4 threes and 6-of-7 frees, with 13 assists and two steals against the 2014 FIBA World Cup silver medallist.

He was simply irresistible in a 33-17 final quarter which belied the unrelenting tension of a contest Australia only led 84-80 inside the last two minutes. But Joe Ingles' three-pointer with 1:46 left cracked it open at 87-80, before Dellavedova created a steal which left Patty Mills and Ingles wide open on the wings. Delly fed Mills who backed himself for a mid-range jumper and at 89-80 this was over.

Rushing now to try and save the game, Serbia came apart and Ingles stroked his second three for 92-80, amid joyous delirium on the Aussie bench. But wait, there was still more as Aron Baynes grabbed a defensive board, Mills leaked out on the break, Dellavedova found him with his 13th assist and Mills completed the layup and three-point play. If the Boomers had enjoyed a better finish to a vital game, few could recall it, the 11-0 run over the game's final 106 seconds something to delight in right across excited living rooms throughout Australia.

It could so easily have gone pear-shaped when Andrew Bogut — dominating the paint like a Croatian colossus — collected his fourth foul with 8:36 left, the Boomers down 64-67. Of course, it had looked worse when Milos Teodosic struck consecutive three-pointers in the third period to bump Serbia 49-42 clear, Dellavedova almost a lone hand in dragging the Boomers back with a triple, two free throws, an assist to Bogut and a three-point play to tie it back up at 52-52.

Early into the last quarter, it was tension personified, relieved greatly when Dellavedova set Baynes up for a dunk. Baynes next drew a charge and Mills somehow made a morale-boosting layup through traffic after fumbling the ball midway through, Australia ahead 68-67.

Dellavedova rewarded Baynes at his earliest opportunity with a lob for 70-67, then an Ingles intercept left Mills open to stroke a three-pointer for a 9-0 run and 73-67 lead. That six-point buffer became huge, trading baskets now only allowing Serbia to reduce it to four each time before that fateful finish which blew Australia headlong into its next match against the USA feeling mighty good about life.

Such a gutsy win came despite Ingles scoring eight of his 10 points in the last quarter, six in the last 1:46 to find his "mojo" as the Aussies battled to cope with atrociously lenient and easily influenced officiating and some of Serbia's physicality and contrasting flop antics. It was extremely bemusing when even the caption on a photo at FIBA's official website showing Serbian centre Miroslav Raduljica taking a free throw said: "Raduljica did a good acting job to get an unsportsmanlike foul called on Aron Baynes."

Like Ingles and Mills, whose shooting midway through the game was alarmingly wayward, Baynes came good when it mattered with big defensive plays and nice finishes, six of his 10 points in the last quarter. Cream rises to the top, Mills finishing with 26 points.

Bogut played true to his reputation with 12 rebounds, nine points at 75 per cent, including a rare three-pointer to beat the shot-clock, six assists, while blocking three shots and intimidating a lot of others. He was vocal, vigilant and completely invested. Dellavedova's 13 assists was the Olympic tournament high for the statistic, topping the previous mark — his 10 against France.

This was a win for the ages, Australia now having beaten two of the medallists at the 2014 FIBA World Cup, with that third medallist — those pesky Americans — next on the schedule. No one was in any doubt the Boomers would have a red-hot go.

A nation stopped to watch, absolutely riveted as Australia's Boomers gave the mighty USA an almighty scare in Rio before the Americans prevailed 98-88 in a game which had everything. Everything except the upset win the Aussies worked so hard to get, let down by a couple of wayward shots which allowed the defending champs to just nudge away sufficiently to salvage a victory, the margin slightly exaggerated by the Boomers needing to foul to stop the clock late.

Even without LeBron James, the US team was imposing, featuring Kyrie Irving (Cleveland), Klay Thompson (Golden State), Carmelo Anthony (NY Knicks), Kevin Durant (Golden State), DeMarcus Cousins (Sacramento), Kyle Lowry (Toronto), DeMar DeRozan (Toronto), Harrison Barnes (Dallas Mavericks), Draymond Green (Golden State), DeAndre Jordan (LA Clippers), Paul George (Indiana), Jimmy Butler (Chicago).

Carmelo Anthony, with 9-of-15 threes in his 31-point game-high, was the thorn, Kyrie Irving also finishing strongly to effect the Americans' great escape. "We expected that," the Melbourne-born point guard said of Australia's superb effort, the Boomers tied 29-29 after one, ahead 54-49 at halftime before being contained to 34 second-half points.

USA coach Mike Krzyzewski pre-Olympics labelled this team as the best defensive side America had selected during his three-Olympics reign and they showed that after the main interval. But even this great defensive team had no answers to the Aussies' 54-point first half as three NBA championship winners — Patty Mills, Andrew Bogut and Matthew Dellavedova — put on a show.

Delly had nine assists by the break as the Boomers refused to be intimidated, Andrej Lemanis using his full contingent of 12 (while USA's Harrison Barnes stayed pinned to their bench) and everyone offered something. Anthony opened with a pair of three-pointers for 6-0 fast start, but Joe Ingles nailed a triple of his own, then a fast-break dunk and it was "game on".

Another Anthony three showed the Boomers where they needed to put their defensive focus, but a Delly-to-Bogey dunk and a Mills three-pointer made it 10-9 Australia. Paul George then got riled up by Dellavedova's harassing defence — and it was nothing more than that — and gave up a technical foul, the Boomers stretching their lead to four.

A 24-second shot-clock violation opened the door for the USA to lead 29-27 but David Andersen (13 points on 5-of-6 shooting, five rebounds) stuck a jumpshot for a tied scoreline. Australia had five turnovers and nine fouls for the period but took the lead again in the second on an Andersen three-point play for 38-36. Patty Mills' three made it 41-36 and the full house at Carioca Arena had found an underdog to support against the NBA's almost-finest.

Just 3:28 out from the main break, Australia led 43-36 before consecutive turnovers allowed the USA back in. By the break, Australia ahead 54-49, viewers already had seen Damian Martin strip a startled Kevin Durant in that way only he could, Paul George cop a flop warning but get away with tripping Andersen on the same play, Aron Baynes and Ingles on three fouls, and some of the best basketball of the tournament.

A 9-0 start by the Americans to the third forced a Boomers time-out, then Mills and Bogut tied it back up at 58-58. It was 63 apiece as Australia would not relent before Durant and Kyle Lowry bumped the buffer to 67-63. Ryan Broekhoff, an unsung hero with some great defensive work, his shooting still not yet there, found Mills on a cut, then knocked a bouncing ball off the rim, opening the door for a 67-67 tie. Not having a memorable game, Baynes received his fourth foul in a double-foul with DeAndre Jordan, Draymond Green pushing the USA out to a 70-67 lead at the last break.

Andersen nixed that with a three to start the fourth and at this point, USA had to be thinking "what is going on here?" Anthony drained four threes in the quarter though and his last made it 88-80, the biggest lead of the game. The Aussies doubled Klay Thompson to leave him wide open in possibly their one misguided strategy of the match.

At 1:58, Mills' layup again cut it to 86-90 before Irving stuck the match's biggest shot, a three-pointer over the outstretched Ingles for 93-86. Dellavedova still sliced the deficit to 88-93 and great defence forced a

US shot-clock violation. When the Boomers could not convert that to a score, the rest was academic, free throws blowing it out.

Five-time Olympian Andrew Gaze described the match as: "one of the all-time great performances by an Australian team," and it assuredly was. Patty Mills mesmerised the Americans once again for 30 points at 50 per cent, Dellavedova 11 points on 5-of-8, 11 assists, six rebounds, Bogut 15 points at 78 percent with three blocks and plenty of keyway intimidation, Australia shooting at 50 per cent.

But while a nation was proud, the players were not as thrilled, summed up succinctly by Bogut post-game. "We're disappointed. We had every opportunity. We still lost the game. Let's not sugar-coat it — we lost the game," he told a slightly startled TV interviewer who seemed more excited by the close finish.

And while the Melbourne Cup rightly is revered as the race that stops a nation, the Boomers brought Australia to a halt, even if they could not stop the USA. The match coverage on Channel 7 peaked with 1.4m TV viewers, and 739k live streams, beating the Melbourne Cup Race record! The Boomers had played their way into mainstream consciousness yet again.

In an online report for News Corp, four-time Olympian Phil Smyth said: "The world recognition for the quality of Australian basketball has gone through the roof. Everyone in the world now knows we can play basketball to this level. It's a huge shot in the arm for Australian basketball and for our own NBL."

Smyth, a member of the first Australian team to reach an Olympic medal playoff — Seoul's 1988 battle for bronze lost to the last USA team suiting only college elite — said he had become a believer in the Boomers' gold chances after watching the match.

The Boomers were like bulls in a china shop as they smashed the Chinese 93-68 to consolidate second place in their pool. Coach Andrej Lemanis had the luxury of resting Andrew Bogut, who had logged many more minutes than anticipated during his hasty rehab from a left knee injury, and also seized the chance to get more time into his benchmen.

As a result, it was Cameron Bairstow leading the scoring with 17 points, from Brock Motum on 15, and Ryan Broekhoff also in double digits for the first time. Matthew Dellavedova played less than half the game for his eight assists and Patty Mills took just four shots for his five points, also playing less than two quarters.

Delly still could have had double-figure assists despite his limited time, but for some missed golden opportunities. But Australia was cool, composed and focused as it steadily wore down the Chinese wall with some great defensive pressure and exemplary team play for 34 assists. Nothing says how well a group is functioning as a team better than its assists numbers.

Kevin Lisch had six, Joe Ingles four, Mills and Damian Martin three apiece, as the Boomers showed individual accolades were not the priority when all eyes are on medalling. The Boomers also smashed China on the boards 35-21, drawing further ahead in every direction the further the game evolved, their biggest lead 27 points.

The clash with Venezuela was rough, it was tough and at times downright ridiculous but Australia survived the physical challenge to move into the Rio Olympic quarterfinals as 81-56 winners. Resting Patty Mills and only playing Matthew Dellavedova for 8:24, coach Andrej Lemanis threw more of the backcourt onus onto Kevin Lisch, Damian Martin, Chris Goulding and even Joe Ingles to an extent, and they responded accordingly.

Andrew Bogut (10 points on 5-of-6 shooting, six rebounds, two assists in 17:55 of court-time) and David Andersen (8 points on 4-of-7 shooting, four rebounds in 16:05) stood up as usual, Aron Baynes solid. Cam Bairstow injured his left arm, possibly his shoulder, and played just 7:56, in what would be the only concern for the Boomers going forward. Goulding finished with a game-high 22 points on 6-of-10 shooting, including 4-of-7 threes as the Boomers squashed Venezuela's morale with a 28-13 final period. Australia was through to the quarterfinals against Lithuania.

From go-to-whoa, the Boomers absolutely blitzed international nemesis Lithuania 90-64, kicking down the door into the Rio Olympic semi finals. Australia gave the FIBA World #3 a thorough lesson in toughness and fair dinkum Aussie grit as it blew away the ghosts of past campaigns where Lithuania had been its stumbling block. This time Australia was a chopping block, severing the head of the Lithos by shutting down prolific scorers Mantas Kalnietis (averaging 19.2, held to 12), destroying Jonas Maciulis (10.2ppg, held to 6 pts, with 5 fouls) and sending Toronto Raptors' NBA centre Jonas Valanciunas into extinction.

Unselfish (30 assists), making great decisions with the ball (nine turnovers) and playing defence with a venom and relentless belief even the 300 Spartans would have found intimidating, the Boomers forced 13 turnovers from Lithuania in just the first half. Defensively, the Boomers were beyond exemplary.

From the opening play in which Aron Baynes took a charge from rampant Lithuanian small forward Maciulus, the Boomers obviously were ready to put their bodies on the line. Then Matthew Dellavedova opened the scoring with the first of back-to-back threes and a 6-0 lead which, incredibly, was rarely truly threatened.

If the defence was magnificent, the offence was truly remarkable for its unselfishness, ability to find open players and for setting bone-jarring screens which released players in the first place. The Boomers headhunted more fiercely than Malaysia's famed Iban tribe and Lithuania visibly shrunk from the challenge.

"With the way we're moving the ball and setting screens, someone's going to get open and that side of the game I was getting some good looks," Dellavedova said.

He finished with 15 points, including 4-of-7 threes, with three assists in just 19:12 of action. Also getting solid looks was Patty Mills who took full advantage to lead the scoring with five three-pointers in his 24-point game-high haul.

Mills took a second charge on Maciulus — it was obvious the Boomers had memorised the scout — before he opened up offensively for consecutive three-pointers of his own. Australia was ahead 16-9, playing its heart out defensively and looking sharp in attack, never more so than with the quarter's final play.

With just 5.0 seconds on the game-clock and Lithuania trailing 17-23, Dellavedova took the inbounds pass, dribbled down the floor, pulled up and sank another three for a 26-17 buffer at the end of the first. Mills on a cut, Dellavedova again from range, then Mills with a triple and Australia was ahead 34-19 at 7:23 in the second.

This was heady stuff, the only dampener when Dellavedova went out and needed extended treatment on what appeared to be his lower back and upper left leg. Damian Martin threw a lob and Andrew Bogut athletically slammed it home for 36-20 as the margin continued to grow. It was 17 at 4:15 when Ryan Broekhoff hit a three-pointer for 39-22, Lithuania struggling to cope with the level of commitment and intensity of the Boomers' defence.

Maciulus copped his third foul with a technical, Dellavedova's runner taking the lead to 18 at 42-24. Joe Ingles knocked down two free throws for 44-24, then stole the ball for a layup and a whopping 22-point lead. A couple of successful last-gasp plays to close the half allowed Lithuania to draw back to 30-48 at the interval but this was as close to a perfect half as the Boomers could have played.

Ingles on a backdoor cut had the lead back to 20 at 50-30 before Lithuania made its one run of the quarterfinal. Maciulis hit a pair of triples in the mini outburst which drew the Lithuanians back to 14 down, their defensive resolve much greater, initially at least.

Once Bogut (six assists) found Baynes for a dunk and bonus free throw, Lithuania's commitment again started to splutter. Such was the ferocity of the Australian focus, Lithuania had nothing to offer in the face of it as Broekhoff dished for another Baynes slam, Mills splashed a three, Broekhoff added two free throws and David Andersen followed an offensive rebound putback with consecutive dishes to Baynes for a 70-43 scoreline.

Another classy Bogut pass to Ingles was just joyous stuff to watch, Ingles with 1:49 left giving the Boomers their biggest lead at 90-58. "We came into the tournament with a goal in mind and we haven't achieved that yet," Ingles said post-game, revealing yet again the team's medal focus.

Bogut said much the same after the USA loss and it was clear Australia's next thought only was for its semi final against the Croatia-Serbia quarterfinal winner. "It's just another step on the journey," Dellavedova said of the landslide win. And what an incredible journey this landmark national team was taking Australia on.

"We're going for gold," Patty Mills reminded everyone.

Sadly, that gold medal goal died in the semi final against Serbia. Devastated. Gutted. Shattered. That was how a nation felt when the Boomers were blitzed 87-61 by the Serbs to drop into the bronze medal consolation playoff game.

But if that was how a nation was feeling, it was difficult to imagine how the Boomers themselves were coping. It would require more masterful coaching from Andrej Lemanis — who tried everything to stall the inevitable freight-train which Serbia proved to be — to restore his team back to the side which belted Lithuania a game earlier. But if Serbia could affect a 41-point turnaround from its 15-point intrapool loss to the Aussies, then nothing was impossible.

It was just that the measure of Serbia's dominance would have been a massive body blow and taken a huge emotional toll on a team which believed to a man it was on a gold-plated mission in Rio. That was now gone, forgotten, finished. Now in the bronze medal game, it would be time to end the reign of Spain.

The challenge, of course, was in the face of such misery, to rediscover all the traits which brought Australia to this pinnacle of unprecedented Olympic success. There still was a medal to be won, history to be achieved. And this still was the team to do it.

Serbia did its homework and executed its game-plan to perfection, Milos Teodosic (22 points, five assists) keeping the ball moving offensively in an 8-0 start which had Lemanis pressing the time-out button at 7:46. The Serbs were brutally physical defensively — as most expected — scragging, bumping, pushing and holding the Boomers, taking them right out of what they wanted to do. Hats off to them, they were brilliant. They jumped into the passing lanes and played defence as men possessed. Then they crashed the boards with similar venom.

It led to second-guessing by the Aussies, bad decision-making, hasty shots as five turnovers and 2-of-15 shooting across the opening period for a five-point total clearly would attest. Having introduced the element of doubt with their fierce and relentless approach to lead 16-5 at the break, the Serbs then capitalised further.

Certainly, the Boomers' start was better, with Ryan Broekhoff sticking a three for 8-16, Andrew Bogut blocking shots on two Serbian offences and Joe Ingles on the break reducing the deficit to 10-16. Here we come, Australia was thinking, daring to hope. But no sooner had Australia escaped on the break than Serbia's coach Sasha Djordjevic called an immediate time-out to again emphasise the game-plan — no Aussie fast breaks, no uncontested passes, no uncontested shots, no respite.

They responded accordingly, Teodosic with a three-pointer to set off another 8-0 Serbian charge. Matthew Dellavedova made some uncharacteristic errors — mainly on defence, surprisingly — but he was no orphan, Ingles and Patty Mills with back-to-back turnovers on consecutive Boomer offences. They stayed off Ingles, inviting him to shoot and they stayed all over Mills, inviting him to pass.

If Serbia's plan was to rattle and unsettle, it over-achieved. Early shots by the Boomers led to Serbia surging and growing in confidence, ahead 35-14 at halftime, containing Australia to its lowest single-half score since it mustered only 18 against Canada in 1956. The Boomers were 6-of-29, 2-of-14 on threes, had 11 turnovers and were outrebounded almost 2-1, behind 15-29 in that halftime count.

It was time to regroup, as only this group could. It was a time to invoke the catch-cry: "The Rock doesn't break and neither will we." In 1988 when Yugoslavia (which was a team comprised mainly of Serbians and Croatians) thrashed Australia by 21 in the Seoul Olympic semi final, the Boomers could not recover from the disappointment, whacked by 29 by the USA for bronze.

In Sydney in 2000, the Boomers were ambushed by France by 24 in the semi — much as they were ambushed by Serbia — and Lithuania capitalised on Luc Longley being injured in that match to win bronze by 18 points. It really was only in Atlanta, in 1996 Australia went into the bronze medal game without any qualms, never expected to beat the USA in their semi and losing it by 28.

"In Atlanta we had the USA in the semi so the loss had very little impact on our morale and is probably a big part as to why we had our best chance at the bronze," said five-time Olympian Andrew Gaze, who three times had been as close to medalling as the Boomers were now.

Bogut was hurting against Serbia and Dellavedova wasn't himself either. The toll was great, the disappointment palpable. This had been Australia's greatest Olympic campaign but there remained the unfinished business of bringing home a medal. Spain was ranked No.2 in the world by FIBA and took the USA to an 82-76 result in their semi. A medal success was not going to be easy, but nothing worthwhile ever is.

It was one of the great games of this or any Olympics but ultimately it was heartbreak again for Australia, beaten 89-88 by Spain on the game's penultimate play.

Of all players, Patty Mills , who led the Boomers with 30 points, was called for what can best be described as a phantom foul as Sergio Rodriguez drove to the basket and was rewarded with two free throws. With just 5.4 seconds on the clock, Rodriguez slotted both to give Spain its one-point lead, the Boomers taking time-out to design their last shot at bronze.

But that shot never came as Joe Ingles passed it in to David Andersen and while he looked to continue the play, Spanish guard Ricky Rubio — who had done nothing of consequence all game — deflected his pass release. The loose ball intended for Matthew Dellavedova was then smartly batted across halfcourt by Victor Claver as time ran out on Australia's gutsy effort.

Tragic, heartbreaking, shattering, the drama was over and evident in Spain's exultations and Australia's devastation. "One defensive stop away from a medal," a disconsolate Mills lamented, but in truth, the call was seriously questionable.

Unfortunately, there already were so many of those in the preceding 39 minutes and 54.6 seconds, Andrew Bogut dismissed it as symptomatic of international basketball. Bogut fouled out with 7:54 left in the third quarter after picking up his fourth foul on the first play after halftime. It was a sad end for the NBA championship winner who worked his tail off to make it to the Games, even flying in his own doctor to assist with his desperate knee rehab.

He sorely was missed out there too as Spain's veteran superstar centre Pau Gasol dominated the contest scoring 31 points at a whopping 80 per cent, with 11 rebounds. Gasol was a giant and Nikola Mirotic also caused early havoc as the Boomers stumbled off to another unsteady start. A 10-0 run to close the first half left them only two in arrears at the main break, down 38-40 and feeling the momentum shift.

It was a welcome recovery from a 28-40 deficit, Gasol continuing to dominate. He and Mirotic controlled the game early with eight points apiece as Spain sped to a 16-9 lead. Australia again was struggling offensively, with two shot-clock violations and a slew of turnovers thwarting any attempts to find the slick ball movement and sure attacks which characterised its intrapool and quarterfinal play.

Some of that credit had to go to Spain's defence but much of it also fell to the Boomers trying too hard and not allowing the game to flow naturally. Andersen's injection ignited the offence, the tall centre-forward making the most of his last game in Olympic competition. He assured the Boomers only would trail 17-23 at the first break and led the early going in the second as Australia closed to 21-25.

A succession of poor plays, including a surprising mid-air turnover from Dellavedova, opened the door again for Spain and it barged through. Gasol had all day to size up a three-pointer from the top of the key, then made a layup on the next Spanish foray for that 40-28 buffer. Triples by Mills and Andersen swung the momentum back as Australia's defensive hustle also appreciably improved.

Fouled on a three-point attempt with 3.2 seconds to halftime, Andersen slotted two of the three freebies and the Boomers left the court in good shape. They still needed Ingles to improve after his 14:21 of the first half returned only three rebounds and 0-of-1 shooting, but the door was suddenly ajar.

The second half was an absolute cracker as Australia tied the game up, Brock Motum magnificent off the bench for 12 points on 6-of-8 shooting, with six rebounds. Ryan Broekhoff also was at his offensive best, his 13 points on a perfect 5-of-5 shooting, including 3-of-3 threes.

Spain led by three with 10 minutes of time-capsule level basketball to go, Rodriguez, who scored 11 of Spain's 22 points in the last quarter, opening it with a three-pointer for a 70-64 lead. Mills and Motum trimmed it back to two before Motum tied the match on an emphatic drive and slam dunk. That was an out-of-your-seat moment.

Australia forced a 24-second violation as Spain briefly lost composure, tech fouls and unsportsmanlike fouls flying around for both teams, the tension unbearable, the lead changing 14 times and tied three times in the pulsating period. Gasol's putback dunk made it 83-82, Mills to the hoop made it 84-83, Rodriguez's jumpshot changed it to 85-84, the drama and theatre at fever pitch.

With 35.3 second left, Andersen slotted two pressure free throws for 86-85. At 28.8, Gasol's free throws took Spain ahead again 87-86. Aron Baynes, who had lost a lot of confidence during the game, found it at 9.7 seconds when his hook shot gave Australia back the lead 88-87.

But it was Rodriguez's night to be the hero, gifted to the stripe on the single most significant call of the Olympics, a nation Down Under watching mystified as its Boomers were denied in the cruellest manner possible. "Obviously disappointed," Patty said in a classic piece of understatement. "We set ourselves a very high goal and we didn't get it done."

What they *did* get done was restore Australia among the world's leading basketball nations, showing fans at home just what great shape the sport truly was in.

CHAPTER ELEVEN
REACH FOR THE STARS

When the dust finally settled and there was a chance to review the Rio Olympic Games campaign in a less emotional light, there remained no comfort in how the bronze medal match against Spain concluded. It was some of the most appalling Olympic end-game officiating since USSR was whistled to gold over the USA in Munich in 1972. But it could not be allowed to dim the Boomers' Rio campaign.

They went with the stated goal of bringing home gold but, in truth, most basketball fans would have been beside themselves with joy if they had scored a historic first medal of any hue. They came home with little around their necks beyond the sweat and desperation of another campaign but were denied in the most gross manner imaginable. Spain twice was gifted to the free throw line in the final half-minute to take the lead twice, the last time for good.

Devastated at the cruel nature of their 88-89 loss, the Boomers had every reason to feel betrayed and outraged — much as a nation at home did — by the orchestration of their demise. The alleged foul against Aron Baynes, which put Pau Gasol to the line, was such a furphy — similar plays repeated at both ends so often throughout the contest that to even contemplate calling it reeked of bias.

Baynes erased the lead Gasol gave the Spaniards and with 9.7 seconds left, Australia's fingers were tingling, so close to touching the medals. The very late foul call then assessed against Patty Mills as Sergio Rodriguez threw himself to the floor after his desperation drive to the hoop, left the team, the fans, the nation nonplussed, shattered in abject disbelief.

It was a travesty, and FIBA's feeble attempt to later explain the call only made it appear conspiracy theorists had it right and this was, in fact, how the game's global governing body paid back Australia for its allegedly false blemish against Angola at the 2014 World Cup. In truth though, that controversy succeeded in sabotaging Australia in Spain two years earlier, leading Turkey 64-59 in their Round of 16 KO match with 62 seconds remaining.

Splitting two huge three-point makes by Turkey's Emir Preldzic with a shot-clock violation, Australia still had five seconds to find a way around its 64-65 deficit. Five seconds left. Did that sound familiar? Fast-forward to Rio and with 5.4 seconds left, once again Australia turned over its final possession and, once again, failed to even get a shot up for a chance to pinch the win. But when a referee deliberately decides the outcome of a game you virtually had in the bag, there's reason to feel inconsolable.

The flop is a staple in Europe. It long ago invaded basketball from its soccer origins and there was plenty of it in the intrapool match against Serbia too. The single criticism fairly levelled at this Boomers' team — our best to date — was that in consecutive major tournaments, it could not get a shot off on its final possession after having a time-out to set it up.

That said, the Boomers in Rio were magnificent, restoring the faith and confidence of even the most grizzled and cynical former follower, delighting the diehards and entrancing a whole new generation of fans. They opened the Games with a comprehensive win over France, their first opening night win since Australia's 1996 campaign in Atlanta.

They staved off Serbia to create their own piece of history as the first Olympic Boomers to win back-to-back matches. (But the 15-point margin was deceptive, given it was four the difference with 1:46 left.) They took the game right up to the USA before ultimately being broken by Carmelo Anthony's wicked shooting. (But the 10-point margin was deceptive, this one more a 3-to-4-point game before Australia had to foul to stop the clock.)

Andrew Bogut's honest post-game assessment that the result was a loss and not something to be thrilled about, reinforced to all that these

Boomers had a focus and were not interested in pyrrhic victories. Taking out China and Venezuela meant Australia finished second to the USA with a 4-1 intrapool record and nemesis Lithuania to face in the KO quarterfinals.

The Lithuanians kept Australia from bronze in Atlanta and Sydney but all the pain was forgotten in a thoroughly emphatic and mesmerising 90-64 rout. Unlike Australia's bronze medal playoff teams of the past though, arrival into the semi finals was not greeted with the glee and relief of those ill-fated campaigns but more with the resolve that yes, the team was where it expected to be.

Those mythical basketball gods though let the Boomers down when Serbia escaped Croatia 86-83 in a rival quarter final. Croatia would have been a second former nemesis the Boomers most likely would comfortably have negotiated, burying another ghost of the past. Instead though it was Serbia again and this time the Serbs had done their homework and came out playing as men possessed, men on a mission. The excellent rotating defence and slick moving offence which had proven so entertaining and successful for the Boomers, came apart at the seams as Milos Teodosic carved up Australian defenders continually caught chasing him around screens.

Andrej Lemanis did an excellent job coaching the Boomers in Rio but rarely was his coaching more focused or intense, ironically, than in this defeat. As crazy as that may appear, Australia beaten by 26, Lemanis tried every player, a number of different combinations and strategies, leaving no stone unturned to try and stem the tide from drowning his Boomers' aspirations.

Ultimately he was unable to influence the result, the Boomers hitting an emotional wall on the one day a nation was tuned in hoping to see history. Boasting arguably the second-most talented team in the tournament and playing a brand of basketball variously described as "beautiful" and "majestic", Spain was going to be a difficult bounce-back in the quest now for bronze.

It always was going to be made more so when the officials entered the equation, quickly hitting Bogut with his fourth foul and finally with his fifth while David Andersen was waiting courtside to check in for him. There was no call between Bogut's fourth foul and Ricky Rubio lunging himself into our best big man before throwing himself on the floor in customary fashion. Despite that, Australia was not going away, Patty Mills hitting 13 third quarter points and Brock Motum burying an emphatic slam dunk through traffic.

Possibly the best half of the tournament, it ended in despair where, clearly, the players were not the ones left to determine the outcome. The Games were at an end. Patty Mills was a class above throughout, and so too was Andrew Bogut, despite the knee injury he battled so heroically to overcome in time for the Games clearly hindering him the longer the tournament went.

Patty averaged 21.3 points per game to finish second among all scorers at the Games. His average was better than the one with which he led the London Olympics in scoring. It was quite the personal postscript, though he gladly would have traded such individual success for that elusive medal.

So too David Andersen, who produced a memorable farewell Olympics. It was sad to see him close this portion of his career without a medallion.

Given the precious nature of the officiating, where even the slightest suggestion of dissatisfaction was penalised by trigger-happy whistlers, there wasn't a lot more that could be done. It was time to sheath the despair and prepare for the next challenge.

Patty Mills did just that when he returned to San Antonio. His three-point blitz lifted the Spurs to a 129-100 win over the All Star-laden Golden State Warriors in their NBA regular season opener. Winning on the Warriors' home court made it an embarrassing night for them, having also added prized free agent Kevin Durant to the star-studded roster. Mills buried two of his three three-point baskets in the first two minutes of the fourth quarter to break Golden State's back. He also was acclimatising to his new teammate… Spanish 7-footer Pau Gasol.

Fellow Aussies Joe Ingles and Dante Exum, in his first game since his ACL tear, started their season at the Utah Jazz with a 104-113 loss to Portland Trail Blazers. Patty enjoyed back-to-back 18-point games in wins over New Orleans and Miami Heat and Aron Baynes, now in the Eastern Conference at the Detroit Pistons, had seven points and seven rebounds in a win over Milwaukee Bucks. Matthew Dellavedova, now starting for the Bucks, had 10 points and five assists. Life was continuing, Rio now very much in the rear-vision mirror.

There was no trick or secret to how Patty Mills sprung wide open for the winning shot over the Houston Rockets in late December. "I have no clue mate," he said. "I didn't do anything other than just stand there. It was a heck of a pass right in the shot pocket." Mills stroked a three-pointer with 12.9 seconds left to lift San Antonio over the Rockets 102-100. The victory was the Spurs' fifth straight and improved its road record to 15-1, while snapping Houston's 10-win streak. NBA Season 2016–17 was travelling smoothly.

While the Spurs may have been enjoying the regular season, Andrew Bogut arrived in Cleveland in March 2017 to join LeBron James and the Cavaliers, only to have disaster strike. Bogut's left leg was broken in a freak accident during his debut with the Cavs. Bogey was closing out to Miami Heat's Okaro White who made a move and as he did, clipped Bogut's left leg high on the shin with his left knee. It was a catastrophe for Bogut, who only was on court for 58 seconds, the impact and crack so loud that television microphones picked it up.

Bogut also could be heard saying he thought it was broken as he sat on the sideline. He was helped off by teammates James Jones and Tristan Thompson, unable to put weight on the leg, the injury later confirmed as a fracture of his tibia. "I heard it break," disconsolate teammate LeBron James said. "It's very deflating. We were excited about the acquisition to bring him in here. It's a tough one, not only obviously for him, but for our ball club." Not to mention the Boomers.

The Spurs completed the regular season with a 61-21 win-loss record, good enough for second place in the Western Conference, behind Golden State Warriors on 67-15. Patty averaged 9.5 points per game across the regular season, plus 3.5 assists and 1.8 rebounds. In the playoffs, he upped his scoring to 10.3 points, with 2.7 assists and 2.1 rebounds.

Patty was a perfect 3-of-3 from the three-point line as San Antonio brushed aside Memphis Grizzlies 111-82 in their opening round playoff game. After averaging 10.1 points through the regular season, Tony Parker had 18 in 22 minutes. It was then another comfortable 96-82 win at home for a 2-0 series lead before the Grizzlies growled twice in Memphis, 105-94 and 110-108 in overtime to lock the best-of-seven series up at 2-2. Grizzlies centre Marc Gasol hit a 12-foot floater with 0.7 of a second left in the five-minute extension to clinch the win, Kawhi Leonard scoring 43 points for the Spurs in a lost cause.

Having failed to trouble the scorer's bench in the first four games, Manu Ginóbili had six points in 33 seconds in the first quarter of Game Five back in San Antonio, hustling his tail off. "He brought that 'grandpa juice' is what I call it, and we all followed," Patty Mills said. "We shouldn't wait for him to do that before we get into gear, but it really is inspiring when you see him dive on the ball putting his body on the line. Hard drives, hard cuts, it gets us all going."

Ginóbili's play spurred Mills, his best friend on the team, Patty scoring a career playoffs-high 20 points on 7-of-10 shooting, with 5-of-7 threes.

"He was incredible," Ginóbili said. "He finished the game. He made four threes in the fourth (quarter), tough ones, quick release. Sometimes you need something like that from somebody. Sometimes it's going to be him, sometimes it's Kawhi, more often. It's good to have a team that deep."

The Spurs shot 14-of-28 three-pointers, just two short of their postseason record. "They're the same shots that we shot in the first three, four games, they just dropped tonight," Mills said. "But definitely a good feeling when you can see some go in."

A 103-96 win in Game Six eliminated Memphis 4-2, the Spurs' reserves tying the Grizzlies' subs with 16 points, thanks to Mills' 10-point game. Game One of the Western Conference semi final against Houston Rockets was an absolute slap in the face for San Antonio, smacked 126-99 on its home court. Game Two revealed a much different mindset as the Spurs reversed the result 121-96, storming home 33-13 in the last quarter.

The win was not without cost though, Tony Parker hobbled by a left leg injury with 8:43 remaining and needing to be carried off by teammates. He had scored 18 points and was looking good when the injury occurred and immediate prognoses were anything but encouraging. "He has that presence, just like T.D. (Tim Duncan) had that presence," Patty Mills said. The series at 1-1, it now looked likely Mills would step into Parker's starting role.

"He was rolling the last month, going back to his old self," Mills said. "But I can tell you one thing, that we're all ready. We're all ready to step up and make an impact." LaMarcus Aldridge and Kawhi Leonard both scored 26 points as San Antonio took Game Three 103-92 in Houston. It marked the Spurs' first postseason game without the injured Parker since 2001, ending an NBA record of 221 straight playoff appearances for the Frenchman.

Coach Gregg Popovich surprised by opting not to start Mills, going instead with rookie Dejounte Murray. Patty responded with 15 points in

30 minutes. Murray scored two in 15, Parker meanwhile having surgery on his quadriceps tear. Houston tied up the series at 2-2 with a rousing 125-104 home win in Game Four, the series heading back to San Antonio.

Tony Parker's surgery meant he would not be returning to the 2016–17 playoffs. Popovich shuffled the deck again, Dejounte Murray back to the bench and Patty Mills inserted into the starting quintet for Game Five. The match was a classic, Popovich screaming at Pau Gasol when the veteran centre chose not to set a screen for Patty on the final play in regulation. Patty eventually banked a three-pointer but time had run out. The mis-read left the scores deadlocked at 101-101, forcing overtime.

"I think I made a wrong read," Gasol said. "It was tough because when they put a small on you, you have a tendency to go in. I saw a switch, but I should have stayed up because (Patrick) Beverley went with LaMarcus (Aldridge) and we could have played off that. I made a bad, bad read on that play." Ultimately it did not matter as San Antonio won a thriller 110-107, despite losing Kawhi Leonard after 38 minutes to an ankle injury.

"I remember saying to a couple of the guys this is what we live for, these moments, to play in these situations," Mills said post-game. "Game Five, at home, you just try to soak it up and play hard. I guess that's where all the passion comes out, at those moments. The diving on loose balls, coming up with whatever it may be; you're throwing your body on the line in those situations."

Patty finished with 20 points, including five three-pointers, only Leonard with 22 scoring more for the Spurs. Danny Green scored seven of his 16 points in overtime, and Manu Ginóbili produced one of the game's pivotal plays. Houston's James Harden had compiled a triple-double with 33 points, 10 rebounds and 10 assists and also had a shot at a potential game-tying three-pointer in the final seconds of overtime. But Ginóbili appeared out of nowhere and blocked the shot, preserving the victory and a 3-2 series lead.

Back in Houston for Game Six and with Leonard now joining Parker on the sidelines, few expected the Rockets to be comprehensively erased but that is exactly what occurred. Stepping up in the absence of fallen teammates, LaMarcus Aldridge produced a 34-point, 12 rebound grand slam performance to steer a thorough 114-75 rout. Aldridge became the first Spur to pair 34 points with 12 rebounds in a playoff match since Tim Duncan against Phoenix Suns in 2008. By halftime San Antonio was ahead by 19 and its 27-11 final quarter put the icing on the cake.

Patty Mills had 14 points and seven assists, and Pau Gasol added 10 points and 11 rebounds, James Harden universally flayed by critics and Houston fans alike for a 10-point return on 2-of-11 shooting. San Antonio was on its way into the Western Conference Championship against Golden State Warriors, though down Parker and with Leonard proppy, the Spurs faced a Herculean challenge.

When Leonard reinjured the ankle during Game One, the Spurs would struggle to hold on, ultimately beaten 113-111 despite controlling much of the contest. Steph Curry with 40 points and Kevin Durant 34 were substantial for the Warriors. "I don't want to talk too much about Patty Mills because the more good things I say, the more we're going to have to pay him," Popovich said before tip-off.

With Leonard now sidelined alongside Parker for Game Two, Golden State took no prisoners, backing a 33-16 first period with a 39-28 second. The Warriors won every quarter for a comprehensive 136-100 demonstration of their greater depth, heading back to San Antonio with a 2-0 series lead.

It was not much better at home for the Spurs, David Lee lost to a left knee injury in the opening quarter as Golden State seized control of the game and the series, winning 120-108. Patty's offensive struggles continued but Manu Ginóbili came off the bench to score a team-high 21 points on 7-of-9 shooting in 18 minutes.

Now down 0-3, Game Four was always going to be a formality. Ginóbili, the majestic 198cm Argentine magician, was shown a mark of respect by coach Gregg Popovich, elevated into the San Antonio Spurs' starting line-up for the match at the AT&T Center. Already missing starters Tony Parker and Kawhi Leonard, plus forward David Lee, the Spurs were not expected to end the Warriors' unbeaten sweep through the playoffs, GSW advancing 129-115 to await the winner of the Cleveland-Boston Eastern Final.

Ginóbili finished with 15 points, seven assists, three steals and a rebound and was afforded a magnificent ovation by the Spurs faithful for 15 seasons of unrelenting commitment to San Antonio. Those came after steering Italy's Kinder Bologna to the 2001 Euroleague Championship where he also was named Finals MVP, on top of two Italian League MVP awards. "Before the game, you think it may or may not be the last game he ever plays in, and I did not want to miss the opportunity to honour him in front of our home fans for his selflessness over the years," Popovich said of his decision to start the veteran.

"I mean, this is a Hall of Fame player who allowed me to bring him off the bench for — I can't even remember now — the last decade or something, because it would make us a better team overall." Popovich said he would leave Ginóbili to make his own decision on his future, not trying to influence him in either direction.

"I do feel like I can still play, but that's not what is going to make me retire or not," Ginóbili said post-game. "It's about how I feel, if I wanna go through all that again." The 39-year-old said he would let it "sink in" for the next few weeks before talking with his wife but was elated he had two "unbelievable options". Those were to keep playing the game he loved for a further season, or spend time as a dad, enjoying life with his wife and children.

Golden State players joined in the applause as Ginóbili was subbed out, one of the sport's international all-time greats still going along and strong and on his own terms. As he sat down alongside Patty Mills, Australia's wunderkind appeared bemused on the bench as to why everyone was delivering the standing ovation. After all, Ginóbili would come back for the 2017–18 NBA season.

Patty Mills inspired and mesmerised a sold-out gathering in a passionate luncheon address at the Lakes Resort of West Lakes in Adelaide in August. The lunch was in support of Adelaide's landmark Aboriginal Basketball Academy, based at Woodville High School. Seated next to him and Alyssa Levesque, I found him as relaxed and engaging as ever, though he did not touch his meal. That wasn't necessarily because he wasn't hungry. He was just acutely aware the time he spent eating would be time that kept him from dealing with the myriad people clamouring for a moment of his attention. Additionally promoting his new range of children's books which chronicled his early life, Mills addressed much of his thoughts towards the Indigenous youth in the room.

Introducing the triple-Olympian, NBA champion and now "$US50million Man" at the San Antonio Spurs, host and (then) fellow *triple*-Olympian Brett Maher opened with a recap of Mills' astonishing career. Perhaps though the star guard's greatest accomplishment was to so thoroughly embrace all that came with being a bona fide role model. Clearly he was accustomed to every moment of it, despite the extraordinary demands it placed on his time and schedule. Mills' Indigenous heritage was recognised with an event-opening of cultural music and dance.

In observing him in this environment, away from basketball, it was clear he was completely comfortable, soaking it up. It may well be this key element that makes Mills so popular. He not only merely embraces his Aboriginal and Torres Strait Islander background to be the quintessential

Australian, he actively promotes and cherishes it. He could not resist joining in with the dance troupe.

"Playing for Australia and wearing the green-and-gold has way more meaning to it than anyone can ever imagine," he told his riveted audience, every eye on him. You could have heard a napkin drop, such was the attention he commanded. Olympic campaigns that ended abruptly at the quarterfinal stage in Beijing and London were always going to be bettered by the previous year's Rio Games quest. "There was a desire for me before this (Rio) campaign started, to make sure everyone on our team understood why we play for Australia," he said. "We definitely gave it a crack. We had a goal of winning a gold medal and we made it to the bronze medal match and unfortunately, it was centimetres and split seconds away from having that in our hand and achieving something that's never been done.

"It burns the fuel even more, it burns the fire even more for me to go on to Tokyo in 2020 and achieve this thing because it means way more to this whole country." Mills' new four-year deal at San Antonio meant greater expectations on him. "I've been in San Antonio for six years now and I've had opportunities to leave San Antonio earlier to go to another team to be the starting point guard," Mills said.

"But for me, I thought the most important thing is to stay in San Antonio, which is such a classy organisation and environment in which I would be able to develop my game, so I decided to stay. So now I'm at the point where I'm setting higher goals for myself. I'm at the point now where I believe I should be the starting point guard for that team, so that's my mindset going into next year.

"Tony Parker is out hurt so he'll miss the first bit of the season but that's the mindset of keep achieving your goals and raising the bar. It's a great environment. I mean Tony has taken me under his wing ever since I got there. We've grown really close. Tim Duncan, for example, is someone that I'm pleased to not only call a teammate but a really good friend as well. And Manu Ginóbili, who I call Gramps because he's older than anyone I've played with, but a person I've looked up to and who has really helped me, not only on the court but off the court as well.

"The (Spurs') system is all about playing the game the right way. It's a value I was brought up with by my mum and dad — you have to respect the game. That's what the Spurs organisation is all about.

"It's a classy organisation, playing the game the right way, representing the San Antonio Spurs the right way and you live with the results." Mills cited the Western Conference Finals as an example of the club doing the right thing when superstar Kawhi Leonard went down injured. Instead of rushing him back and risking his long-term health, the Spurs allowed him to heal properly, safeguarding his future.

Asked about the fact Boomers teams for major internationals such as FIBA World Cups and Olympic Games mainly now comprised Australia's NBA and European players, Mills said it was a positive problem to have. "You've got the Commonwealth Games coming up next year that will be played over the NBA season so there's a chance for not only the NBL players but younger guys too to pull on the green-and-gold," the recently appointed Commonwealth Games ambassador said.

While the pride on Alyssa Levesque's face never waned as he spoke, Patty addressed much of his thoughts towards the Indigenous youth in the room. "You kids need to reach and aim for the top — the most highest point in whatever field you are. It doesn't just stop at basketball. It could be in the classroom or in the science lab," he said. "You've got to reach for the stars and if you fall short, then you're still up there.

"My advice is not to reach for anything short of the best."

Mills' own example of playing in the NBA and at the highest international levels he said reflected on his career choice of basketball. But aiming for the summit was the only course, regardless of the field.

"I was lucky enough to be born into a basketball family," he said. "Where I'm at now, it wasn't handed to me on a silver platter. I'm not this superhero some people try to make me out to be. I'm exactly like you guys, at your age and younger.

"And it was all just because of hard work and sacrifices and support, which all you guys have right here today. I was in the exact same position as you. I'm no-one special, but I was just determined, I was motivated. I wanted to represent my people the right way. The first Indigenous person to represent Australia at the Olympics and World Championships was Michael Ahmatt.

"The next one, my uncle Danny Morseu, and then I was the third. You know that's too big of a gap. The goal is to shorten that 30-year gap between me and my uncle Danny Morseu. But the first thing you kids have got to realise is I'm no one special."

We all knew and understood what he meant — that it was dedication, hard work and focus which got Mills to where he was. But no one special? That may be the only thing Patty Mills had 100 per cent wrong. He is most certainly a very special human being, a credit to himself, his family and to the First Nation peoples he represents with such grace, passion and dignity. We are all lucky to have him and to call him ours.

The luncheon formalities over, Patty then settled back to pose for selfies and sign autographs for the 260 delighted Aboriginal children who sat spellbound throughout his address, sparing time for everyone. It was no surprise then he was running late for the 36-kilometre drive to Colonnades Shopping Centre to the south of Adelaide to promote his children's books. "He didn't miss a single kid," said Scott Whitmore, a board member of the Aboriginal Basketball Academy who helped organise and coordinate the event. (The ABA programme is for Year 10, 11 and 12 students, embracing Aboriginal culture and has as one of its goals students achieving their SACE certificate.)

"It's no wonder he was late to his book signings at Colonnades… and he didn't forget the ABA either. The following year he sent us three big duffel bags full of Under Armour gear to give to the kids — shoes, training gear, just a lot of stuff." Patty's "Game Day" books were a fantastic and fun basketball series designed to entertain young readers, inspire kids to achieve their goals through sport, while showcasing his pride in his Indigenous heritage.

CHAPTER TWELVE
A VERY BIG YEAR

FIBA, basketball's global governing body, changed the method of qualifying for its four-yearly World Cup, requiring in-season "windows" when nations in various regions could play home/away fixtures to determine rankings and qualifications. Drawing Australia, New Zealand and the rest of its Oceania region into its larger Asian Zone, it now was left to the Boomers to reach the 2019 World Cup — the Worlds also were moved from the even years between Olympics to the year prior to the Games — via this home/away system.

It effectively ruled out NBA players being available to drive World Cup and Olympic qualifying campaigns and threw the onus back onto Australia's burgeoning National Basketball League to provide Boomers candidates. As national men's coach Andrej Lemanis put it, the NBL players did the "heavy lifting" now to confirm Australia's participation in the major international tournaments. What FIBA's new methodology also did though was offer consistent exposure on home courts to national teams around the world.

The machinations also meant Australia (and New Zealand) now additionally could compete in the FIBA Asia Cup, the Boomers sweeping all before them in Beirut in their first such tournament and claiming its gold medal. Australia beat Iran 79-56 in the gold medal game and Brad Newley, controversially omitted from the Rio Olympic Games team, starred with 18 points. Newley showed yet again that nothing beat wearing the green-and-gold of Australia.

Patty Mills, named NAIDOC (National Aborigines and Islanders Day Observance Committee) Person of the Year, was preparing for the 2017–18 NBA season. It would be the last time Tony Parker and Manu

Ginóbili played for the Spurs, while Kawhi Leonard and Danny Green were traded following the season to the Toronto Raptors. San Antonio's 47-35 win-loss record was good enough for seventh seed in the Western Conference, which drew it into a best-of-seven first round conflict with the second-ranked and defending champion Golden State Warriors.

Averaging a career-best 25.7 minutes and 10 points per game, Patty was a non-factor in Game One, Golden State handsome 113-92 winners. Patty scored 21 points in Game Two but to little avail, the Warriors again too talented, winning 116-101. Patty's 14 points helped keep San Antonio competitive in Game Three at home, but again it was in vain, Golden State ahead 110-97 at the siren. Game Four brought the Spurs back to a 1-3 deficit, Mills with three three-pointers and an equal team-best five assists in a 103-90 victory.

But it was over, 99-91 in Game Five, despite LaMarcus Aldridge scoring 30 points and snaring 12 boards and Patty Mills adding 18 points. Season 2017–18 was being packed in mothballs and Patty now the longest tenured Spur on the roster. He and Marco Belinelli were the only remaining Spurs from the 2014 championship team still on San Antonio's active player list.

At home in Australia, Brad Newley claimed his second Commonwealth Games gold medal as the Boomers crushed Canada in the final at the Gold Coast Convention Centre. Chris Goulding led all scorers but importantly for the Boomers, Nick Kay continued his growth as an international player, an opportunity the NBL stalwart may never have received had FIBA not altered its qualifying strategy for its major events. Commonwealth Games and Asia Cup gold medals served to reinforce Australia's prestige and standing within those confines. But it meant precious little in the *real* world. World Cup or Olympic medallions were the true gauge of success.

Despite major roster changes, Gregg Popovich still was able to guide his San Antonio team back to the playoffs for an NBA record-tying 22nd consecutive season, matching the mark set by the Syracuse Nationals/Philadelphia 76ers from 1950–1971. San Antonio's 48-34 win-loss tally again gave them the seventh seeding in the Western Conference, this time setting up a best-of-seven first round series against #2 ranked Denver Nuggets.

But undoubtedly the season's greatest moment came on March 28, the night the Spurs retired the #20 playing singlet of Argentinian superstar Manu Ginóbili. An hour-long ceremony after San Antonio hosted the Cleveland Cavaliers was emotional and moving in equal measure. But the event was off to a fairytale start as the Spurs battled the Cavs to a standstill prior to the Ginóbili tribute. As Ginóbili, one of Patty Mills' firmest friends from the ball-club, sat with fellow championship stalwarts Tim Duncan and Tony Parker, the match wound down to a classic close finish.

With seconds to play, DeMar DeRozan, who the Spurs scored from Toronto in the trade for Kawhi Leonard, drove into the keyway, drawing three Cavaliers defenders. Airborne, he threw a picture-perfect pass into the left corner of the court where Patty Mills caught the ball in sweet rhythm and released it with that trademark arc. The ball had no option but to swish through the middle of the hoop and Patty had scored the match-winning three-pointer. His exuberance and delight clearly were evident as he danced to mid-court, teammates mobbing him, Marco Belinelli a second after DeRozan.

It could not have been scripted any better. The perfect finish from the perfect player to finish it, in front of the three stars who won four championships together and including Ginóbili, the man with whom Patty conspired in that fateful third quarter some five years earlier to clinch the NBA crown. Ginóbili is one of only two players in history, Bill Bradley the other one, to win a Euroleague title, an NBA championship and an

Olympic gold medal. To have his uniform retirement ceremony launched from such a high note, and to have it provided by Mills, is the stuff which creates legends and stories to be passed along the generations. These are the moments when fans believe in those mythical "basketball gods".

Just two weeks or so later, those gods still were smiling on the Spurs as they stole Game One of their playoff series in Denver 101-96. Game Two went a little differently, the Nuggets tying it 1-1 with a 114-105 home win, Denver's Nikola Jokic two assists shy of a triple-double. San Antonio pulled off a surprise Game Three win 118-108 at home to again seize the series initiative. And Denver had it all "back on serve" when it won Game Four 117-103. Torrey Craig, who played in the NBL for Cairns Taipans and Brisbane Bullets as an import, had 18 points as a starter for the Nuggets.

Ahead 3-2 after winning 108-90 at home, Denver now had two chances to seal it, either in Game Six in San Antonio or at home in Game Seven. It would take all seven games to provide a victor as the Spurs smacked Game Six 120-103, then fought it out but went down 86-90 to end their 2018–19 on-court NBA commitments.

Popovich still had a busy northern summer ahead, preparing the USA team for the FIBA World Cup in China, but Patty Mills' off-season was going to be extra-special. First and foremost, he had proposed to Alyssa Levesque and the couple were due to marry. Then there was the other little matter, the 2019 FIBA World Cup and another shot at that elusive international medal. The Boomers had qualified and, equally importantly, Andrew Bogut spent the 2018–19 season playing for Sydney Kings in the NBL, claiming league MVP honours in the process.

He was ready and willing to anchor down the middle for the Boomers in China and was in such good form, Golden State Warriors threw him an SOS and he returned to the NBA to complete the season with his former club. Bogut added 30 games for the Warriors, including the NBA Championship Series against Kawhi Leonard and the Toronto Raptors.

Chasing a rare "threepeat", Golden State fell short 4-2, Leonard winning the Finals MVP to join Kareem Abdul-Jabbar and LeBron James as the only players to win it with multiple teams.

Patty and Alyssa Levesque married on a gorgeous northern summer day in Oahu, Hawaii in a beautiful ceremony and, in the words of his Spurs teammate and wedding guest Boris Diaw, those present were "spoiled with a great cultural diversity of food, music and traditions." Yet instead of revelling in a lavish honeymoon, Patty and Alyssa spent the week delivering water to drought-stricken outback towns in New South Wales.

The town of Walgett, about six hours from where Patty was born, was without any rainfall for more than a year. Compounding problems in the small rural town of about 2,000 was the fact its solitary supermarket burned down a month earlier, stretching food and water supplies. The drought stranded Walgett without water as early as January.

Without drawing any undue attention to his gesture, Patty Mills financed rescue water to the area, including necessary drinking water to the community. His presence brought untold joy and had his legion of fans seeking photos and autographs, Mills obliging everyone with his usual humour and abundant good nature.

Life was travelling particularly well for Patty. He had been recognised by the NBPA, winning the NBA's ultimate "glue guy" Backbone Award for San Antonio Spurs. Traditionally the award goes to those "heart-and-soul" players on NBA teams, and Mills best exemplified it in 2018–19 at the Spurs. "They pick us up, push us forward, never let us down," the promos for the Backbone Award exulted.

The Spurs continued to consistently make the NBA playoffs and Mills, 30, now was the eight-year-long constant in that process and San Antonio's "elder statesman". It was a role he was handling with typical aplomb, wisdom, insight, sincerity and charm, making him a crucial sounding board for the Spurs younger brigade. The exciting Aussie also had shown he was durable, playing all 82 regular season games for the second season in succession. In 2018–19, he averaged 9.9 points, 3.0 assists and a career-high 2.2 rebounds per game.

He was second on the Spurs in three-point makes with 159, and his 9.9 points also was second in bench scoring as he further solidified his reputation as the ideal teammate. "He's one of the greatest teammates ever," coach Gregg Popovich told NBA.com. "He's always ready to help out, to make people feel comfortable and he's just continued that. He's always ready to play the leadership role and helps us in every way that he can."

Ahead of the FIBA World Cup in China, Australia secured exhibition games against Canada and the USA in Perth and Melbourne. It was a coup on two fronts. For starters, the Boomers had drawn Canada, Senegal and Lithuania in their group in China so to have a couple of good looks at the Canadians was a bonus. Coming off an NBA championship coaching the Toronto Raptors, Nick Nurse joined Steve Kerr (Golden State Warriors, 2015), Tyronn Lue (Cleveland Cavaliers, 2016), Pat Riley (Los Angeles Lakers, 1982) and Paul Westhead (Los Angeles Lakers, 1980) as NBA championship-winning coaches in their rookie season as a head coach. Appointed as coach of Canada's national team, there was acute interest in how his team would play.

The second coup was landing matches against the USA on Australian soil. The event was deemed so big that Melbourne's Marvel Stadium was booked as the venue for the two showdowns. The AFL's prized football stadium, with its retractable roof, would be reconfigured to accommodate a basketball court in the middle of the ground and some 50,000 spectators. This was going to be a massive event — *two* massive events — and no one was in any doubt Melbourne's sports mad public would flock to see our best against the NBA's select.

A Ben Simmons controversy developed as Australia's second No.1 NBA draft pick had just signed a new $US170 million five-year contract extension with Philadelphia 76ers. Originally available for the Boomers' World Cup team, he then withdrew, and if his employer wanted him back in the States working on his game, no one could really blame him. Irate fans who purchased tickets to the Australia-USA games believing Simmons would be a Boomer, took their complaints to social media and the furore raged. Simmons subsequently made himself available to play the two exhibitions before it was determined he would not.

Andrej Lemanis' team for China was laden with surprises and shock omissions. Aron Baynes, Andrew Bogut, Matthew Dellavedova, Chris Goulding, Joe Ingles and Patty Mills were "no-brainers" and the men behind the culture of the team. Jonah Bolden, Xavier Cooks, Cameron Gliddon, Nick Kay, Jock Landale and Nathan Sobey completed the line-up.

Bolden was on the Philadelphia 76ers roster and brought good size and athleticism. Cooks was the 2018 Big South Conference Player of the Year, earmarked for an NBA career eventually. He performed admirably in Germany with SIG Strasbourg and enjoyed a strong NBA Summer League series with Golden State. Nick Kay revealed himself to be a solid meat-and-potatoes "big" with an extraordinary engine driving his relentless work rate. He was one of the "finds" via the process of NBL players representing Australia in the qualifying rounds. And Jock Landale was playing at Zalgiris Kaunas in Lithuania and showed out at the NBA Summer League with some eye-catching performances for Milwaukee Bucks.

The selections of Gliddon and Sobey, who both joined Lemanis at his Brisbane Bullets' club, were received with some degree of suspicion as a result of their NBL transfers. The omissions of Rio Olympian Brock Motum and Mitch Creek, another of the "finds" in the qualifying matches, also were not received overly fondly.

The Simmons controversy having died down, a new issue emerged when Xavier Cooks suffered a meniscus tear, forcing him to drop out of the team. His loss was a huge blow and the Boomers reached out to Ryan Broekhoff, now in the NBA but unavailable for this campaign because his wife was giving birth to their first born. When Broekhoff did not materialise as an option, Mitch Creek was promoted into the line-up.

Basketball Australia boffins, again publicly declaring this Boomers team as the "strongest ever", had a sobering reality check when Canada won the opening exhibition match at Perth's RAC Arena 90-70. Australia's first opponent at the World Cup dished out a stunning performance, coach Nick Nurse keeping it simple for Canada, extracting the ball movement he wanted, his shooters making the ones that mattered to send the Boomers into a night-long game of catch-up.

Canada's defence was disruptive, but it was more the Boomers' lack of offensive sync which made that look so much better. In contrast, Australia's defence, for so long a staple of any international success it enjoyed, was akin to road-cone refuse. That was the hardest aspect to explain because defence is mostly about effort first, technique second. The offence looked great early, Joe Ingles-to-Jock Landale for an opening dunk, Patty Mills-to-Andrew Bogut, Bogues-to-Ingles, were all morale-lifting scores.

Remarkably though, Ingles' bucket for 6-4 was Australia's only lead, Canada responding with three three-pointers before forcing Boomers coach Andrej Lemanis to take time-out at 5:35 in the first when the lead blew out to 15-6. It was Landale, impressive in his starting power forward role — Aron Baynes was rested from this one — with 18 points at 57 per cent and eight boards, who finally broke the drought.

Consecutive triples from Patty Mills (game-high 20 points, four assists) had the Boomers in touch at 20-22 before trailing by five at the first break. By halftime, Canada doubled that to 10 at 46-36. A Bogut shot rejection which spurred a Boomers fast break with Mills flicking it to Landale, saw the Arena crowd come to life in the third. A Mills three in transition and a Chris Goulding triple tied it at 57-57. But while the Boomers were taking time to enjoy pulling the contest back to an even keel, Canada kept going with a 7-0 run before another Mills three-pointer.

Australia's last hurrah was pretty much a Mitch Creek basket off a Landale feed for 64-69 in the last quarter before an 11-2 Canadian avalanche buried any Boomers aspirations. Matthew Dellavedova looked rusty, going 0-for-9 despite six assists, while Sobey (13 minutes, 0 points, 2 rebounds, 2 turnovers) and Cam Gliddon (10 minutes, 0 points, 1 rebound, 1 foul) predictably looked off the international pace.

Lemanis rested Mills and Bogut from the second match with Canada, a game which saw Jonah Bolden unearthed as another diamond and Australia getting the job done 81-73. Jock Landale again also was a standout with team highs of 13 points and nine boards in a far more committed effort from everyone all over the floor, particularly without the ball.

The shockwave came after the match when Bolden, possibly aggrieved that as an NBA player he was coming off the Boomers bench behind Landale, withdrew from the team for "personal reasons". It was another unforeseen setback and sent an SOS to Brock Motum, who already had returned from the Boomers' camp to his professional gig in Europe. Motum gave jumping back on a plane the thumbs down so Lemanis turned to veteran David Barlow, who had not even been in his final 18-player selection squad. It meant the Australian team now had three players who were unlikely to see much action in China.

Gregg Popovich, Patty Mills' veteran coach at San Antonio Spurs, and his USA team arrived in Australia to much fanfare. Joe Ingles was photographed with Utah Jazz teammate Donovan Mitchell, and Boomers assistant Luc Longley with his championship teammate at the Chicago Bulls and now US assistant coach Steve Kerr. The American team also was beset by withdrawals but it was still the USA. Since first playing the US at the Tokyo Olympic Games in 1964, Australia had lost on all 25 occasions the two great nations met in basketball combat. It came within a point in an exhibition loss in Melbourne in 1978 and at the 1990 FIBA World Championship.

Ahead of their first exhibition match-up at Marvel Stadium though, Patty Mills and Joe Ingles were capturing headlines for different reasons than basketball. Patty had not only embraced his Indigenous roots and been a peerless role model, but also done important tangible work in remote Australian communities. There was little he could do of greater value than what he already had done far from the hardwood.

His latest project was a partnership with Australian Indigenous Basketball and Zero Mass, a company which made SOURCE hydropanels, bringing clean drinking water to six remote communities in Australia. Mills officially launched the project as part of the 2019 International Indigenous Basketball and Cultural Showcase, part of which included the "curtain-raiser" for the Australian team's first exhibition game against the USA.

Australian Indigenous Basketball's All Stars were scheduled to play the Kingdom of Hawai'i, and also entertain with traditional songs and dance before the big exhibition. "Being a basketball player and having a platform, using it the right way to be able to tackle the real issues in the world," is how Mills saw his role.

Dampier Peninsula in WA, Blacktank Bore (NT), Cunnamulla (Qld), Walgett (NSW), Wilcannia (NSW) and Oodnadatta (SA) now would produce more than 5,000 litres of drinking water per month as a result of his initiative. "We partnered with a company from Phoenix called Zero Mass Water," Mills said. "They have created a solar hydro panel to be able to use the moisture and sunlight and humidity to be able to create clean drinking water. So we've taken these panels and we've placed them in six different very remote communities within Australia — places where they don't have water, and if they do, it's not accessible or they can't use it. So it was an important trip to be able to improve the lives of Indigenous Australians.

"And to see the emotional feedback from the community members and the kids was something that was very emotional, something that I'm very pleased that we had the opportunity to do it. Water is important and access to clean water is a human right which these people don't have. So improving this lifestyle meant a lot to me." The reactions to Mills' arrival within these communities was beyond heart-warming.

Patty's fellow Olympian at Beijing, London and Rio, Joe Ingles, and Joe's Australian Diamonds netball star wife Renae, discovered in January when it was diagnosed, that their three-year-old twin son Jacob had autism. The Utah Jazz swingman said the in-stadium sensory room created through the partnership between Marvel Stadium and the Ingles now provided an accessible and inclusive environment for all fans.

The sensory room was the latest in a number of Marvel Stadium additions which reflected the couple's goals of inclusiveness and accessibility. Championed by the venue and Joe and Renae — supported by the National Basketball Players' Association (NBPA) Foundation — the sensory room was unveiled in the week leading into the Boomers-USA matches in Melbourne.

The Marvel Stadium sensory room now is a quiet and safe space enabling children and adults with autism, dementia, PTSD and other similar conditions to deregulate from sensory overload, while still being able to enjoy a game-day experience. "It will be great knowing Renae, Jacob and our daughter Milla are all able to watch the game in an environment where they are all comfortable," Joe told Australian Leisure Management magazine.

Despite very different personal circumstances and backgrounds, Mills and Ingles had grown into their roles as selfless young "true blue" sportsmen, the type to make all Aussies proud to be Australian.

Meanwhile the Australian media also was finding the sometimes-irascible Coach Popovich in good spirits at USA practice, especially when asked about Mills. "Patty brought me their game-plan yesterday because I threatened him with his contract if I didn't get that," Popovich joked. "He was great. He brought everything. Coach Lemanis wasn't happy about it. I copied it and sent it to all the players."

Game One of the two-game exhibition was a watershed night for basketball in Australia with a record crowd of 51,218 in attendance at Melbourne's Marvel Stadium to see the USA beat the Boomers 102-86. It was a very "American" event too, with some patrons paying $1,500 for their seat. The crowd number and ticket price made it seem like a fantasy-come-true for those with hoops in their veins. And even more so for those who watched Australian teams barely fill 3,000-seat venues such as Adelaide's Apollo Stadium for a Boomers-USA game ahead of the 1978 World Championship.

Marvel Stadium looked awesome and the atmosphere flooding into lounge-rooms across the nation via SBS-TV was something very special and unique. No one was sure how many people were watching this in the comfort of their own homes, but if 50,000-plus were in attendance, it is safe to presume interest did not peter at Victoria's borders. This was a huge night for basketball and USA coach Gregg Popovich and his team played their role completely appropriately.

The pre-show provided by the Australian Indigenous Basketball and Kingdom of Hawai'i sportsmen and women was significant in making the night the event that it was. Then the Boomers put it to the Americans for a half and when Andrew Bogut pulled his fake-handoff, spin to the hoop throwdown dunk for a 25-22 lead, Aussie fans could not have been happier.

Of course the US response was instant and significant, requiring another fightback capped by Patty Mills' triple to close within 43-44 at halftime. After the interval, Kemba Walker was magnificent, the USA's 32-18 third period making the final quarter academic. But Australia had much to like, especially Chris Goulding (19 points, 4-of-6 threes) responding to his role as a key off-the-bench shooter and some of Bogut's five assists, which were gob-smackers.

Goulding and Mills jointly led the Boomers' scoring, Jock Landale also not out of place as a starter, having previously opened against Canada twice, but once when Aron Baynes did not suit, then a second time when Bogut was in street clothes. This was his first start in a full Boomers team and he handled it well. However the USA winning the boards 54-36 and able to shoot at 48 per cent against what was a better Boomers defensive effort for the most part, hardly was thrilling.

As the first such event staged at Marvel Stadium, there naturally were teething problems with some of the seating and sight-lines. The issue was sufficiently topical to prompt Basketball Australia to release the following statement post-game:

"Last night was the biggest basketball event ever staged in Australia, which is likely to be surpassed on Saturday when the Australian Boomers and USA Basketball battle it out again at Marvel Stadium. Over 51,000 fans attended the event and it is worth noting the feedback to us has been strongly positive. Clearly there have been some fans that feel their expectations were not met on their purchased seats.

"TEG Live and Marvel Stadium worked with a number of fans at the game to make alternative arrangements. Of the 11,000 fans who purchased floor seating to last night's game, only 200 people were relocated. They were relocated promptly without issue and just two refunds were requested. Tickets for the event started from $69.90, which is reasonable and typical for a major international event. Ticket prices on the floor started from $149.90 in the rear sections, increasing in price the closer the seats were located to the court.

"We appreciate that it was a different viewing experience than many basketball fans are used to because the event was staged within a traditional football stadium. There were 14 massive video screens to augment the live action, including providing action replays, statistics and video pieces to keep the audience entertained.

"These games feature the best available players that have been selected to represent their respective nations at the 2019 FIBA Basketball World Cup in China later this month. The action on the court was fantastic as the Boomers took it up to USA Basketball for most of the game but the class of the current World Champions shone through in their 102-86 victory.

"The pre-game entertainment was exhilarating and created a concert-style atmosphere, setting the scene for the on-court battle. Basketball Australia and TEG Live are looking to a further history making encounter tomorrow at Marvel Stadium in front of an expected record crowd for a basketball game in Australia."

That was the official statement. Oscar-winning Aussie actor Russell Crowe who was at the game begged to differ, tweeting: "Having attended a few outdoor rock concerts outside on plastic chairs at Adelaide's Botanic Park and paid heavily for the privilege, last night's discomfort, in itself, was no surprise. But at least at the concerts, the acts were on an elevated stage so sight lines were never compromised."

Then in Game Two on August 24, 2019, it finally happened. The brilliance of Patty Mills, the smarts of Andrew Bogut and the guile of Joe Ingles underpinned a sensational 98-94 victory for Australia over the USA in front of a record 52,079 roaring fans at Melbourne's Marvel Stadium.

The Boomers' historic first-ever win over the US national team after falling short 26 times since first crossing swords at the 1964 Tokyo Olympic Games, also ended a 66-game winning streak for the Americans when using NBA talent and dating back to the end of the 2006 FIBA World Championship. It was a glorious day for basketball in Australia and a monumental performance — a 20-point turnaround against a team which won the series opener by 16.

The Americans threatened to do it again too, leading by 10 during the third quarter. Starting point guard Matthew Dellavedova was hampered by foul woes and Aussie coach Andrej Lemanis turned to Mills to run the show earlier than usual. But one of the keys was when Ingles comfortably ran the point, the laconic swingman with a game-high seven assists, while also picking his moments en route to 15 points at 50 per cent.

Aron Baynes was a huge keyway presence but it was Bogut's willingness to attack offensively which threw the US onto a back foot. Bogut's 16 points came on a tidy 7-of-8 shooting, and he added nine rebounds, four assists and a steal, while also maintaining his intimidating defensive presence. His former championship-winning teammate at Golden State Warriors, Harrison Barnes, was instrumental in the visitors' great start as USA coach Gregg Popovich also tried a few different combinations.

Kyle Kuzma (ankle) did not suit but Kemba Walker and Donovan Mitchell were constant threats, even as the Boomers again pulled the deficit back to a point at halftime, just as they had in the series opener, this time down 48-49. And just as they did then, the Americans pulled away in the third, drawing clear by 10 despite the great hustle plays by a Nick Kay more in tune with the match tempo than he was in Game One.

Australia battled back strongly, Mills prominent and Jock Landale again showing he would be a key component of this team for years to come. Mills' shooting was inspired in the second half, with 23 of his game-high 30 points after the interval and 13 in the last quarter to seal it. Calling the game on national TV, Australia's most seasoned basketball commentator John Casey may have been overstating it when he said the last five minutes would be the most important in the Boomers' history — the last five in Olympic Bronze Medal matches in Atlanta and Rio may still have been a tad more relevant — but he encapsulated the raw emotion which accompanied this sizzling finish.

Ingles' three-ball gave Australia the lead for keeps with 3:35 to play on a step back for 88-87. From there the Boomers played exemplary defence, Bogut and Ingles both combined exceptionally with Mills who hit big shot after big shot as the lead stretched out to six. Whether he was beyond the arcs, guiding the mid-range jumper or taking it to the hoop, Patty Mills was outstanding.

Lemanis threw Mitch Creek on for the game's final defensive stands and he responded as expected. "I need to start by congratulating the Boomers," Popovich said post-match. "The Boomers were really great tonight. They did a great job. It's really a testament to how long they've stuck together to get this accomplished tonight, so I've got to give them big credit, both ends of the court they were competitive.

"They executed really well and they came up with the victory. That needs to be said." Then tongue-in-cheek, he added of his San Antonio Spurs star Mills: "And as I told you all after the last game, Patty's a pain in the arse."

The Boomers drew great confidence from the performance, which was in stark contrast to their opening 20-point World Cup preparation loss to Canada in Perth. The win was a historic watershed moment but the Boomers did not wallow in it, knowing their medal goal in China was the real challenge.

"We're actually a better team than at the start of the game because of the knowledge that we gained so, you move on," Popovich said, explaining his team is still relatively new and not consistent yet. "Some of it is expected with a new group that's trying to learn about each other and learn about a system. It's not surprising, but the Aussies gave us a great lesson about where you want to be and how you want to play in this kind of competition."

Over two nights at Marvel Stadium, 103,297 basketball fans attended this Boomers-USA series, a phenomenal achievement for the sport and a magnificent springboard for the Boomers into the FIBA World Cup and for the upcoming NBL season. It most definitely would be a milestone day to remember, the "culture club" of Patty Mills (30 points), Andrew Bogut (16 and nine rebounds), Joe Ingles (15 and seven assists) and Aron Baynes (13) showing the way.

CHAPTER THIRTEEN
A WORLD OF HURT

Matthew Dellavedova produced his greatest shooting performance in an international game for Australia as the Boomers weathered a Canadian storm to open their FIBA World Cup campaign with a 108-92 win in Dongguan. Never possessing a shot release anyone would describe as a "thing of beauty", Dellavedova spent much of the off-season working at improving it and it paid handsomely as he went off for a game-high 24 points on 9-of-13 shooting, with 6-of-10 three-point baskets.

Any time the ball left his hands with its new higher arc, it was money and the Boomers cashed in after receiving a hell of a fright when Canada went off for 37 points in the third quarter. Chris Goulding was perfection in his sixth man scorer's role, with 16 points on an efficient 6-of-7 shooting, with 2-of-3 threes in just 17:50 of action. Andrew Bogut similarly stood tall with his 12 points also from 6-of-7 shots.

Joe Ingles too was magnificent with 13 points, five rebounds, nine assists — although he originally was credited with 10 — three steals and a block, the Boomers' offence down the stretch looking far more polished with the ball in his hands. Not coincidentally, all six of the Boomers' Rio Olympians finished in double-figure scoring, Canada's great effort to snatch the lead after trailing by as many as 17 points, leaving it gassed as Australia stepped up a gear.

Dellavedova scored Australia's opening basket after a Jock Landale free throw with a drive to beat the shot-clock. When Ingles backed that with a three-pointer, it was a 6-2 start. Ingles-to-Bogut for 10-5 looked even better for Australia as Canada's NBA playmaker Cory Joseph collected his second foul with 5:01 on the game clock. The margin blew out further on a Landale triple, then a Patty Mills (15 points, 6 assists) three-point play before Canada rallied and dragged it back to 20-22 on a Brady Heslop three-pointer.

Free throws by Ingles, then Aron Baynes and a Goulding three-pointer had Australia ahead 29-20 after one. Joseph kick-started Canada after the break and when he went coast-to-coast, Boomers coach Andrej Lemanis called time-out at just 9:21 into the second period. Soon after, Canada's coach Nick Nurse was penalised with a technical foul, Mills bulging Australia's lead to 35-26 before Joseph picked up his third foul. Mills then made it a double-digit break at 37-26, in a second quarter highlighted by emphatic Landale and Bogut dunks.

Australia just powered on with Ingles turning an unsportsmanlike foul into a 48-35 buffer, Mills-to-Bogut making it 50-35, Mills-to-Nick Kay pushing it to 52-35. From there, Australia's offence dried up, Thomas Scrubb with a triple before Melvin Ejim conned the refs into a foul on Ingles by falling to the floor in front of him. Kyle Wiltjer further trimmed the deficit to 40-52 at the interval.

Canada scored 40 in the first half and 37 in a withering third quarter but the Boomers did not lose their composure or self-belief. Baynes and Goulding quickly made it 80-77, Mills iced two free throws — he was 9-of-9 from the line — Ingles lobbed to Bogues for a slam and Canada was taking time-out, down 77-84 and with Australia on an 8-0 mini-run.

Joseph finally broke through for Canada but Ingles-to-Dellavedova for three was a back-breaker. Then Mills-to-Dellavedova against what looked like a fairly flaccid zone defence made it 90-79. When Bogut took it out to 92-79, it was a second 8-0 outburst in a 16-2 masterwork that left Canada now needing to beat Lithuania and Senegal to advance, barring any other misstep.

Mills in a spin move for a dish to Kay was sweet, Ingles also still with time to swish a three-ball and flick another great pass to Dellavedova for a three-pointer. Australia led by as many as 21 points, a few late Canadian buckets trimming it to 16 which, hopefully, would have no bearing on a points spread later in the tournament.

Canada identified Mills as Australia's hottest gunslinger, playing a box-and-one defence on him and even face-guarding him at times. It was ironic then they were gunned down by The Maryborough Kid, Matthew Dellavedova. It was a fair call to go after Mills after his 30-point demolition of the USA at Marvel Stadium, but the Boomers' electrifying spiritual leader still supplied 15 points and six assists.

Australia also had to deal with the Chinese fans riding Bogut all game. He was subjected to relentless booing and derision in Dongguan for his tweet about Chinese swimmer Sun Yang, convicted of doping in 2014. Of course he handled it all with customary aplomb but that white noise was to be a tournament constant for the Boomers. "Swimmers who medal vs Sun Yang should break the podiums with hammers," was Bogut's tweet, referencing the Chinese swimmer smashing a vial of his blood during a random drug test, the tweet typically inviting a reaction.

Against Senegal in its second intragroup match, this time Australia needed a Joe Ingles near-triple-double to inch to an 81-68 win in a lacklustre performance. It was anything but an impressive outing against a Senegalese team thrashed by 54 points in its opener against Lithuania. Obviously humiliated after scoring just 47 points in that match, Senegal came into this contest with real purpose and focus, knowing its tournament was on the line.

How much of the way this story played out was as a result of their desperate resilience as much as Australia's occasional indifference was up for debate. But grabbing 13 offensive rebounds against some ordinary defensive aptitude or desire by the Aussies spoke volumes as to why this contest still was alive inside the last three minutes. That final 13-point margin was deceptive, the Boomers made to play to the bell.

Ingles finished with 17 points at 75 per cent, including 4-of-6 triples, with 10 rebounds and nine assists, to go within one dish of the coveted triple-double. For good measure, he also blocked two shots. But just as another African qualifier — Angola — destroyed Australia's 1986 FIBA World Championship campaign with an upset win, Senegal hung around all night, threatening to do the same.

Patty Mills found his range for a game-high 22 points at 50 per cent, with three threes, and Nick Kay had a positive game after Jock Landale had his worst since donning the green-and-gold for the first time in Kazakhstan. Landale was pointless and had four turnovers in 14:37 in his most uncharacteristic effort, one of his only two shot attempts blocked. Fortunately it was just an aberration for the burgeoning young star.

Mills hit his first basket — a three-pointer — at 4:43 in the second period and when he followed up with a jumpshot, it appeared the Boomers might start pulling away. Instead, Landale's third turnover saw Senegal snatch the lead back at 32-31 as Australia continued to be messy. A Goulding triple made it 36-33 at halftime. In a combined 25 FIBA World Cup/World Championship or Olympic Games campaigns, the Boomers had started 2-0 just twice in their history. The first was at the 1994 Worlds in Toronto where they matched their best WC result (of 1982) by finishing fifth. The other was at the 2016 Rio Olympics where they played off for bronze.

With its 92-69 win over Canada, Lithuania joined Australia on 2-0 win-loss record to jointly top their group. Both countries were guaranteed to move on from Group H, although the Lithuanians looked far more impressive. They had thrashed Senegal 101-47 and their 23-point win over the Canadians also carried more cred than the Boomers' 13-point escape from the Africans and 16-point beating of the Canucks.

Even though the smart money was on Lithuania, a relentlessly focused Aron Baynes and some Patty Mills late-game heroics sent Australia flying through to the second phase of the World Cup with an 87-82 victory over its archrival. Baynes finished on a double-double, combining 21 points at 53 per cent, including 3-of-5 three-pointers, with a game-high 13 rebounds in arguably his best-ever game in the green-and-gold.

Patty came through with 23 points at 50 per cent, leaving his best until last. His jumpshot with 1:42 left gave the Boomers a 78-76 lead before his three-pointer — over the outstretched arm of Lithuania's 213cm NBA centre Jonas Valanciunas — made it 83-78 with 33 seconds remaining.

It was the biggest single shot of the tournament for the Aussies, though there still was plenty of drama in the last half-minute before Group H officially was claimed with the 3-0 clean sweep of Canada, Senegal and Lithuania. The win also marked the first time in 25 FIBA World Cup or Olympic Games events Australia had won its first three games. The success over Lithuania also brought their all-time win-loss record against each other to 5-5.

It was a fitting victory for Australia, built on a memorable first half which kept the Lithuanians chasing for much of the contest. Patty's first three-pointer started a 9-0 Boomers surge which concluded with a Jock Landale slam dunk and forced the Baltics into a very early time-out. When Lithuania nudged the deficit back to 25-27, it was Andrej Lemanis' turn to call time-out.

But revisiting their first Boomers sojourn together at the 2012 London Olympics, it was Dellavedova-to-Baynes for a dunk, then Dellavedova-to-Kay for a rare three-pointer from the Perth Wildcats' big-man. Baynes was a man obsessed, with another dunk and another three-ball forcing a further Lithuanian time-out. Ahead 52-41 at halftime, the Boomers were bounding but knowing full well Lithuania would be making a run. Fortunately, they weathered it to storm into Group L with Lithuania, France and Dominican Republic for the tournament's next stage.

Probably the best news though was that by progressing on into the FIBA World Cup's second round, Australia also now automatically qualified for the 2020 Tokyo Olympic Games as the leading nation from the Oceania region. When Greece broke New Zealand's heart 103-97 to put the Tall Blacks into the 17-32 positional playoffs, the Boomers became the region's higher placed finisher, meaning they joined host nation Japan as the second team confirmed to compete in the 12-team Olympics.

It now was Patty Mills' turn to load the Boomers onto his shoulders to narrowly hurtle past a plucky Dominican Republic 82-76 in Nanjing. The win marked a history-making fourth straight at a FIBA World Cup, putting Australia on the brink of its quarterfinals. Mills continued to show he now belonged in any conversation about Australia's greatest players after slotting a game-high 19 points at 50 per cent, with a game-high nine assists, four rebounds and two steals. When the game needed to be won in the last quarter, it was Mills who stepped up and delivered it, with several co-stars also grabbing the spotlight, Chris Goulding's 15 points including 6-of-6 free throws, Jock Landale's 13 at 83 per cent including 2-of-2 big threes.

His first came with 9:19 left to play and gave the Boomers some breathing space at 60-54. Mills pulled the lead to 61-54 after sticking the tech foul free throw on Victor Liz's outrageous flop. He then buried a three-pointer for 64-56. At 7:03, he drove to the hoop for a clever basket and at 6:38, he drew the pressure again, dishing to Landale for the big man's second three-bomb and 69-60.

A Joe Ingles steal led to Mitch Creek lobbing the ball for Landale to slam home and Australia had its biggest lead of the game at 71-60. A huge dunk from Eloy Vargas and a three-pointer from Eulis Baez showed Dominican Republic was not ready to drop its collective head, though Andrew Bogut's sweet runner for 73-65 stung.

Bogut, Landale and ever-reliable Nick Kay were pressed into greater service when Aron Baynes fouled out in just 16 minutes, taking 10 points at 63 per cent, five rebounds, two assists and a block to an early seat. Throwing down a massive slam dunk off a Matthew Dellavedova (6 points, 7 assists, 2 steals) feed with 6:15 to go in the third, Baynes fouled out 11 seconds later and just over a minute after his departure, scores were tied 46-46.

Bogut then showed yet again why he was considered among the best passing big men of all time with a dish to Mills' cut, before throwing a pass from the opposite side of the keyway to Mills arriving in the far corner for an all-swish three-pointer and 51-46 lead. Bogut (8 points, 8 rebounds) also forced Joe Ingles to score off one of his six assists, the Utah Jazz swingman strangely reluctant to fire up any shots, missing his only shot of the first half and finishing with 1-of-4 in a few clicks under 30 minutes.

Australia's unselfishness was exemplary, with 30 assists on 30 made shots and 15 free throws, but Ingles took it a little too far for a shooter of his ability. The Boomers also won the boards 40-30 but 16 turnovers, especially a couple of loose ones, did nothing to deter Dominican Republic from staying on task for another upset.

Australia's record now in Group L with France, Lithuania and Dominican Republic was 4-0, the quarterfinals within striking distance. The Aussies next kicked open the door to the medal podium with a stunning 100-98 win over France in Nanjing, setting up a quarterfinal matchup against Czech Republic.

In securing arguably their most important match since their 2016 Olympic Games bronze medal playoff, the Boomers set a record for their fifth straight win, avoided USA in the quarter (and semi) finals, with a showdown in the semis against the winner of Spain-Poland, provided they first cashed the Czechs.

Patty Mills again was sensational, scoring 30 points at 56 per cent but it was his solitary steal of the game which clinched it, Australia leading 99-98 with 4.4 heartbeats left. France took time-out, advanced the ball and had Evan Fournier (31 points) or Nando De Colo (26 points at 69 per cent) as excellent end-play options.

But it never got to that as Mills, defending De Colo, leapt to intercept Andrew Albicy's inbounds pass to his man, flicking it across court where Mitch Creek caught it and threw up a prayer well inside France's half. Fournier had a brain fade and grabbed his arm — unsportsmanlike anyone? — so Creek still had three free throws to come with 0.9 of a second remaining. After sticking the first, he missed the second, then aborted the third, giving France no chance to salvage the contest.

It was a memorable win for the Boomers in one of the highest quality matches of the tournament, Australia shooting at 58 per cent, France at 57, yet both teams working their tails off defensively. Mills certainly staked his claim as World Cup MVP with his game, Joe Ingles also finding his shooting touch, delivering 23 points at 53 per cent, while Aron Baynes was huge. Apart from scoring 21 points including 5-of-6 threes, the new Phoenix Suns centre also had five defensive rebounds and two assists. But biggest of all, he laid his body on the line in that frantic final quarter, taking three big charges in the period, making himself personally responsible for half of France's six turnovers.

Ingles' offensive aggression was critical in keeping the scoreboard ticking and maintaining the pressure, especially after Dellavedova was called for his third foul just four seconds into the third quarter. Mills was superb, with a 13-point third period matching his first half output. He swished three free throws after erroneously being fouled on a three-point attempt, the Boomers down 46-50.

Delivering a three-point dagger next, he tied it at 52-52, then drew all the defensive heat to feed Baynes for a three and a 55-52 lead. Next he drove and it was 57-54. But with 5:10 left, Fournier again conned a foul out of Dellavedova, the Aussie's fourth, before Chris Goulding and Andrew Bogut also collected fouls for being in Fournier's vicinity.

Frustrated briefly, the Boomers faltered as France produced a 9-0 run to go 70-61 clear. Again, this was another defining moment in

Australia's resolve to claim a medal in China, Ingles and Mills splashing three-pointers and by the last break, it was back to 71-75. Creek's back cut followed by Baynes' three-pointer put the Boomers in touch before Baynes' inside move meant Australia led with 6:57 left. Ingles' layup forced a French time-out, the Boomers now 82-79 ahead.

Dellavedova-to-Creek inside for a three-point play nudged the buffer to 85-80 but Fournier levelled it again at 87-87, shortly after Bogut fouled out, the big man leaving the game with seven points, six rebounds, three assists and a block in 13 minutes. Albicy gave France a 92-90 lead with his only triple of the night and again 94-92 after a midcourt steal.

But Ingles tied it from the stripe, then gave the Boomers the buffer when he drove through traffic for 96-94. With 46.7 seconds to go, De Colo tied it again with a jumpshot, something he did again at 98-98 after Dellavedova knocked down two free throws as French centre Rudy Gobert fouled out. With 5.7 seconds remaining, Dellavedova again was at the stripe, made his first for 99-98 but missed his second. Baynes collared the offensive board but stepped on the line with 4.4 to play.

Albicy only made one turnover for the game and Mills only one steal, but it absolutely clinched the match and made the Boomers winning their historic first-ever medal a tangible reality.

Patty Mills once again was "the man" for the Boomers and in beating Czech Republic 82-70 in the quarterfinal, he was simply sensational. Patty carried Australia offensively through early woes across the first half, before delivering the three-point dagger with 47.8 seconds left to make it 80-70, ending any fleeting Czech hopes. It was a step-back triple as the clock ran down and a statement basket if ever there was one.

The medal job was not yet complete but many were tempted to put champagne on ice as the Boomers advanced to the FIBA World Cup semi finals for the first time to already equal Australia's greatest performance at an international event. In beating Czech Republic in Shanghai, the

Aussies continued on their history-making way by making it into the Final Four of the tournament and eclipsing their previous best World Cup/World Championship results of fifth placings in 1982 and 1994.

Andrej Lemanis' team, with six Rio Olympians, had come to China on a mission and in taking their record to 6-0 with their quarterfinal Czech-mate, already had surpassed their predecessors. Mills finished with 24 points at 60 per cent, with 6-of-9 threes and six assists, his jumpshot to close it ensuring Australia kept its semi final appointment with Spain. After the controversial finish to their 88-89 bronze medal playoff loss to the Spaniards at the 2016 Olympics, their semi final opponent was one these Boomers took particular joy in facing.

Realistically, the chance at some international revenge/justice remained very much a secondary consideration to its real importance, the match representing a doorway into an unprecedented crack at the gold medal.

There are insufficient superlatives to describe Patty's performance, but in a game-changing third quarter, Andrew Bogut showed off his basketball skills and IQ, the NBL's reigning MVP instrumental in a 14-0 run which turned a 43-43 contest into a 57-43 masterclass. If Bogut was Batman, Chris Goulding was Robin, as Australia's dynamic duo pushed the Boomers to a 17-point lead at 63-46, a 20-3 run in all.

Playing with abandon and great self-assurance at their first World Cup, the Czechs caused Australia consistent problems throughout a torrid and clumsy first half, the Boomers ahead 33-30 at the main break. The Czechs quickly jumped to a 34-33 lead after the interval before Mills stuck a three-pointer at 8:39. Aron Baynes drew a charge before the Czechs swung into a zone defence, Tomas Satoransky tying the game at 41-41 with 5:49 left in the third. Satoransky went within a rebound of a triple-double, with 13 points and 13 assists but had to work hard against a succession of Aussie defenders, including Matthew Dellavedova and Mitch Creek.

Inside the final five minutes of the third, Dellavedova stroked a three-pointer to break the 43-43 deadlock, before Joe Ingles got the ball to a breaking Mills who steered it to Jock Landale for a massive slam dunk and a Czech time-out. That was Bogut's cue to go to work, feeding a pass to Goulding for a triple before putting his body on the line to check a Czech charge.

Next he dished to Nick Kay for a double-digit lead at 53-43 before Creek showed some typical Horsham hustle to secure the Boomers another possession. When Bogut scored off a lob at 2:39, the Czechs were forced to take another time-out but it made no impact as Bogut scored off a low-post hook shot. Then it was Goulding's turn with consecutive three-pointers and 63-46 before the Czechs scored the last basket of the period.

The Czechs made their last run and cut it back to 70-77 with 1:11 left. Mills then simply took control, watched as the clock counted down, and stuck that brutal triple to end any doubt. If Bogut and Goulding were Batman and Robin, Mills was Superman.

He went into halftime with 16 points on 6-of-9 shooting with 4-of-5 triples, Goulding and Dellavedova his only teammates with two field goals. Australia started poorly, looking tight and anxious and it was almost two minutes before Mills drilled a three-pointer to open its scoring. But turnovers, rushing in offence and missing easy shots dogged the entire first half, the latter possibly exacerbated by the officials' generosity in how much physical play they allowed.

When you are whacked on a shot for no call, you tend to shoot the next shot harder, so if there's zero contact on that one, you've over-shot and it's usually a miss. The Boomers shot at 36 per cent for the half and only looked to be in any sort of modest control within two minutes of the interval when Bogut threw a sweet dish for Dellavedova's cut and a 31-28 lead. A Landale fast-break dunk at 20.7 seconds took the buffer to 33-28, matching Australia's best lead at 13-8. But the Czechs ran a play to close the half which again pulled them back to 30-33.

Playing without fear and with great tenacity, the Czechs disrupted the Boomers who were carried almost exclusively by Mills. But Lemanis had the luxury of sitting his superstar during the third period when several of the support cast merrily stepped into the spotlight. The Chinese crowds routinely jeering Andrew Bogut were increasingly silenced as he showed off his best form in the quarterfinal win. Australia's world-renowned international supporter group known as the "Legion of Boom", also entered the fray by chanting "An-drew Bo-gut" with accompanying handclaps to further send the Chinese fans into frustrated hibernation.

The Boomers now literally were on the threshold of a gold medal. France drew a great game from Utah Jazz centre Rudy Gobert and all of its usual suspects to upset the USA 89-79 in their quarterfinal. With Argentina KO'ing the other tournament favourite Serbia, it left the run to the gold medal wide open and a very realistic prospect for the Boomers if they could get past Spain.

It largely was Pau Gasol who cost Australia a bronze medal at the Rio Olympics but in China his brother Marc buried the Boomers in an epic and heart-breaking 95-88 double-overtime semi-final in Beijing. Gasol went off for 33 points after a four-point first-half — all free throws — and shouldered Spain into the gold medal match by scoring them at 58 per cent, with three massive three-pointers, plus six rebounds, four assists and two blocks.

Spanish playmaker Ricky Rubio finished with 19 points after scoring nine in the opening period, and added 12 assists, seven defensive rebounds and four steals to break Australia's heart after the Boomers led by as many as 11 and controlled the game across regulation. Australia absolutely was valiant in defeat but never before had its pathway to gold been so clear and attainable, and sadly this was a golden opportunity wasted, literally.

A whopping 22 turnovers — a stat which haunted the Boomers across their incoming six-win streak — and the disappearance of key players when the furnace was roaring at its hottest, cost Australia dearly. Patty Mills was sensational again, as he was throughout the tournament, still scorching a match-high 34 points despite heavy off-the-ball treatment. But the little man with the giant heart was expected to do too much as Australia's other offensive options dried up or lost self-confidence.

And that was less about Spain's defence and more about the glare of the spotlight blinding some key Boomers. Nick Kay though was not one of them, coming off the bench to play 31 minutes, scoring 16 points at 50 per cent, with 11 rebounds, every one of his seven offensive boards hugely significant. Andrew Bogut's 12 points came on an efficient 6-of-8 shooting, with nine rebounds in 24 minutes, his presence on the court a calming influence.

But after that trio, Australia's scoring pretty much was non-existent, Chris Goulding playing just 14 minutes and cold by the time the second overtime period rolled around and unable to make the impact he otherwise may have. Joe Ingles played 43:56 of this spine-tingling 50-minute extravaganza, gathering 10 defensive boards and seven assists. But he shot just 1-of-9 from the floor for his four points, and his three turnovers stung, especially 20 seconds into the first overtime when he drove for an open layup, tried to pass it instead and turned it over.

Matthew Dellavedova's six points came on 2-of-9 shooting, and while his nine assists were quality, many of his six turnovers were calamitous. Mills had seven turnovers but subjected to double and triple-teams — and a couple of non-calls when he clearly was fouled — half of his were forgiveable.

Jock Landale also struggled and Aron Baynes' six points was off two three-pointers, his second one coming with two minutes left in the second overtime. In late-game scenes reminiscent of the Rio officiating, Bogut and Gasol tussled for a rebound off Sergio Llull's missed triple, with the Aussie big called for a foul. With 8.7 seconds left in regulation and the Boomers having led since 45 seconds into the second quarter, Gasol went to the stripe and coolly converted both free throws to put Spain 71-70 ahead.

But on the Boomers' last play, Mills drove into traffic and forced the officials to call a foul on Spain, putting him to the line with 4.7 seconds remaining. His first tied it at 71-71 but his second caught iron and the game was going into a five-minute overtime extension. Yes, had he made both, Australia would at worst have collected a silver medal and no-one felt the anguish more than Patty. But it was through no fault of his own, Mills having been played to exhaustion by Lemanis who throughout the tournament had to leave Nathan Sobey, Cam Gliddon and David Barlow pinned to the bench. They had shown they simply were not up to this level but that threw so many more minutes into Lemanis' "Olympic six" and Nick Kay, Jock Landale and Mitch Creek — the latter not even an original team selection.

Those selection decisions came back to haunt the Boomers as the game wore into its five-minute overtime extension, Gasol inside, then Gasol outside quickly rushing Spain to a 76-71 lead. Mills pulled back the deficit by stroking a three-pointer. Dellavedova flew out of court to miraculously save an offensive rebound, flicking it back to Kay for a basket and it was 76-76.

Ingles tied the game 78-78 by knocking down two high-pressure free throws and when Mills converted two super pressure free throws with 14.7 seconds left on the clock, Australia was ahead 80-78. Considering the past and the history of Europe-centric FIBA, anyone who did not expect a foul to be called on the Boomers on Spain's last play either was new to the international game, or naïve.

With 4.6 seconds to go, Gasol again strolled to the free throw line to tie it up 80-80. With no time-outs left, Dellavedova took a running shot which never really looked like dropping and it was off to a second overtime. Bogut started it with a tip in but 82-80 sadly was the Boomers' final fling. The game was so incredibly intense, Andrej Lemanis was subbing freely early in the contest to maintain extraordinary pressure on the Spaniards.

But by the second overtime, the rotation shrunk and it was clear there was little left in the tank when Kay flubbed a layup, Llull nailed the first of two back-breaking triples and Gasol scored in between them for an 8-0 run which broke it wide open. But where there was devastation in Rio, there was no time for that in Beijing, an unprecedented bronze medal still within reach.

Patty Mills played more than 45 minutes and Joe Ingles 43:56 and it was clear the longer this game went, the more it became a war of attrition, featuring a number of supremely fatigued combatants trying to make the least mistakes.

On that front, Spain definitely had the edge. The bogus foul on Andrew Bogut with 8.7 seconds left in regulation to put Marc Gasol on the stripe with the Boomers leading 70-69, was so reminiscent of the bronze medal playoff loss to the Spaniards at the Rio Olympics as to be uncanny. It even prompted an enraged outburst from Bogut as the Boomers headed for the change-rooms post-game of: "Google where headquarters of f--king FIBA is." (Switzerland, if you were wondering.) "F--king disgrace." And if that did not adequately sum up how the players felt, Boomers assistant coach Luc Longley had *this* take.

"We've got to find an altar somewhere and burn a sacrifice to the basketball gods, because they're not kissing us on the dick yet, like they do Spain," Longley said. "I feel like Spain are kissed on the dick by the basketball gods every time we play them. It's gut-wrenching for the guys. They've been so f--king good, so consistent and played so hard and I felt like they deserved to win that and it doesn't feel like that's the right result." It was gut-wrenching, to be sure.

And then came the sledgehammer. France produced a 46-29 second half to claim its second FIBA World Cup bronze medal, denying Australia its first 67-59 in a sad end to what was an absorbing and exciting Boomers campaign in China. Turnovers, shooting options drying up and its discredited persistence in how it played the pick-and-roll all came back to haunt Australia as it not only ran out of gas the further the game went, but was surviving on the smell of an oily rag by the siren.

In the end, Australia had nothing in the tank to curb a French advance led by Nando De Colo, Nicolas Batum, Evan Fournier and Andrew Albicy, even though the Boomers came out firing and keen to put a match-winning buffer between the two teams early. Joe Ingles rediscovered his shooting touch with 17 points on 7-of-11, plus five rebounds, three assists and a steal in 34:15.

Asked to do so much for so long, Patty Mills was off to a flyer, faded, but still finished with 15 points at 50 per cent. But the man with the heart of a lion was running on empty long before the siren sent France to the medal podium. There was no lack of effort or intensity from the Boomers, but they did hit the wall, despite taking great momentum into the early stages of the third quarter.

A Nick Kay three-point play and a rare Dellavedova make on a drive had the Boomers leading 35-23 in the third. Kay then was hit with an offensive foul for a screen which was nothing more than a fancy French flop. Undeterred, the Boomers pushed on, Ingles driving the baseline for a basket and an additional free throw, drawing a third foul on Utah Jazz teammate Rudy Gobert.

When Ingles knocked down the bonus, Australia was 38-23 ahead with

7:00 to play in the third. But Ingles hit the floor on his next drive, a huge bloody scratch across his back, the referees though assessing it as "France ball". Bogut flipped a nifty behind-the-back pass to Mills who — clearly tired — missed his second layup for the contest. Mitch Creek blocked De Colo on a fast break before Aron Baynes picked up his third foul for absolutely nothing.

At 4:55, Chris Goulding was assessed an unsportsmanlike foul when Fournier bounced off his back at the sideline. After Fournier's made free throw, Batum knocked in a three-pointer and France was coming. Goulding got to the hoop with a great move, but missed, Vincent Poirier with a dunk at the other end for 34-42. Ingles' layup pushed the lead back to double digits but consecutive De Colo baskets had Australia breathing hard, its lead reduced to 44-38.

Baynes threw a poor pass to Jock Landale which Batum leapt to save at the sideline, throwing it out off the Aussie forward and France was feeling the momentum. Goulding drew a French charging foul but within five seconds, Ingles was called for a midcourt offensive foul on another fancy French flop.

Fournier's floater trimmed it to 40-44 before Creek copped a phantom foul as Batum did a quality tumble and half pike. Another Poirier dunk and it was 42-44, France on a morale-boosting 14-2 run since trailing 28-42. Dellavedova hit a runner and Mills blocked De Colo's shot to send the Boomers into the last quarter ahead 46-42.

But De Colo opened the final period swishing a three-pointer within 10 seconds as France began a quarter-long exploitation of Australia's pick-and-roll strategy of no help from the defender of the screener. De Colo from the stripe gave France the lead 47-46 for the first time in the match with 9:01 to play. His three then bumped France's lead to 50-46 as Australia's offence dried up, its focus distracted.

A Kay reverse and a Mills jumper tied it at 50-50 with 6:56 left, and

Mills-to-Bogut put the Boomers up 52-50. Albicy then swished the first of three three-pointers he stroked for the period to give France back the lead, which then seesawed until Kay's tap-in at 3:49. But 56-55 was Australia's final moment of glory.

At 3:27, Albicy's second three gave France the lead for keeps, Gobert scoring his only basket with 2:06 left to make it 60-56. The Boomers looked cooked and they were, Albicy's next three-pointer chocolate on their eclair. Mills' three inside the final 40 seconds for 59-64 briefly suggested a flicker of life where there was none, no miracle shining Australia's way this day.

Having shown diminishing faith in his bench during the 88-95 double-overtime semi final loss to Spain, Boomers coach Andrej Lemanis was far more adventurous from the tip-off when he sent out Bogut and Kay in place of Baynes and Landale in the starting quintet. Much to the Chinese fans' delight, Bogut immediately was assessed an offensive foul on Australia's first possession as he handed the ball to Mills and a Frenchman got caught on his back.

Kay opened the scoring with a back-cut and feed from Dellavedova, then Ingles-to-Mills for a three-pointer made it 5-0. Dellavedova was working himself to exhaustion shadowing Fournier, and Gobert collected an offensive foul hipping Delly to the floor, followed by a technical. At 4:40, Mills' back cut made it 10-4 rubber ducky, before it was Fournier's turn to deck Dellavedova.

When Baynes banked a three-pointer, the lead was 13-6 and it was up to eight at 16-8 on a Bogut bucket, Ingles rewarding the centre with a sweet assist after the NBA championship-winner drew an offensive charge call at the other end. But again the Aussies played their last pick-and-roll of the quarter poorly, with Bogut dropping back into the key for De Colo to stick a wide-open three-pointer.

Australia's 16-point first quarter matched its lowest single-period return of the tournament, France's 11 also its lowest. That was, until halftime. The Boomers led 30-21 at the break having kept France now to 10, but only scoring 14 themselves.

Ingles finally broke off his self-imposed shooting shackles with a three-pointer to start the second quarter scoring and by the main interval, had a game-high 12 points on 5-of-7 shooting, with four rebounds, two assists and a steal. Australia kept France shooting at 25 per cent to the break, Lemanis doing a far better job distributing the minutes among a fatigued rotation still out there busting their butts. But by the last quarter, the Aussies only could muster a paltry 13 points — their lowest single quarter return of the tournament — as bronze again slipped from their grasp.

Patty Mills was the Boomers' standout by far, averaging a team-best 22.8 points per game at an amazing 49.6 per cent. When you consider the level of game-by-game pressure to which he also was subjected, there can be little doubt he was the World Cup's real Most Valuable Player. Mills was the main man, ultimately worn down by his lack of consistent offensive support.

In the meantime, what did this campaign positively give Australia? Firstly, it was impossible to ignore 52,000-plus people seeing the Boomers defeat the USA for the first time in history at Melbourne's Marvel Stadium, or that more than 100,000 fans saw the two pre-World Cup matches. Beating Canada, Senegal, Lithuania, then the Dominican Republic, France and the Czech Republic saw the Boomers play some inspired and convincing basketball.

Matthew Dellavedova, Aron Baynes, Jock Landale, Joe Ingles, Andrew Bogut, Chris Goulding all joined Mills in having their own big game, or two. And Nick Kay and Mitch Creek showed they could be relied upon to do jobs, as required. The semi final against Spain was a double-overtime classic but the Boomers ran out of running mates for Mills, Kay working hard for a double-double. It was an epic game, won and lost several times, sweeping every Boomers supporter through a roller-coaster of conflicted emotions.

And recovering from that shattering disappointment to beat France for a second time — the Boomers historically struggle to beat the same team twice at a major international — was going to take just that bit more than the national team had left. Australia was left with an overwhelming sense of pride in what these men achieved for our country of passionate basketball fans, albeit still a small sporting community.

The Boomers discovered Kay could play at this level and Goulding, in the role usually reserved for Ryan Broekhoff, could flourish too. That was the glass-half-full and accurate portrayal of what was achieved in China. Of course, if a glass is half full, it also is half empty.

Australia was seconds away from beating Spain in regulation and if it had, the likelihood is fairly compelling it would have won the gold medal. To ponder that for a moment is to become truly wistful as the Boomers may never again have an opportunity such as that one. Spain smashed Argentina by 20 in the gold medal game. That was the same Spanish team which took two overtimes to shake off those pesky Boomers, not that such form is necessarily a reliable guide. But in all honesty, Australia had the golden goose... and turned it into goose cutlets.

The Tokyo Olympics were only a year away so there still was plenty to be excited about. But dampening that excitement was the knowledge the USA would not be sending its "Team C", that Canada would not be suiting its "Team B" and while the Boomers were full of anticipation at who else from Australia's growing NBA stocks might finally suit in Japan, there were more than a few other nations with NBA reps preparing to step up in 12 months also.

Plus Australia had some real issues to address. In three international events since stepping up from the role of Brett Brown's assistant at the 2012 London Olympics, coach Andrej Lemanis had brought home a

12th place from the 2014 World Cup, a fourth at the Rio Olympics and a fourth at this World Cup.

Believe it or not, it was a better record than his three predecessors Brown, Brian Goorjian and Phil Smyth, none of whom got anywhere near medal rounds, a feat previously achieved by Barry Barnes at the 2000 Olympics. The pick-and-roll strategy needed revisiting as it was exploited by teams with good mid-range shooters. And the team for Tokyo could not include any passengers incapable of making a relevant contribution at this level. Seriously, this team showed such great heart, fight and mateship that to again fall short was borderline tragic.

But the basic defensive and offensive strategies — remembering how often the offence dried up if Mills was handcuffed or manhandled — and the handling of today's new breed of player, were essential areas to address ahead of Tokyo. Either that or the Boomers again ran the risk of being only the latest in a long line of "our greatest team ever" outfits to fall tantalisingly short of the podium.

CHAPTER FOURTEEN
GOLD VIBES ONLY

That was not going to happen again on Patty Mills' watch. He told the *Sydney Morning Herald*'s Phil Lutton: "I made the team for the 2008 Olympics and you're playing the USA in the quarterfinals and it's like, this is awesome, this is a great feeling. We lose the game and as a young kid like you don't understand really what that means, you just got your backside handed to you by all-time greats.

"Then you jump to the 2010 World Cup quarterfinal against Slovenia. Lose that again. So now that's two major tournaments where we lose at that point. Now we're in London 2012 and playing the USA in the quarterfinals, Kobe (Bryant) is having a flurry in the third quarter. Game over.

"It's (Boomers' forward) Matt Nielsen's last time being with us, and I remember sitting at the end of the lockers and it's taking me so long to come down off this sheer anger and disappointment. This is three times in a row now. I remember Matt coming over to me and he could feel that I'm not over this thing yet. He sits down next to me and he's trying to comfort me and I just remember snapping back at him and swearing and saying: 'This ain't it. This is not good enough'. I think that's where I said to myself that we have to do something here to create this thing."

It was no great surprise when Andrej Lemanis decided the 2019 World Cup campaign was his last, stepping down as coach of the Boomers. Cruelly denied a medal at the Rio Olympics and again at the Worlds, the pressure of the role and growing disquiet at his perceived poor relationships with NBA players such as Ben Simmons, Thon Maker and Jonah Bolden started making the job seem untenable. There even was speculation players such as Patty Mills, Joe Ingles and Andrew Bogut were keen for a new voice at the Tokyo Olympics in 2020. Whatever the truth of the situation was, Lemanis' decision to step away was his own and accepted by Basketball Australia.

The federation then turned back the clock and offered the role to Brett Brown, now head coach of the NBA's Philadelphia 76ers where Simmons was a starter for him and Bolden on the squad. Brown accepted the position. BA planned a joint announcement featuring Lemanis and Brown via a video teleconference link, but the story broke on ESPN so the federation, as always, instead went into self-preservation mode. "Basketball Australia would like to advise that at this time, no comment will be made in relation to the speculation surrounding the Australian Boomers," it said in a statement. Shortly after, Brown was announced as Lemanis' successor. Go figure.

"When the opportunity to coach the Boomers next summer in Tokyo came up, I was reminded of my deep history with Australia and Australian basketball," he said. "I felt a duty to try and help in any way that I could. The spirit of the country and the athletes of the country exemplify on a day-to-day basis the passion that is Australian sport.

"That passion is respected and recognised throughout the world and I'm very excited to be a part of that again. This is our mission and my message to our team — we're going into the 2020 Olympics to win a gold medal. I understand the magnitude of this statement. I would feel irresponsible having any other goal but this."

The Tokyo Olympic Games were due to begin on July 25, 2020, Andrew Bogut likely to play on to again give the Boomers that reliable centrepiece. Most pundits expected that would be his playing swansong, Bogut still on top of his game leading Sydney Kings into the NBL's 2019–20 grand final series. A medal with the Boomers in Tokyo would be a fitting finale to his stellar career.

Except in December 2019, the Coronavirus disease first was identified from an outbreak in Wuhan, China, and the world was about to irrevocably change. COVID-19 would burst into a full-blown global pandemic, the like of which had not been seen for a century. For a while, the planet was in a shutdown, local lockdowns occurring everywhere as governments sought to curtail the spread. Most of those efforts were akin to standing on a shore trying to stem a tidal wave with an umbrella.

Sporting competitions worldwide were put in a type of "holding pattern" as the world wrestled with the "new normal" of face masks, quarantining and social distancing. The AFL went into a recess, then reconvened and finished utilising "hub" options.

On March 11, 2020, the NBA season was suspended, then revived with a reformatted regular season, eight more games scheduled for 22 qualified teams going to the league's "Bubble" in Orlando, Florida. The regular season resumed play within the bubble on July 30.

Meanwhile in Louisville, Kentucky, mass protests erupted in May over the March 13 police killing of 26-year-old Breonna Taylor. Soon after Taylor's story captured worldwide attention, there was the horror of the May 25 murder of George Floyd in Minneapolis, Minnesota. Footage seen around the world saw Floyd screaming: "I can't breathe" and crying out for his mother while his neck stayed forcibly pinned under the knee of a white police officer for nine minutes.

The Black Lives Matter movement became an international phenomenon as protesters first took to the streets in US cities before it spread globally, including Australia. Amid the burgeoning movement, Patty Mills announced he was donating his NBA salary while in the Orlando bubble, to social justice causes in Australia. His salary specifically went towards Black Lives Matter Australia, Black Deaths in Custody and the "We Got You" campaign.

"I'm proud to say I'm taking every cent from these eight games that we're playing — which for me will turn out to be $1,017,818 and 54 cents — and donating that directly back to Black Lives Matter Australia, Black

Deaths in Custody and to a recent campaign that's called We Got You, dedicated to ending racism in sport in Australia," Mills said in a video posted by the Spurs.

"So I'm playing in Orlando because I don't want to leave any money on the table that could be going directly to black communities." Earlier in the year, Patty had launched Indigenous Basketball Australia (IBA), a programme of pathways for Aboriginal and Torres Strait Islanders to play basketball in an environment free of discrimination and exclusion.

"My love of basketball has come from the fact that it has brought me happiness, joy, health, education, and knowledge, with a greater appreciation and perspective on life," Mills said. "At the end of the day, a platform was created for me to carry and be seen as my true identity as an Australian, an Indigenous man of the land. When I combine those experiences, I become aware of the positive influence I can have on my own people in Australia who are continuously oppressed.

"It makes me want to work harder at finding ways to provide better opportunities to make a real impact on the lives of my people."

When Brett Brown was released by the Philadelphia 76ers as coach after the 2019–20 NBA season, his life would be impacted on multiple fronts. Suddenly the thrill of coaching Australia's men's national team again, gave way to the reality of what an uncertain future now held for him. While Glenn "Doc" Rivers was being announced as the new coach of the 76ers, Brown was informing Basketball Australia he no longer could commit to the Boomers and Tokyo due to uncertainty around his professional future.

Those hopes Brown's connection with Australia's impressive list of NBA products would be the missing link to lead them to a maiden medal at the 2020 Tokyo Games, now also were dashed. And as the year wore on and the pandemic showed no sign of relenting, the Olympics tentatively were moved to 2021, with no one completely confident they would go ahead at all. NBA boss Adam Silver stated his league's next season could run straight through the proposed July–August Games window, leaving NBA players and coaching staff with an eye on the Olympics treading water.

"Whilst I have a deep and long-standing passion for Australian basketball, I am currently unable to commit to coaching the Boomers at next year's Olympic Games," Brown said. "The uncertainties around the direction of my professional future unfortunately mean that I cannot commit to the time and preparation that this job deserves and requires.

"The difficulties around travelling internationally with my family during the pandemic have also contributed to my decision. It is important for me to give Basketball Australia, the coach, and players, the necessary time for a full and thorough Olympic Games preparation in the event that the Games do proceed."

Delaying the Games by a year had a further consequence for the Boomers. Andrew Bogut, prepared to prolong his career to include the 2020 Tokyo Games, did not believe he had another year of playing at the highest levels in him. Much to the dismay of Sydney Kings fans but much more to the fans of Australia's Boomers and their medal aspirations, his decision to retire from the sport was a devastating blow.

Now the team not only had no coach but had lost its primary interior presence. Fortuitously, Brian Goorjian returned to Australia from more than a decade in Asia, mostly in China. Accepting the job as head coach of the Illawarra Hawks in the NBL, Australia's most successful basketball coach suddenly was an option. But jumping back into the role he first took for the Athens Olympics in 2004 and finished with at the Beijing Olympics of 2008 did not have huge obvious appeal.

"The hardest thing, I think the biggest decision I ever made in my life, in my profession, was that Boomers job," Goorjian told Andrew

Johnstone for *News Corps Code*. "My gut told me, 'No, don't do this'. I'm at an age now when opportunities come up, I go by my gut. I didn't want to do it because there's good jobs and there's bad jobs. I thought under (Andrej) Lemanis and (Luc) Longley they were amazing. I thought what they were doing was amazing. The team played an amazing brand of basketball, they punched above their weight and everyone watching them thought they were wonderful.

"Now they've (the coaches) walked away from it and the only thing that you can do is medal. That's a bad job. That's a bad job, and I don't need that shit." The team's leaders — Patty Mills, Joe Ingles, Andrew Bogut and Matthew Dellavedova — had other ideas and told him as much. Goorjian coached Mills, Ingles and Bogut at the Beijing Games. "I was like, 'Wow, these guys, it's unbelievably important to them'. The next move from their standpoint is they're familiar with me," Goorjian said.

"We go back to Beijing together and I'm the right piece for their comfort. And that flipped me. 'I'm in'. I completely understood. I'm not a foreigner coming in. I'm not a guy from outside. I understood the enormity of this, the pride for these guys after 12 years. And the whole country is in on this, wanting a medal." Publicly, Goorjian said if his country called, he would answer. "My thought process has always been that it's like the military. If you are needed then I'm here." Australia called.

The new issue now was caused by the dates of the NBA season, the Finals scheduled to end a day before the Games began on July 23. That meant any quarantine requirements could compromise those NBA players competing in the post-season joining their national teams. In a Zoom meeting with his potential NBA Boomers, Goorjian was struck by their response and Patty Mills' unwavering determination to be leading the way to a medal in Tokyo. "It shocked me," Goorjian told *NCA Newswire's* Matt Logue. "I've been away from the Boomers system and I saw it (NBA players playing at the Olympics) like everyone else — it is a big ask and these guys are going to try.

"But that is not what came from them at all, and Patty led the way. He said, 'No man, I'm there, we're in and we are doing this, and we are getting that gold medal'. It was strong, and powerful, and there was no 'if this happens' or 'what if we make this'. No, man, I'm playing and that is it."

The programme for Tokyo 2021 now was starting to take shape. San Antonio finished 10th in the Western Conference and under the new "play-in" rules, had a one-and-done clash with Memphis Grizzlies to advance into the playoffs-proper. The Spurs lost 96-100, Patty Mills scoring nine points on 3-of-6 three-pointers in what would be his last game in a San Antonio uniform. It was May 19, two months short of the Tokyo Olympics.

But there still was time for a further setback, Ben Simmons deciding to withdraw from the Boomers squad for the Olympics to focus on honing his craft. It was not quite the body blow some believed, because the 210cm playmaker once favourably compared to Earvin "Magic" Johnson, had yet to genuinely commit to a serious Boomers international campaign. Already taking heat in Philadelphia for his fadeout in the finals, the decision to skip the Olympics generally was not well-received. But Patty Mills had a different take and revealed it.

"As a teammate, as a fan, and as a supporter, we all want to see our best players putting on the green and gold and for me in particular, having that thought even to be able to share the court with Benny at some stage in the green and gold, is something I am always going to look forward to and unfortunately now is not going to be the time, and that is OK," Mills said.

"This place right here, and the programme we have developed, and how strong our culture is, this is one place for him that is always going to be here with open arms because we are mates. We are teammates, we are a brotherhood and to be able to represent the green and gold, that is the culture that we have.

"The number one fact and characteristic of our group is how we support each other through the good, bad and ugly, whatever it may be, and Ben isn't an exception to that. No matter what he does, myself and the team will continue to support him because this is a safe place — everyone needs to know and understand that now more than ever, we need to support Ben on his journey."

When the final 12-man team for Tokyo was named, it had its constants and its surprises. Patty Mills, Joe Ingles, Aron Baynes, Matthew Dellavedova, Dante Exum, Chris Goulding, Nick Kay, Jock Landale and Nathan Sobey all had worn the green-and-gold before. Exum finally was fully fit and back in the fold while Sobey had blossomed into one of the NBL's leading players. He forced his way onto this team by sheer weight of performance. Duop Reath, Josh Green and Matisse Thybulle were new faces. Burgeoning young talent and NBL Rookie of the Year at Adelaide 36ers, Josh Giddey, and fellow future Boomer Xavier Cooks, were kept in the group through the preparation phase for Tokyo to fully sample what would one day be theirs.

Duop Reath was born in South Sudan, a versatile 211cm physical specimen who grew up in Australia, played college basketball at Louisiana State University and was playing professionally in Serbia before impressing at the Boomers' training camp. Josh Green was born in Sydney to an Australian mother and American father, whose basketball skills eventually took him to Arizona Wildcats and on into the NBA at Dallas Mavericks.

Matisse Thybulle arguably was the most interesting player of the new faces selected. At 196cm and outrageously athletic, he was an Australian-American, meaning he occupied the one naturalised player spot available on a national team. American shooting guard Bryce Cotton was setting records in the NBL with Perth Wildcats and when word spread he was seeking citizenship, many presumed it a formality he would be in the green-and-gold in Tokyo. But his naturalisation did not come through in time and, in fact, still was not finalised when this book went to print.

Instead Thybulle became the revelation of Australia's Games campaign. Indirectly part of the Boomers' Rio Olympic preparation as a member of the Pac-12 All Stars who played Australia in the "Farewell Series" before the trip to Brazil, he won myriad admirers with his regular video-logs of the Tokyo journey.

Gathering in Los Angeles for their training camp, the Boomers' "elders", led by Patty Mills but also comprising Joe Ingles, Matthew Dellavedova and Aron Baynes, indoctrinated the newbies into fair dinkum Aussie-ness. Whether it was Australian music with Jimmy Barnes, Kylie Minogue or Cold Chisel blaring in the bus or at shoot-around, eating pies, pasties or a goody bag laden with Milo bars, tasty shapes or a jar of Vegemite, Patty was making sure everyone knew what it meant to be a true blue Aussie.

While he was busy ensuring everyone was on the same page and the catch-cry "Gold Vibes Only" — meaning bring only a gold medal standard of behaviour to this campaign — was understood and adopted, Patty Mills received his own accolade. He jointly would carry the Australian team flag at the Tokyo Olympic Games' opening ceremony with swimming star Cate Campbell. Patty, 32, would be the historic first Indigenous Australian to carry the flag and the third basketball star, following in the footsteps of Andrew Gaze in 2000 and Lauren Jackson in 2012. It was totally appropriate but made even more poignant for Tokyo, where at the 1964 Olympic Games, Michael Ahmatt was the first Indigenous Aussie sportsman.

"We got some pretty cool news the other day," Joe Ingles told the team as it prepared to take the court for practice. "Patty has been named the flag-bearer." The response was immediate and wildly supportive. "Obviously very well deserved, as we all know for not only what he's done in his basketball career but for what he does off the court. He's the first-ever Indigenous Australian to carry the flag, I think there's about 33 sports teams, teams going for Australia, so he's the one they chose out of 33 teams, which is pretty cool. And then, it's the second-largest team that's ever gone to an Olympic Games so, everyone's proud of you. Congratulations and hold the flag properly," Joe concluded as the team again burst into spontaneous applause.

For Patty, this was further acknowledgement of the role he now was playing in the very psyche of his nation. "It's obviously an absolute honour and a privilege and it's so iconic that it's going to be hard for me to really wrap my head around this moment," Mills said via video conference.

"I could probably try my hardest to describe what it means, but the answer is, what does it mean to everyone else, what does it mean to everyone throughout Australia, the team, the thousands of ex-pats that live across the world, the next generation, the young ones that are coming through, the ones that have come before us, what does it mean to them? Because at the end of the day, that's who I represent.

"To be able to make them proud about going about our business and trying to achieve our dreams is what it's really all about. At the end of the day, I think it's about identity, it's about being proud of who you are and really showing that and being passionate about that, so it's obviously an honour."

The five-hour bus trip from LA to Las Vegas for exhibition games ahead of Tokyo was a further chance to spread Australiana and even Slim Dusty songs among the new faces. All of the new players felt welcomed and travelled emotionally from happy-to-be-here to beyond-rapt-to-be-involved. "We're here, gold vibes only," coach Brian Goorjian recalled, watching as the team's elder statesmen taught the new faces what it meant to be "a Boomer". "It's time, it's right now. You look at Josh Giddey being touched by it. You look at Josh Green, Jock Landale, Dante — those guys haven't really been tight in the thing like it is now.

"They (the elder statesmen) made such an awareness of the kangaroo and what a boomer is. Patty did such a good job on 'culture night' of what a kangaroo is. It's a unique animal to Australia and it never takes a step backwards. And every one of the players adopted a kangaroo and Patty had all that organised. I was sitting in the back just watching the enormity of this and how it was touching everybody."

Opening their match practice against Argentina, it was the irrepressible Patty Mills who pulled out a scorching, high-arching three-pointer at the buzzer to secure a clock-beating 87-84 win. Rookie Matisse Thybulle was the game's other big talking point, on top of Ash Barty overnight claiming the Wimbledon women's singles crown.

Mills was inspired by Barty's majestic performance as she became Australia's first women's singles champ at tennis' biggest event, since Evonne Goolagong Cawley in 1980. And it marked 50 years since Goolagong Cawley first won the Grand Slam tournament in 1971. There was a symmetry about it all and when Mills was called upon to break the 84-84 deadlock with Argentina, he did just that, sinking a match-winner in the same way he did against Russia, and by now, probably a dozen other morale-busted opponents.

Boomers boss Brian Goorjian took time to draw up a play and with 2.5 seconds left, Mills inbounded the ball to Jock Landale who handed it back for his match-winning triple. Matisse Thybulle and the flexibility and depth of the Aussie team were the day's main takeaways, the Philadelphia 76ers defensive stopper showing a tremendous offensive upside few knew existed. Duop Reath also was value for minutes, the core of this unit — namely Mills, Joe Ingles, Matthew Dellavedova and Aron Baynes — leading a charge quickly embraced by Thybulle, Landale, Nick Kay, Dante Exum, Chris Goulding and Nathan Sobey.

Truthfully, they looked surprisingly cohesive… until they didn't. Then

Argentina, with evergreen Luis Scola, 41, en route to a match-high 25 points, ran up an 11-point buffer. Once again working far more smoothly together than should have been expected at such an early stage, Australia turned that on its ear to create a double-digit lead of its own in the second half.

Then came the rush to the finish line where Mills already was waiting to be embraced by his jubilant teammates. Xavier Cooks and Josh Giddey being part of the bigger picture as squadmen also showed just how right Goorjian had it, their peripheral involvement giving them the type of culture exposure to make them key elements of future campaigns. At this early point, this campaign looked in solid shape.

The two big questions though came out of Nigeria's earlier shock three-point win over the USA. First, how tough was Nigeria going to be, given it suited seven NBA players and had highly-regarded NBA veteran Mike Brown coaching? Nigeria was in Australia's Group B in Tokyo and the Boomers' first tournament opponent. (The Boomers also drew Germany and Italy. Group A comprised the USA, Czech Republic, France, Iran. Group C was host Japan, Spain, Slovenia and Argentina.)

The second question was, is the USA really this vulnerable? Maybe, maybe not. Coach Gregg Popovich only had his US team together four days, one of which involved only a walk-through. And they only had three days of scrimmages, not all of which were full on. It showed, as the Americans were rusty on offence and missed many open looks. Clearly it was far too early to draw any conclusive conclusions, other than the fact the Aussies most assuredly would be in the medal mix.

Falling in behind Australia's Olympic flag-bearer Patty Mills, the Boomers next marched straight past the gold medal-defending USA 91-83 for a morale-boosting Games exhibition win in Las Vegas, only the Boomers' second ever success over the sport's standard-bearers. That was two-in-a-row now as well, coming on the back of Australia's win in Melbourne ahead of the 2019 FIBA World Cup in front of a record 52,079 fans at Melbourne's Marvel Stadium. On that occasion, it again was the brilliance of Mills and the guile of Joe Ingles which underpinned the 98-94 upset.

Andrew Bogut also was invaluable in that match, the microscope now on Aron Baynes to fill his big shoes in Tokyo. But here was the odd thing. Baynes cracked knees with Bradley Beal early in the match and did not resume, icing it on the sidelines as USA raced 11 clear just ahead of halftime courtesy of consecutive Boomers turnovers. But Australia owned the third period, Chris Goulding big in a 19-6 finish that had the Boomers on the brink of victory. His long-range missile to close the term was particularly inspirational.

Kevin Durant and Damian Lillard ensured the match would go to the wire but down the stretch, the defensive hustle and scramble of the Aussies was impeccable and impenetrable. That was despite Matthew Dellavedova being hit with two fouls within 44 seconds of the last quarter's start and the USA helpfully in bonus from midway through the quarter.

Matisse Thybulle continued to impress but Australia's defensive emphasis ultimately was the difference. Jayson Tatum put USA ahead on a fast break 82-80 with 4:34 left, but it was an 11-1 run to the siren for Australia, Mills en route to an equal game-high 22 points, with four assists including a stinging zinger of a pass from the top of the key to a cutting Thybulle. Lillard finished with 22 points, Durant 17 and Beal 12.

This was glorious to watch and while it was true the Americans still had three key players to add — the trio locked up in the NBA Finals between Phoenix and Milwaukee — it marked their second loss in successive games. Beaten by three by Nigeria to open this exhibition series, the USA now was counting down the days until it could assemble its true line-up.

In the meantime, Nigeria routed Argentina to show its victory over USA was no fluke and that it could more than successfully compete at this international level. Those pencilling in a certain win over Nigeria in Australia's Games' opener now were rummaging through drawers for their erasers. The flexibility in Brian Goorjian's line-up was exciting to behold, with players such as Thybulle and Duop Reath revelations.

Thybulle (12 points, 3 steals, 3 assists, 2 blocks), Ingles finishing with 17 after stroking three consecutive three-pointers in the first quarter, and Chris Goulding (11 points), showed the Aussies also had their share of offensive options. It was now a mere 10 days from the opening ceremony... and excitement in Australia was growing.

There was no hint of it abating either when Chris Goulding struck gold with an imperious 7-of-7 threes, helping the Boomers sink burgeoning Nigeria 108-69 in their final pre-Olympic exhibition. The result rocked Las Vegas bookies and further dared Australian basketball fans to dream, albeit it tentatively.

With satisfying wins over Argentina and the USA already under their belts, the Boomers chose to rest their "Four Horsemen of the Apocalypse" — namely Patty Mills, Joe Ingles, Aron Baynes and Matthew Dellavedova — instead letting their colts run wild and they did, seizing the initiative and never relenting. Bear in mind, this Nigerian team came into the match also owning the scalps of the USA and Argentina, beating the Argies by 23.

Sharing Group B berths in Tokyo, the game presented the perfect opportunity *not* to reveal too much strategically, although Australia's defensive brilliance again was on show, containing Nigeria to a 29-point first half as the Boomers swept 20 clear. Jock Landale (14 points, 5 rebounds) was joined in the starting five by Nathan Sobey (15 points, 4 rebounds, 5 assists), Dante Exum (6 points, 3 rebounds, 5 assists and a highlights package drive to the hoop), Matisse Thybulle and Nick Kay.

The insertion of peripheral pair Josh Giddey and Xavier Cooks, not to mention Josh Green (11 points), along with the continued emergence of Duop Reath (17 points, 3 rebounds, 2 assists) meant Boomers fans had the opportunity to look into Australia's international future. And it looked blindingly bright.

Compiling 14 points, four rebounds and three assists, Giddey successfully quarter-backed the side but it was Goulding who shot out the lights, leaving no-one in any doubt about his role in this team. The Boomers bamboozled Nigeria and absolutely were a delight to watch from tip-to-toe, connecting on 18-of-29 threes. Their commitment to defence was through the roof. Nigeria scored 90 and 94 in its previous games before being stifled to 69. And the Boomers' unselfish offensive play was a pure joy.

But just as Aussie fans knew coach Brian Goorjian kept some cards close to his chest, not showing his full hand, there was no reason to believe Nigeria was showing its full deck. The Boomers were flying to Tokyo, gold vibes only.

Defence tenacious? Tick. Patty Mills alight? Tick. An unexpected contributor or two? Tick. Australia's Boomers opened their Tokyo Olympic campaign by locking in and safely tucking away an 84-67 victory over Nigeria, ticking all the boxes. Ahead 58-52 with a period to play, the Boomers' rampaging 26-15 final quarter placed them at the head of Group B, Italy beating Germany 92-82 in the pool's earlier match.

Mills led all scorers with 25 points and six assists, his tally including 5-of-8 three-point makes. As usual, Nick Kay was a solid contributor off the bench with 12 points, eight rebounds, three assists and a block, offering big-man relief where Jock Landale was hampered by foul trouble and Aron Baynes by soft hands. Nigeria opened with the game's first two baskets before Joe Ingles peeled a casual triple off his money-wad. Yet at times Ingles resembled the Rio Olympics' "second-guessing" version of himself when the cool "I enjoy kicking your butt and smirking at you" version was the one Australia needed for this campaign to be successful.

Hopefully it was just a case of first-game nerves because that secondary scoring option to Mills remained a vacancy yet to be filled. Dante Exum worked hard for his 11 points but the ball stuck in his hands far too often when he took it to the hoop and a few of his five turnovers were avoidable.

He made up for it defensively in a promising first game and while Matisse Thybulle's numbers may not have read particularly spectacularly — seven points, four rebounds, two assists, five steals — he was an X-factor all over the floor. His energy level and commitment to every play was heady stuff and the Boomers needed it after leading 21-14 early, only to be tied at 23-23 after one. Thybulle already had thrown down a powerhouse dunk as Australia pulled its offence together after trailing 28-32, producing an 11-2 response.

Leading 43-40 at halftime, threes by Matthew Dellavedova and Mills to start the second gave the Boomers the buffer required to keep Nigeria at a safe distance. Australia's copybook defence meant Nigeria scored its first basket of the second half at 4:41 in the third quarter, but it finished strongly to trail 52-58 going into the last.

Focus shifted quickly into a case of "Sacre bleu!" as France formally threw the Games' competition wide open when it ended the USA's 25-game Olympic winning streak with a glorious 83-76 victory built on Evan Fournier's 28-point excusez-moi. Hopes of another USA gold medal understandably had drifted wildly, the Americans instead laying a golden egg as France came from behind, played with great desperation and made all the big shots.

It was the USA's first men's loss in Olympic basketball since the 2004 Athens Olympics and while it would be crazily premature to imagine the Americans would not still progress to the medal rounds, any air of invincibility they flaunted had well-and-truly been sullied. Every other national team now had the Americans in their crosshairs, France content with others bowing to their "merci beaucoup".

Italy never was going to be an easybeat for Australia, but the Boomers' gritty 86-83 win thrust them through to the second round and within range of that historic first medal. Their intragroup record now stood at 2-0, only Germany to play before the quarterfinals. A win over the Germans meant Australia would finish on top of Group B with a 3-0 record, the most desirable of results. But even a surprise loss could not keep the Boomers from advancing.

This time around they had their array of "bigs" to thank for escaping Italy's clutches, Jock Landale leading the way with 18 points at 64 per cent, Nick Kay with 15 at 86 per cent, and Aron Baynes 14 at 56 per cent. All three hauled down seven rebounds apiece, Australia crunching the boards to the tune of 44-30.

Patty Mills opened the game with a seven-point first quarter but Italy worked hard to smother him offensively and keep him from maintaining his usual influence. It worked to a degree but he found other ways to contribute, his 16 points, six rebounds, five assists and a steal all part of a solid stats line.

And while the Italian defence did force him into some tough shots and a few rushed ones too, when the result was on the line in the last half-minute or so, he was Superman-Patty as always. His drive with 31.8 seconds left gave the Boomers back a five-point lead at 82-77 and with 8.8 seconds left, his free throws clinched it.

Joe Ingles' 14 points included a match-high four three-pointers, leaving Italy scrambling for who else it could shut down. Australia also committed half the turnovers it had against Nigeria, down to 11, Dante Exum the main offender with four. Unlike the match with Nigeria where he drove to the hoop repeatedly and rarely looked to pass, against Italy he drove and rarely looked to shoot, often finding himself in no-man's land. If he could get the balance right, good results would follow.

Australia also again received great service from Matisse Thybulle, whose energy and hustle were proving symptomatic of the Boomers' culture. It was growing difficult to believe this was his international debut. Tied at 25-25 after the first period, Nathan Sobey was exploited by flame-haired Italian guard Nico Mannion, who bumped Italy to a 30-25 lead by attacking him, Sobey missing two shots in response.

It turned into an expensive 99 seconds of court-time but later proved an invaluable learning curve. Mannion became a real headache, having his way with Matthew Dellavedova too before Exum's length was able to disrupt him to some degree. Down a point at halftime, Australia's ball movement brought it back from a six-point deficit, a 14-2 run turning 44-50 into 58-52 to force an Italian time-out. Defence again was the key.

Ahead but stuck on 71-67 for four consecutive plays, the Boomers' offence finally was rewarded when Landale went to the free throw line. He made his first, missed his second, but Kay regained the ball, it swung back around to Landale who then struck a three-pointer to create a four-point play backwards. Now ahead 75-67, the Aussies had no time to enjoy the lead before Simone Fontecchio swished a three and was fouled by Ingles, his bonus freebie trimming it back to 71-75.

Kay swished an important shot and after another good defensive stand, Landale tipped an offensive rebound to Ingles for the triple and Italy would need a miracle. Australia played the final minute perfectly, its strategies holding Italy at arm's length for a satisfying victory, with more improvement shown and the promise of more to come. It also showed great character to play such a focused second half after losing stalwart Aron Baynes during the three-quarter-time interval.

Baynes, one of the Boomers' "strong quartet" with Patty, Joe and Delly, suffered a neck injury after rushing to the change-rooms during the break and causing consternation when he did not return. He was found on the floor, the injury sufficiently serious to require his hospitalisation.

The injury was so bad he immediately was ruled out of the rest of the tournament, then subsequently also missed the 2021–22 NBA season. An MRI showed internal bleeding that was putting pressure on his spinal cord. In hospital, Baynes could not communicate fluidly with the Japanese nurses or doctors. The COVID-19 pandemic meant Tokyo was in a state of emergency so he also could not have anyone from the team with him.

"Aron is a big part of our team and we are all hurting for him, but we have great depth in our squad and I have every confidence in the 11 remaining players. We will all stay focused on the task ahead," Boomers coach Brian Goorjian said. "Unfortunately, injuries can happen but this team is resilient and we will adapt".

This was a bitter pill for Baynes and a huge blow for the Aussies, despite the Boomers rallying in support of their fallen comrade and remaining fully committed to the goal at hand. First it was no Bogut but now no Baynes, and to lose him mid-tournament had the potential to derail the quest.

Typically, it was Patty Mills who marshalled the troops as Australia bombarded Germany 89-76 to sweep Group B, marching into the quarterfinals full of confidence. Baynes' absence always was going to be challenging but Jock Landale and Nick Kay responded with their best games of the tournament. Landale opened the match with a three-pointer and a dunk to give Australia an immediate 5-0 lead, continuing on to finish with 18 points at 70 per cent, plus three rebounds, three assists and a block.

Kay's 16 points also were delivered at 70 per cent, with four rebounds, four assists and a steal. He was most definitely proving to be the team's "Mr Reliable". Of some concern was the fact the Boomers were flogged 45-28 on the boards, but this was compensated by forcing 18 turnovers while conceding just six.

After initially shooting erratically, Mills found his groove and led all scorers with 24 points, adding six assists. In the last quarter, Joe Ingles also became more active offensively, drilling both of his three-pointers in the final stanza as the Boomers finished all over the Germans.

Matthew Dellavedova was fortunate an accidental poke he took in his eye early in the second wasn't millimetres across from near the bridge of his nose, as he was cut, bleeding and had to check out. As expected of Delly, he would return unfazed. Nathan Sobey relished his sudden opportunity and with it, earned more time later in the game to be a valuable contributor at both ends.

Boomers coach Brian Goorjian was unafraid to "go small", often running with three guards and Ingles at the power forward as Australia's team play took it to a 44-40 halftime buffer. Mills opened the second half alight, his drive taking the lead to 46-40, then after a defensive rebound, he took it up the floor, stroked a triple and was fouled on the shot, adding a bonus free throw.

This was vintage Patty, Australia up 50-40 but sparking a 10-0 response from Germany as a few poor decisions and turnovers forced Goorjian to call time-out. Kay then iced a three before the energetic and always active Matisse Thybulle stole the ball and took it in for a slam dunk.

Germany again dragged the scoreline back to 55-55 before Duop Reath, seeing some action in Baynes' absence, stole the ball and threw down a fast break dunk of his own. Dante Exum kept his feet on his drives, pushing the lead to 61-55, Landale's three-pointer making it 64-57 and another Thybulle steal closing the quarter with the Boomers beaming 66-59.

When Ingles started rolling offensively in the last, Germany was fighting a rearguard action, but the Aussies were attacking on all fronts. Mills created chaos, either nailing threes or drawing defenders and creating sweet plays for grateful teammates. As the result became self-evident, Germany's desperation to keep the deficit manageable — keeping it in the hunt for a "best third-placed finish" advance to the quarterfinals — led to a bizarre barrage of three-point missiles. Suddenly there were more threes than in the last Miss Kyrgyzstan Beauty Pageant, to little avail as the Boomers bounded on.

The whole unwieldy idea of three groups of four and having the top two teams from each, plus the best third placegetters qualify for the eight-team quarterfinals, was to prevent any form of sand-bagging or match-fixing by any team trying to manipulate the draw in its favour. If you didn't know who you might be playing in the quarterfinal round, then surely that ensured the integrity of intragroup play?

It should have and maybe it did. But for FIBA officials to then produce the quarterfinal draw behind closed doors that the world at large was unable to see or attend was dubious, at best. Australia drew Argentina as its quarterfinal opponent, with the chance to advance to an Olympic semi final showdown against the winner of the match between the USA and Spain. This was typical of anything-but-transparent Eurocentric-FIBA. The other half of the draw featured four European teams, guaranteeing one would be competing for the gold medal.

What made this "fair" draw laughable was that one half of the draw had USA, Spain, Australia and Argentina. Why was that suspect? Because FIBA's world rankings of the top four teams in the world were USA 1, Spain 2, Australia 3, Argentina 4. The top four teams in the world, as ranked by FIBA, all on the *same* side of the draw? And on the other side, four European teams, ranked by FIBA as France 7, Italy 10, Slovenia 16, Germany 17. To paraphrase Andrew Bogut: "Google where FIBA headquarters is."

Australia was in Tokyo to win a gold medal. It had no qualms about the task it faced, or of knowing any trip to gold ultimately meant having to go through the USA. And they were meaning business as Argentina discovered when the Boomers unleashed a staggering 37-11 last-quarter blitz in a 58-26 second half extravaganza. Their emphatic 97-59 rout of the world #4 saw Australia smash open the door and storm into the semi finals.

Gold medallists at the Athens Olympics — the first time Brian Goorjian coached the Aussies at an Olympic Games — the Argentines were no match for the relentless defensive pressure and hustling rotations he drew from his totally focused and committed outfit. After a tight opening period, Australia charged into its semi final match against the gold medal-defending USA with three quarters of perfect Boomers basketball — ball pressure, doubles on the onball screens, swift rotations, great ball movement and superlative unselfish offence.

The Boomers produced 33 assists on 35 made field goals, all 11 players scoring and by the end, having fun doing it, the pressure of qualifying having dissipated. Australia contained Argentina to 11 second-quarter points, 15 in the third and 11 in the last which it opened by peeling off 19 unanswered points to lead 79-48.

Dante Exum's steal and coast-to-coast drive gave Australia a 60-48 buffer with a quarter remaining before he opened the last with a driving dunk, leaving Argentina in no doubt of the mountain it would need to climb to stay in sight of the Aussies. Frankly, Argentina never made it out of base camp as Matisse Thybulle swished a three-pointer, Joe Ingles followed a layup with a triple and Chris Goulding iced a three for 73-48.

Argentina's time-out did nothing to stem the tide, Nick Kay (10 points, 10 rebounds) making it 75-48 before Jock Landale pushed the lead out to 29 and Patty Mills to 31 at 79-48. Argentina made its basket breakthrough with 4:38 left in the contest, the game truly completely on the Boomers' terms straight after halftime.

Landale opened the third with a three, and his second soon after gave Australia its first double-digit lead at 47-37. Gabriel Deck offered some token Argentinian resistance before he quickly leapt to four fouls after Mills and Kay took charges from him on consecutive plays. Australia went into the halftime break nursing a 39-33 lead built on a terrific 21-11 defensive quarter. Argentina controlled much of the first period to lead

22-18 but with Thybulle setting an example defensively, the Boomers grew in stature.

He had three steals and a block before the main interval and was active at both ends of the floor. His three-pointer to start the second quarter was a positive sign as the Boomers' early shooting from long-range was haphazard at best, after Matthew Dellavedova opened the quarterfinal scoring with a three bomb.

Working the ball around, Argentina had its lead out to 18-10 at one stage while the Aussies still were finding their groove at both ends. Goulding's three-pointer tied the game at 24-24 with 8:01 to go in the second quarter, Mills' layup for the lead forcing an Argentine time-out. Thybulle with another sharp steal saw Ingles open on a wing and he drilled a three for 29-24.

A Mills triple meant the lead was out to 32-26, the Boomers on a 14-4 run from the first break. Landale stretched the lead to eight and Mills to nine, the only downer Exum collecting his third foul ahead of halftime. But even that was compensated somewhat when veteran Olympic superstar Luis Scola collected his third foul 42 seconds out from halftime.

The 41-year-old international champion was subbed out with 51.4 seconds left in the game and received a standing ovation from the players on the court, the Australian bench and the spectators permitted to be in attendance as Argentina's last active contributor to its Athens gold medal left the hardwood for the final time.

The Aussies? They showed they would be back and in no uncertain terms. They now were playing some of the best basketball seen from teams wearing the green-and-gold, and no-one in Basketball Australia called them the "strongest" or "greatest" or anything else. No-one wanted to risk jinxing this quest in any way at all.

CHAPTER FIFTEEN
OUR DREAMTIME TEAM

When the 2020–21 NBA season ended, Patty Mills became a highly coveted free agent. With the San Antonio Spurs destined for a period in a rebuilding mode, the franchise was happy for him to pursue better opportunities as he moved into his career twilight. Among the many clubs keen for his services, according to *Athletic*'s Anthony Slater, were the Golden State Warriors. Slater quoted Warriors coach Steve Kerr saying of Patty: "Seems like our kind of guy. I'm a huge fan. Great player, leader."

As assistant coach to Gregg Popovich in the latter's role as USA head coach, Kerr saw close up how capable Patty was of ripping even the best players in the NBA. He also saw his qualities as a leader of the Boomers' culture and their never-say-die attitude. Kevin Durant, a star at Oklahoma City, Golden State and with the Brooklyn Nets, also had seen Patty up-close-and-personal while he led the USA. They had long history, dating back to the 2006 Nike Hoop Summit in Memphis when Patty was a member of the World Select Team that competed against the USA National Junior Team. Durant now was one of the "big three" at the Nets, along with Kyrie Irving and James Harden. Brooklyn had a potential championship roster.

Joining the Nets for a run at another NBA title made sense to Patty, negotiations with his management still ongoing into the Olympic Games. "It was such an extraordinary circumstance with free agency being in the middle of the Olympics," Mills said. "Knowing where my head was in the trenches so to speak, of trying to win a first Olympic medal and knowing free agency was going to be in the middle did make it quite tough."

With Patty's immediate priority to break Australia's medal drought, he prepared as best he could before entering the Olympic Village. "For me, being able to be prepared for a lot of things is something I take pride in," he said. "It was one of those things where I prepared before I entered the national team realm. From my standpoint, I did all that I could, did the research I needed to do which gave me confidence to go into the national team and be there. When it came up and the information came through when I was in the village, by that stage it was almost obvious and a calculated decision, combined with what the gut was feeling… but it was hard.

"Knowing that you're all in for a championship and you have that mindset and feel throughout the group, every day it's working towards something. That's an exciting feeling to know when you walk in the gym, or in the weight room, it's for a championship. A lot of it starts in the locker room, off the court. This is a great opportunity for me to insert myself in a group that's already established. What I'll be able to bring is that leadership and that experience of coming from a winning culture environment."

Mills' conversations with Kevin Durant confirmed he made the correct career move. "It's exciting for me to know there is a different opportunity to see how I can fit," he said. "The conversation I had with Kevin was so pure and so genuine. Being able to understand that he is such a genuine hooper and go back-and-forth about basketball specifics. It was exciting for me to know there is an opportunity there for me to try and be who I am, like who I am with the national team."

Who he was with Australia's national team was a leader and a winner. Warming up for the semi final game with Durant at the other end of the court among the USA outfit, his long-time coach Gregg Popovich and the man who wanted him, Steve Kerr, standing on the sideline, did not faze Patty Mills. Winning, which meant a gold medal — or at worst a silver medal — was the only thing on his mind.

With Australia following on from its quarterfinal rout of Argentina by playing some of its finest international basketball, the USA's reluctance to play any fully committed defence or to use the ball selflessly played right to the Boomers' strengths. Joe Ingles opened the match with a confident three-pointer, following it with a second triple in transition for a 6-2 lead.

Patty Mills (team high 15 points, 8 assists) missed his first four shot attempts, three of them drives, then turned the ball over in what seemed an anxious start by the Boomers' magician. But his runner after a Dante Exum three-pointer bumped the lead to 16-8 and a dunk by Nick Kay kept the margin at eight.

Durant was simply unstoppable and singlehandedly kept the USA's offence ticking as it closed to 18-21. But Chris Goulding's triple to close the first quarter had Australia ahead 24-18. He opened Australia's scoring in the second the way he closed the first and Australia's lead was 27-20, then 29-20 after two more Goulding free throw makes.

Kay was tripped as he wheeled to go to the hoop for a no-call which ignited a rightfully indignant Australian bench, but only earned it a technical foul. Coach Brian Goorjian wisely took time-out to settle his troops, Exum then twice putting the Boomers ahead by 10. Once was at 33-23 when he took a charge, then drove, the second again at 36-26 when he calmly slotted a triple. From a defensive rebound, Mills threw a long pass to Matisse Thybulle for a three-point play and it was 39-26 to the Aussies.

Australian fans scattered among living rooms throughout the nation, others watching at work, others on their phones, iPads, computers, in bars and hotels were feeling their excitement and anticipation growing. The Boomers twice had beaten the USA in relatively recent meetings. France had beaten the USA at these Games. Could we dare to dream? Exum with the lob pass to Jock Landale for the slam dunk produced a 15-point lead and time-out by the Americans.

Trailing 26-41, the USA was on the ropes, those boxing kangaroo Boomers seen on all those yellow flags across the years, ready to deliver the killer blows. But that isn't what happened. The game actually turned from that moment as the USA walked back onto the hardwood. They stiffened their defence, Thybulle picked up an unsportsmanlike foul, the Aussies turned over the ball, their offence now spluttering and needing a Mills rainbow three-pointer just to steady the ship.

NBA champion Jrue Holiday was active at both ends and Australia missed several good open looks as the US drew steadily closer. Durant's jumpshot brought USA to 40-45, Thybulle turned the ball over, Holiday driving for 42-45. Matthew Dellavedova, who endured a hardly memorable 12 minutes, then turned over Australia's last possession of the half and even though Tatum's shot for the tie missed, the mood in both camps was vastly different heading into the change-rooms.

Four poor minutes to the halftime break brought the Boomers back to earth with a resounding thud and once the Americans sniffed a weakening of Australia's belief, they were ruthless. Their 16-4 run into halftime saw the Boomers' buffer sliced back to a single long shot at the break. The Aussies were left lamenting a golden lead surrendered with some unusually wayward decision-making.

The Americans now knew they had taken the Boomers' best shot. They knew they weathered the storm. They could handle business from here. Everyone sensed the game's momentum shift and it was now more hope than confidence with which Aussie basketball lovers greeted the Boomers as they returned to the pine. The officiating also did Australia no favours, play stopped when Devin Booker lost a shoe with the Aussies going into offence, and several phantom no-touch fouls called on bewildered Boomers.

Ultimately though, that was small potatoes. The Americans simply made a meal of the Boomers with a devastating 32-10 third period, dining out on fried kangaroo. Patty Mills opened the second half with two missed shots, suffocating under some furious defensive pressure. Joe Ingles too went MIA offensively, Holiday with consecutive scores giving USA the lead at 46-45 as it just became progressively worse.

The best team in the world — until rival semi finalists France or Slovenia could prove otherwise in the gold medal playoff — was off and running. Even threes by Mills for 50-56 and Kay for 53-59, which offered some light at the end of the tunnel, quickly fell into darkness as Booker, Tatum and Zach Lavine punished Australia for every hesitant play. Its confidence shot, Australia stumbled badly, another turnover leading to a USA fast break dunk, Landale muffing a dunk and it was Showtime.

Australia still led by 10 (45-35) 1:45 out from halftime, but its inability to retain that buffer was all the USA had to see to know if it took its game up another level, the Boomers could no longer go with them. Kevin Durant carried the USA on his shoulders until it weathered the best Australia had to offer, before turning the Boomers' gold medal dream into a convincing and nightmarish 97-78 beating. The USA was going to be defending its gold medal and Australia, so full of pluck and excitement motoring to that 41-26 lead, was off to another bronze medal playoff.

For a quarter-and-a-half everyone saw how good Australia could be. For two-and-a-half quarters, everyone saw how great the USA was. This was the Boomers' fifth loss in an Olympic semi final and they came up empty in the bronze battle on the previous four occasions. Gutted, they quickly needed to regroup to buck the trend and bring home the nation's maiden men's basketball medal.

Devastation. That was the prevailing sentiment in the Boomers' change-room. The shot fired at a gold medal opportunity turned into a blank. Australia's national men's team would not be coming home with the gold medal. It was a shattering fusion of emotional despair and realisation they had failed again. But had they? Had they *really*? Did "gold vibes only" mean "gold medal only"? Or did it mean a gold standard of culture, of behaviour, of camaraderie, of commitment, of focus?

"There was disappointment, there were tears because our goal was gold," Mills told Phil Lutton at the *Sydney Morning Herald*. "This is where I believe all the credit has to go to Goorj and his unbelievable ability to get his team to a point of understanding what we needed to get done. It was like he was (former Canberra Cannons' defensive star) Simon Dwight and just swatted all of the disappointment out of the locker room.

"We jumped back on the bus, it was the only time throughout the whole campaign we had a bus ride with no music. But it was all Goorj, he hit the parts he needed to bring everyone together and refocus." Up and until that point, Goorjian's assistant coaching staff of John Rillie, Matt Nielsen and Adam Caporn each had very definite designated roles in the Australian team environment, a genuine coaching "team." But after the semi final loss, Goorjian stepped into the spotlight.

"The strongest my voice was, was after that USA game," Goorjian said. "We lost the game. There was a definite 'we want gold, we want gold' — they, Patty, Joe… that group — expected gold and were dropped to the knees with the loss. And I walked in the locker-room, there was tears, it was like 'this is done — we're done'. I came in and 'hey, 0 and 11 at this point, you've been great. This culture has been strong. You performed outside the boundaries. You've been a bust here. We ain't got nothing done'.

"I went down that path — head up, back straight, be proud. Boxing kangaroo — we don't take a step backwards. Now we're going to showcase, and the whole nation is going to be watching this game. And it's no good if the culture is just in this room, with 15 guys. We're going to showcase this. There's a special place you have to go after you get kicked in the teeth and nobody does it better than an Aussie."

And while Goorjian unquestionably played his strongest role for his team between the semi final loss and bronze medal playoff, he was adamant Mills drove the passion. "This guy was on a mission. I just sat back and steered the energy into the areas I wanted it and it was just an epic performance and I enjoyed it and it goes down in history," Goorjian said. "I got back to the room and there was a message sent loud and clear, and we had a meeting and I sat with Joe and Patty."

At the Sydney 2000 Olympics, Aboriginal sprinter Cathy Freeman lit the flame at Sydney Olympic Stadium before later delivering the iconic moment of the Games when she won gold in the 400 metres. She carried the hopes and dreams of every Australian in that epic race — a huge additional weight of expectation — then celebrated by carrying the Aboriginal flag around the track. "That moment was — I get shivers just thinking about it," said Mills, who was 12 when he watched it. "I ran track, and my pet event was the 400 metres, and I wanted to be like Cathy Freeman. The whole country was (riding) on Cathy's back during that race.

"Everyone was clued in during that race, seeing her cross the line and how she handled herself, not only on the track, but before and after, because she had so much pressure." Patty Mills wanted to serve his nation and be a similar inspiration. Cometh the moment, cometh the man. France outlasted Slovenia 90-89 in the other semi final, making the playoff for gold between the French and Americans. Australia would be facing Slovenia for bronze.

"After the USA game, there was a meeting and it was basically driven by the coaching staff on-board, but Patty and Joe Ingles said 'put the ball in our hands here and let's get Matisse (Thybulle) on Luka (Doncic) and I can go 40 (minutes),' Goorjian said. 'Don't worry about rest, this is it'.

"It was something that was discussed and his performance, the ball being put in his (Mills') hands and also Joe, it was discussed prior to the game and there was a determination in there from the opening tip that he was going to get to the spots a la Kevin Durant in the game prior against us." If Australia was going to win a medal, Patty Mills and Joe Ingles would be doing everything possible to achieve it. And if it didn't, it would not be for want of trying.

Patty Mills was Cathy Freeman sprinting to immortality and more in the bronze medal game. He was Nova Peris-Kneebone winning gold with the hockey team in 1996. He was Lionel Rose becoming the world bantamweight boxing champion in 1968. He was Andrew McLeod winning two Norm Smith Medals in Adelaide Crows AFL premiership teams. He was the personification of a nation, determined and single minded for that ultimate appreciation. And he did it.

Opening the match with Matisse Thybulle inserted into the starting line-up for Matthew Dellavedova, Australia looked laser-focused from the outset, Ingles scoring twice and Mills with his first three making it 9-2. Patty had seven points in the first quarter and an unbelievable 19 in the second, his play overshadowing Slovenia's megastar Luka Doncic (22 points, 8 rebounds, 7 assists, 8 turnovers), Australia winning the second period 33-26 after taking a 20-19 lead into the first break.

From 31-33 down in the second quarter, the Boomers went on a 14-2 tear to lead 45-35. Some of their play was simply sensational, Ingles-to-Thybulle-to-Landale just pretty to watch. Thybulle's third dunk of the half closed it with Australia ahead 53-45 and Patty Mills taking an Olympics-career high 26-point single-half return into the interval.

Jock Landale had 10 at the break on 5-of-6 shooting, the Boomers weathering the best Slovenia could muster after worrying signs only minutes earlier. Patty was keeping the Slovenian defence on its toes, allowing him to also dish four assists, his pass to Landale for a dunk, followed by a fast-break basket from the super-quick mesmerising magician creating the 10-point lead.

That forced Slovenia into a time-out and a quick basket, a stop and a Doncic three-pointer had it back to 40-45 in the blink of an eye. Slovenia was at 43-47 when Mills drew a charge from Doncic, who also earned a technical foul after that play. That again ignited the Aussies who were looking clearly on top going into the interval.

The third quarter started with a bench tech against Doncic for some halftime banter and Slovenia's composure was becoming questionable. Attending its first Olympics, it had trouble coping with the Boomers' relentless play and the many little but significant "one per centers" players such as Nick Kay (game-high four steals) consistently contributed. The lead was at 12 just 4:46 from the last break but back to six (66-60) when Klemen Prepelic completed a four-point play after a poor foul on his three-point make.

Consecutive Patty Mills jumpshots had the lead back at 10, two triples by Ingles to close the third ensuring Australia won another quarter and had a 78-67 buffer going into the last. An early three from Goulding meant the lead briefly ballooned to 81-67, an 8-0 run including a turnover and an unsportsmanlike foul in its favour, suddenly swinging Slovenia the momentum.

At 75-81 it was back in it and with 6:18 left, Doncic's drive sliced the deficit to 80-83. It was a horrific time for Jaka Blazic to pick up a foul manhandling Mills, then choosing to shove him to cop an extra unsportsmanlike. Horrific for *Slovenia*, perfect for Australia.

Patty's free throws at 6:05 took the lead back to five, Dante Exum drew a by-the-numbers charging foul, then coolly slotted a triple from a Mills feed for 88-80. Kay's steal for an Exum fast break dunk pushed the lead back to 90-80, successive Doncic threes drawing Slovenia to within 86-92. That, however, was its last gasp.

Ingles sank a three, then grabbed another defensive rebound releasing Mills for a layup and with 3:22 left and ahead 97-86, the bronze was within reach. Free throws from Exum and a Mills feed to Kay for a three-pointer made it 102-86, a 10-0 response and this was over.

There still was time for a further Exum three-ball and another Thybulle dunk — that stuff *never* grew old — and a team which set out to return home with Australian men's basketball's historic first medal at Olympic level, finally could stamp "Mission Accomplished" on that aspiration.

It had been an interminably long wait but on August 7, 2021, the Boomers, led supremely by the NBL's coaching doyen Brian Goorjian and a fully-committed purposeful crew of assistants and helpers, finally had the job done. The team of Aron Baynes, Matthew Dellavedova, Dante Exum, Chris Goulding, Josh Green, Joe Ingles, Nick Kay, Jock Landale, Patty Mills, Duop Reath, Nathan Sobey and Matisse Thybulle blasted its way into history as Australia's greatest ever on a night to remember forever.

Patty Mills carried the flag, the Boomers following him to immortality as Australia's historic first men's medal-winning team, claiming the bronze with a 107-93 victory. After 65 years of many great and memorable moments but no ultimate team glory — and four defeats in bronze medal playoffs — with 42 points Mills planted the Aussie flag early, declaring any Slovenian win had to deal with him.

A man possessed, he led this now immortal "Dreamtime Team" with his highest Olympic Games point-scoring return — second only to Eddie Palubinskas' 48 points in an overtime victory for Australia over Mexico in Montreal in 1976 — but the most scored by any player in a medal playoff in Games history. And basketball first was played at the 1936 Berlin Olympics.

But Mills was not just scoring and running rings around, through and in between frustrated Slovenian defenders with his exceptional range in change-of-pace moves — he also fed out nine assists. Joe Ingles thrived on his kick-outs with four three-pointers and a game-high nine rebounds to figuratively claim the Oscar in a best supporting role capacity. But it also was the contributions of Olympic debutants Matisse Thybulle, Dante Exum, Nick Kay and Jock Landale which had every Boomer, past and present, punching their fists in jubilation, exultation, relief and joy.

Not to mention a hungry national public which followed the exploits of Brian Goorjian's amazing team through all of its many highs in this campaign — and even its one low against the USA — to the ultimate celebration that a bronze medal finally was achieved. With three wins in the Olympics build up followed by four straight wins before the loss to the US, then claiming the medal prize, this Australian team went on an unprecedented 8-1 win-loss journey.

Four Olympic campaigns by Mills and Ingles, three by Matthew Dellavedova and the unfortunately absent-through-injury Aron Baynes, and two by Chris Goulding finally bore fruit that every Australian basketball fan equally could savour for its "rose gold" sweetness. And make no mistake. After the pain of a one-point loss to Spain for Bronze in Rio five years earlier, this could not have been much sweeter.

Patty Mills' performance — one for the ages... and that's *ALL* ages — became the immediate benchmark of self-belief, belief-in-the-team and belief in the maybe-not-so-impossible dream. The USA beat France to claim gold — apparently its birthright — as much a joy as a relief for head coach Gregg Popovich, for so long Patty Mills' NBA sensei.

After a decade in San Antonio, Popovich had lost Patty Mills on a two-year $12million deal to the Brooklyn Nets, then his USA outfit eliminated him from the gold medal game. Neither made Pop particularly happy and he felt for his former star player and friend. "Thrilled with the victory, obviously," Popovich said after the US comeback which relegated Australia to the bronze game. "But when I looked him in the eyes (post-game) I felt badly. They do have great camaraderie and history and culture and want it just as badly as any of us. That was a little bit sad, but that's what we all do, we all try to win."

Patty Mills came out of the Games campaign as every bit a winner and his success resonated right across Australia. Five-time Olympian Andrew Gaze was moved to tears on Network 7's television coverage, embodying the feelings of every basketball follower in the nation, if not every sporting fan.

"It's a tribute to resilience," Gaze said when they crossed to him in the studio. "It's easy to go in there and say this is too hard. When you're in there and you're in the trenches and you see that resilience being rewarded in this way — and it hasn't been for a long, long period of time. So for me, selfishly I feel a part of it and to see Patty and the boys…" he began, his voice trailing off. Gaze was on court for the heartbreaks of 1988, 1996 and even at his Sydney 2000 swansong. Opportunities lost.

"They're beautiful journeys. You don't have to win a medal to have a beautiful journey. It's about what we want to stand for in representing Australia and representing a sport. And I think those that have been along for the journey, they have their DNA on this. There's so many that you look back on that toiled — when you don't get a cent for playing the game, when you build in stages, you're building a sport; you're trying to generate it and, for me, I am so grateful, incredibly grateful.

"Before the game, I called up my dad (five-time Olympic coach Lindsay Gaze) and just to hear him talk about what this means to the sport, and the humility and — nothing to do with him — just about how this is going to be good for Australia and Australian basketball. And (it is) another tangible bit of evidence to say that we have arrived as a sport, both our men and women.

"And he started when there were 200 registered players. And he toiled away as a coach and an administrator, to build facilities, propagate the game, take it to the people and the whole way, it was about the Olympics. The values of the Olympics, the spirit of competition were instilled in me at a very early age. It's all about getting on that podium and showing the friendship and love and making sure that you do the right thing by the game and the nation, and the pride that comes with pulling on a green-and-gold jersey.

"Tonight we saw 11 athletes, a beautiful man in Brian Goorjian, John Rillie, Matty Nielsen — who's pulled on a green-and-gold jersey to play —

get a reward that has come from the generations that worked beforehand. For those people, the Phil Smyths, the Ian Davies, the Eddie Palubinskas, the Larry Sengstocks, the Danny Morseus, Keith Miller, Ken Watson — for all they have done for the game that culminates in this reward here tonight is spectacular.

"I'll have a bit of a sook now," Gaze said of his emotion-charged assessment, "There'll be more sooking when you hear Patty Mills because, 42 points tonight — it doesn't happen without his incredible efforts. And all the guys, every single one of them, and what they put into this journey. And as I said, it's the resilience, the hardship." Gaze spoke also of the hardships of falling so tantalisingly short of a medal, even referencing the Rio Olympics and the adversity of losing Andrew Bogut when COVID shifted the Tokyo Games from 2020 to 2021.

Patty averaged 23.3 points per game and his 6.3 assists was third best at the Games. Matisse Thybulle's 3.0 steals per game led the Olympics in that category. There was the ceremony where he finally was able to relish the joy of the medal at long last, before returning to the Athletes Village to be welcomed like rock stars.

"That's our guy. He's going to get the ball into spots and he's either going to make a play or get the ball to the right person that can make his play, and along with those 42 points was nine assists," Goorjian said of Patty. "That's another 18 points.

"What he did was an epic performance of any Australian in any sport, and the fact that he carried the flag, all that came with that, representing the Aboriginal community, bringing all of our cultures together. There's a tremendous responsibility. That meant a lot to him. I don't think anyone has played in a medal-round game and scored more than he has in Olympic history.

"It's not just scoring points and accumulating points — it's in the most important game in Australian basketball history and he's done better than anyone else ever in the world."

Patty was the difference in the match and played a whopping 38 of the possible 40 minutes. Joe Ingles played 35 minutes as the duo completed the journey they began together in Beijing. Their emotional on-court hug of love, delight and relief celebrating winning Australia's first men's Olympic basketball medal became the most memorable image of this long and bumpy journey.

Artist Scotty Marsh captured the moment perfectly for a painting on the walls of the AUSA 24-7 basketball facility in Alexandria in Sydney. The painting drew significant praise from politicians to Basketball Australia and even rival sports revelling in Marsh's rendition. Both Mills and Ingles took to social media to express their delight to the artist. This was a classic encapsulation of a defining moment for Australian basketball.

"The way it happened, it was like destiny," Goorjian told Andrew Johnstone for *News Corps Code*. "People ask, 'Do you think about the Boomers? Do you remember the Boomers?' Yes. Every day I think of the Boomers. That is just the enormity of it. The bond is forever. So happy for the country. So happy for basketball. It resonated with so many people. When it finished, the people that I care about, Lindsay (Gaze), people that we've named all through this, all contact me and even to this day… we (Illawarra in the NBL) play, we lose to Tasmania and I'm walking down the hallway with my head in my hands.

"The (Tasmania JackJumpers) assistant coach comes up and gives me a hug and says, 'Man, thanks for the Boomers. All these years of my life I've been dealing with the juniors. Thank you so much'. I know that's there, so that one was a life changer. Life changing."

Goorjian's admiration for Mills the man and Mills the leader grew throughout the campaign. He was not only the captain of the Boomers — the first Indigenous captain of an Australian men's basketball team — but also captain of the Australian team competing at the Games.

"The responsibility that Patty carried was second-to-none," Goorjian said. On the bus back to the Village, the music again was blaring and more than a few eyes were no longer dry when *I Am Australian* came on.

"We are one, but we are many

And from all the lands on earth we come

We'll share a dream, and sing with one voice

I am, you are, we are Australian"

Then it was fisting pumping delight at Rose Tattoo's *We Can't Be Beaten*.

CHAPTER SIXTEEN
A VERY DIFFERENT ROLE MODEL

Benny Mills wore a half smile when he said: "COVID has a lot to answer for." At the time, Patrick's father was addressing the delays the global pandemic caused Indigenous Basketball Australia in tipping off its historic first National Indigenous Basketball Tournament in 2022. But it did not end there. "The Tokyo Olympics were the first one I missed," Benny said. "I was at the Beijing Olympics, and also in London and Rio to watch Patrick. But because of COVID, I couldn't go to Tokyo." Of all the Games to have to watch on your living room television!

While neither Benny nor Yvonne could be in Tokyo to see Patrick in live action for the Boomers, they were evident in the attitude and athleticism of their son. If ever a set of parents had reason to feel proud of how positively and purposefully they raised a child, it was Mr and Mrs Mills.

Patty turned 33 four days after he led Australia to victory in Tokyo, the culmination of a journey begun in Tokyo in 1964 with Michael Ahmatt. What Patty showed Australia in Tokyo was the human embodiment of all that is good in the world; of love and inclusiveness, of compassion and understanding, of tolerance and playfulness, of commitment and forgiveness, of ascending and achieving.

The manner in which he led from the front was and will forever be the stuff of legend. Patty Mills personified what it is to be Australian, taking his country along on a thrilling, emotional, exhilarating and ultimately glorious journey. Now it was time to share the joy with Boomers of the past, like his uncle Danny Morseu. Unfortunately, COVID restrictions across Australia meant a special day Patty planned for past and former Boomer Olympians was restricted to Queensland.

A Very Different Role Model

"I'm sitting at home one Saturday afternoon and I get a phone call from some weird number," Brian Kerle recalled. Kerle is one of the great personalities of Australian basketball. As a 206cm centre, he represented Australia at FIBA's 1970 and 1974 World Championships and in between at the 1972 Munich Olympic Games. He was an assistant coach of the Boomers team which missed on a medal at the 1988 Seoul Olympic Games and also assisted at FIBA's 1986 Worlds. In his own right, he won the first two NBL championships with St Kilda in 1979 and 1980, and two more with the Brisbane Bullets. He was the NBL's first great coach named Brian.

"I'm looking at this phone number and I think this must be some sort of spam so I didn't answer it. A little while later I get a text from the same number saying: 'Mr Kerle, I'm Patty Mills. I tried to call but you didn't answer.' So now I'm curious but not sure. I ring the number and someone answers with: 'Patty Mills here'. I'm still not sure it's him so I say: 'How's your mum? Oh, I've forgotten her name.' And he replies, 'It's Yvonne. And it *is* me, Patty Mills'. Then I realise that yes, it is him so now I'm apologising profusely and he's laughing, saying: 'I can add that to my resume — Brian Kerle wouldn't talk to me.' We talked for about 40 minutes… and he was ringing from the US."

Mills invited Kerle to attend a very special day in Brisbane, along with other Olympians in Queensland. "We gathered at the Eatery on the Brisbane River. There was a boat pontoon and we met there," Kerle said. "Patty's hired this massive yacht, it has four-or-five bedrooms below, and we all meet there." The roll call of past Boomers included Danny Morseu, Larry Sengstock, Leroy Loggins, CJ Bruton, Robert Sibley, Nate Jawai, along with Patty, Nathan Sobey and Chris Goulding from the Olympic bronze medallists.

"We all get on the boat, Benny (Mills) is there too, we're all presented with a commemorative T-shirt and we go down the river, into the city," Kerle said. "There's drinks and food on the boat but we pull up at another pontoon where there are several cars waiting for us. We get into the cars and are given a police escort — front and back — and do a lap of the city before we arrive at a park."

The Boomers' "golden oldies" are greeted with traditional islander and Aboriginal music and dance. "Then each one of us is presented with an Akubra hat, with our Olympic number on it," Kerle said, the memory again bringing with it a flood of delighted emotion. The number on each Akubra reflected where the recipient was selected as a Boomer Olympian. "I mean, the work, time and effort that's gone into this," Kerle said, shaking his head in admiration. "Aron Baynes arrived too at the park, in a wheelchair. Then we were back in the cars for two more laps of the city, police sirens blaring, lights flashing, horns going."

Returned to the yacht, the entourage next was shipped back to the Eatery where a private room had been arranged and the celebrations raged until 1:30am. "We arrived for the day at midday and at 1:30am, Patty is asking me if I'm going on and out dancing with the rest of them," Kerle laughed. "No, that wasn't happening but it was a sensational day and a sensational night and Patty paid for everything. I know the boat would have cost at least $10,000 on its own, not to mention the rest, the food, drinks.

"It was a fabulous and memorable day for all of us. It was fabulous. It was my birthday the next day and trust me, that was very much the undercard. I must admit, I was quite emotional and the day went like clockwork. We all know about 'island time' so I had to ask Patty: 'Are you sure you organised this trip up the river, because everything ran on time'. He had a good laugh."

The day was no less astonishing for Patty's uncle and dual-Olympian Danny Morseu. "I had nothing to do with it," he said of organising the event. "I had calls from Benny and Patty just asking me for a few phone numbers of people like Larry (Sengstock), (Robert) Sibley and Leroy

(Loggins) and I was just told the time and where to be. Patty rang them all to invite them. It was just such a fabulous day." Danny's Akubra hat was emblazoned with his arrival as an Olympian, #56.

"Winning that bronze medal — everybody who played (for Australia) was watching that game, right throughout the country," Danny said. "Everyone was over the moon." Danny was on Thursday Island with close family and friends watching as the match played out on TV. "Someone shot the ball and Matisse (Thybulle) grabbed it and we had won the medal. I was up and jumping around.

"We'd waited 56 years and we finally had it. All of us that had gone before, we all felt part of it. I was crying, tears running down my face. It was about all of us — we were all part of this 56-year-long journey. I was jumping around all over the place and crying." Rarely has a nation been more excited, more thrilled or delighted with the winning of a bronze medal. It felt as if all of Australia had been along for this amazing ride. All of Australia was Patty's family.

Brooklyn and the NBA's Nets beckoned. Having averaged 8.9 points on 38.8 per cent three-point shooting during his 12-year NBA career that began at the Trail Blazers, Patty Mills was ready for a greater role. "Obviously, the Olympics is one thing with the role, the leadership, the position that I'm in with the Australian team," he said. "I think after a good Tokyo Olympics campaign, being able to ride the momentum and carry it into Brooklyn is something I'm looking forward to."

And playing under as successful a playmaker as Steve Nash also excited the Aussie champion. "That style and freedom of what Steve does such a great job with, being among some of the best players in the world is just an exciting opportunity that I think I'll be able to thrive off. People ask when I was younger in the league who my favourite player was to play against and it was Steve Nash. It wasn't necessarily that I was guarding him or he was guarding me — it was more so getting to see up close and personal how he plays and how he approached the game. That was very exciting for me.

"I may or may not have been a part of the game in a slight way that ended his career in Phoenix, so that's a memory that I thoroughly enjoyed. I don't know that if he did. I've worked closely with him in the past, to be able to really dive into the details of what it takes to be able to continue to learn about the game and continue to learn about your body. For me, it was that I'm not the biggest player in the NBA or the strongest so finding little things here or there to continue to get better. That's stuff you get out of his book, you get out of Manu Ginóbili's book.

"I've been in the NBA for a few years now and been in San Antonio for 10 of those seasons. You know I think it was an opportunity for me to turn the page of a new chapter. And speaking about Brooklyn and everything that I have learned on the court, off the court, the culture of the city — I think it was something that was very attractive to me and my wife. So to be able to make a next step in our life was very exciting for us. The familiar faces around the organisation is something that was very comfortable as well."

Kyrie Irving's refusal to have a COVID vaccination left the first-choice point guard out of Brooklyn's line-up until the season's final third when vax and quarantine rules were eased across the USA and NBA. It meant Patty was off to a flyer. He played 34 minutes, scoring 23 points as Brooklyn held out visiting Minnesota Timberwolves. He dropped a record-equalling 34 points against LeBron James and the Los Angeles Lakers on Christmas Day. His eight three-point makes against the Lakers were the most in a Christmas Day fixture in NBA history. After a mere 33 games for Brooklyn, he already ranked fourth all-time for the Nets in three-pointers off the bench.

By January 2022, Patty Mills well and truly had proven his worth and opposition teams had him on their game scout. In career-best form and promoted into the starting line-up, his shooting prowess made him arguably Brooklyn's third best player. When he fouled out in the fourth quarter against the LA Clippers, his on-court absence was pronounced. He had 17 points, including five three-pointers when he departed, the Clippers surging in the final minutes to snatch a memorable 120-116 road win.

James Harden had a triple double (34 points, 13 assists, 12 rebounds) and Kevin Durant scored 28 points. Nonetheless, Brooklyn's two big guns firing was insufficient to get the win. Durant said when Mills fouled out, Clippers players were shouting that the Nets only had two shooters, allowing them to double-team Durant and Harden. "It was a huge absence, you know," Durant said.

"When he went out, all they kept screaming was, 'Now they only got two shooters out there'. That's what they were saying. We knew double-teams were coming and they were going to forget about their defensive scheme and just bring two to James and myself for the last six minutes of the game."

Patty's influence also could be seen elsewhere. Philadelphia 76ers-based bronze medal-winning teammate Matisse Thybulle was ebullient in his praise for Patty in a *Daily Telegraph* article by Matt Logue. "We have multiple chats," he said of his national team friends in the NBA, such as Joe Ingles, Josh Giddey and Jock Landale. But he singled out Patty. "Playing with Patty was such an interesting shift for me. Having such a dynamic and interesting scorer and being able to get him open; it has been interesting to try to carry that over (to the NBA) and how I can find different forms of success.

"It has been massive, not only for helping me take on a bigger role, but also in terms of developing my basketball IQ." Thybulle was enjoying maintaining and developing his relationships with all of the Aussie players. "It is such a cool group because there is a solid core of established guys who have been playing for a long time. Between Joe Ingles and Patty, they've put together a lot of years in the NBA and playing pro ball. Now they have this young core of guys coming in who are really establishing themselves on the scene in the NBA — it is really exciting."

The accolades did not end with an Olympic bronze medal for Patty Mills. In December, he was named the recipient of the coveted The Don Award by the Sports Australia Hall of Fame. The award is named after legendary cricketer Sir Donald Bradman and considered the highest honour in Australian sport, awarded annually to an athlete or a team that most inspired the nation through performance and example over the past year.

Mills said from the US: "I go about my craft as a professional and learn ways to get better, trying to carry myself in a way that I think can inspire others. Being recognised in this way to me isn't about who I sit alongside, it's about how I can inspire others with my journey. I never set out to win awards like this, I go about my craft as a professional and learn ways to get better and do so in carrying myself in a way I think I can inspire others. The honour isn't necessarily about me, it's about the impact on unity, identity, being proud of who you are and expressing that passionately."

John Bradman, son of Sir Donald, confirmed Patty personified the qualities his father most valued in sport. "He's not just a champion player, he's a champion person, a leader, a star on and off the court and most of all, an inspiration to us all," he said. Benny and Yvonne Mills again had reason to feel proud of their son. "(It's) very special," Benny said of Patrick winning The Don.

Nominated also for the 2022 Australian of the Year, as the Australian Capital Territory's Australian of the Year, Patty Mills was prominent on the list of the final eight nominees.

A Very Different Role Model

Dylan Alcott, a Golden Slam tennis winner and former basketball player with the Australian Rollers men's wheelchair team, was named the 2022 Australian of the Year. As the events of the Tokyo Olympics evolved just months earlier, Alcott also rode the ups and downs of the Boomers' campaign. "I was tearing up," he said of watching the Aussies claim their bronze. "One thing that I love about the Boomers and the Australian basketball community in general is — you know what you see of these guys on the court, on TV, Patty Mills, Joe Ingles — they are exactly like this behind closed doors.

"They are some of the best people, not only some of the best basketballers, that you'll ever see. I remember when I was like 15 years old. I was a nobody at the AIS. Patty Mills was a couple of years older than me. I was training trying to get picked for Beijing. Patty Mills just walked up and started rebounding for me. He was a 17-year-old kid you know."

Now very much an established player, Patty's three-point shooting since joining the Nets was so deadly he was invited to participate in the NBA Three-Point Contest at its annual All Star Game. Patty joined the eight-player field against Zach LaVine (Chicago Bulls), Karl-Anthony Towns (Minnesota Timberwolves), Fred VanVleet (Toronto Raptors), Trae Young (Atlanta Hawks), Desmond Bane (Memphis Grizzlies), guard Luke Kennard (LA Clippers) and guard CJ McCollum (Portland Trail Blazers).

"I'm just excited to have fun with it tonight, more than anything," Mills told a packed press conference pre-shootout. "A lot of people in Australia will be tuned in for this. It will be early in the morning while everyone's having their morning coffee and breakfast. There's a lot of kids, and in particular my IBA (Indigenous Basketball Australia) League that's kicking off at the end of the month.

"There's going to be about 800 kids with 200 coaches, volunteers, officials. So I think about them a lot when it's something like this. That's who I represent. This is why I do what I do." Although he didn't win the competition, Patty still was the first Australian to compete in the event.

His return to San Antonio to face the Spurs for the first time as a member of the Nets was made memorable by his former club with a moving video tribute, both for him and LaMarcus Aldridge. The video recalled Aldridge's arrival in San Antonio and his response to which Spurs player he most was looking forward to playing alongside. "Patty Mills," he said. They now were teammates at their third club.

"We didn't know what we were getting when we got him," coach and Mills guiding light Gregg Popovich said in the video. "As a basketball player, he's gone off the charts with development, but as a human being and a member of our society, and a leader on our team, he's been fantastic."

Mills finished his time in San Antonio as the Spurs' second all-time leader in three-pointers made (1,171) behind Manu Ginóbili (1,495) and ranked 13th all-time on the Spurs career points total with 6,218. He is 12th in assists with 1,597 and tied for sixth alongside Avery Johnson and Matt Bonner for most seasons played (10) with the organisation. He was beloved by the San Antonio community, taking an interested and active part in it. And that famed "Game Day Bala" catchphrase of his was embraced and became hugely popular.

Playing 665 games for the Spurs, Patty averaged 9.4 points and 2.4 assists. The debate rages still whether his #8 uniform should be retired into the rafters by the franchise. The reaction, welcome and ovation of the fans for him in San Antonio probably answered that question.

When the Nets crushed Oklahoma City Thunder 120-96, led as usual by Kevin Durant with 33, right behind him with 29 points in 31 minutes was Patty, including shooting 9-of-12 from behind the arc. He had to play extended minutes as Joe Harris, who was playing at small forward or off-guard for the Nets, was forced to leave the game in the second quarter with an ankle injury.

In February, Brooklyn met James Harden's demand to be traded by sending him to Philadelphia 76ers for versatile Australian guard/forward Ben Simmons. The big Aussie had been estranged from the Sixers since the disastrous end of their 2020–21 playoff campaign and at times it had gotten ugly.

"I've got his back," Patty said. "I've always had his back and now I have an opportunity to be with him, so you know I've had his back from afar and I wish I was with him earlier in his career but, being able to do what I can from afar. So I'm excited to be able to be with him in this aspect and help him in any way necessary. That's how it's always kind of been but at the end of the day, I'm excited for this and I know he is as well.

"For us to come together, I think it's going to be great for both of us. For me, to continue to learn things and I think for me to share with him as much as I can as a professional and as an athlete." And Mills was positive about Simmons' likely impact when talking with *ESPN*'s Nick Friedel. "He's going to be a threat either way," he said. "On ball, off ball — whether he's handling the ball, whether he's off the ball as a screener, I think he's such a threat that he's going to draw a lot of attention. So I think given his IQ and the way he can pass the ball and handle the ball, that makes us better at his bare minimum.

"So obviously, where he's the biggest threat is in an open-court situation with people, especially shooters around him. But, like I said, a bare-minimum Ben Simmons makes this team a whole lot better as well. We're doing a lot of talking, a lot of conversations, meaning the group, a lot of film, a lot of walk-through stuff. So he's there for all of it; he's there for the entire practice. And then he's doing his part with his shooting coach and physio and whatever that looks like. But as far as every team thing goes, he's at everything."

Within a few weeks, an injured Simmons still accompanied his Brooklyn teammates to a regular season game in Philadelphia. He received the vitriolic, bitter and hostile reception most expected when he appeared at the Wells Fargo Center, home of the 76ers. Fortunately, he had his big little brother Patty Mills as a calming influence, Sixers fans ruthlessly trolling Simmons.

During the game, even a loud "f--- Ben Simmons" chant erupted. Philly fans earlier congregated around the hotel where the Nets were staying, verbally abusing Simmons as he walked to board the team bus. When he emerged from the tunnel at the game, he was accompanied by Mills and shadowed by him through the pre-game shootaround. Simmons rebounded for Mills.

Patty's class in sticking with his Australian buddy did not go unnoticed, either. NBA reporter Nick Friedell: "Patty Mills has said repeatedly he wants to be there to support Simmons in any way he can. It's no accident that Simmons came out at the same time as Mills and has been rebounding for him and throwing Mills some passes to get him ready for tonight."

NBA writer Austin Krell: "Simmons has essentially served as a ball boy for Patty Mills in this warm-up." Journalist Bilge Ebiri: "Nice to see his Mills walking out there with Simmons, sticking by his countryman & teammate." It was a memorable night on the court too for Patty, scoring 10 points and notching up his 200th three-pointer for the season in the 129-100 road victory.

On July 30, 2020, Patty Mills first announced the formation of Indigenous Basketball Australia, the IBA seeking to instil basketball skills, values, and wellness in the next generation of Aboriginal and Torres Strait Islander youth across Australia. This ambitious programme followed on the heels of Patty's growing activism which saw him donate his salary while in the NBA's Orlando bubble, towards social justice programmes and campaigns in Australia.

Patty established IBA to overcome the many challenges and barriers Aboriginal and Torres Strait Islander people faced in Australian basketball's existing systems and structures, by creating pathways and opportunities at the grassroots level. The programme was designed to create better chances to advance and succeed on the elite stage. IBA's focus was fundamental skills development and competitions by facilitating programmes in regions across Australia. These were designed to engage and empower Aboriginal and Torres Strait Islander youth to unlock their full potential.

And IBA programmes would provide a safe environment, free of discrimination, criticism, judgment or exclusion, while creating a sense of belonging within the wider community. It also would serve as a platform to educate and address the socio-economic disadvantage, with IBA's programmes underpinned by culture, education, health, safety and wellbeing. Indigenous youth would retain cultural practices, with the goal to strengthen and promote their individual cultural identity and lead healthy lifestyles.

Ambitious? Audacious even? You bet. But Patty Mills was presenting a pathway for participation and success, designed to take Indigenous youth from community level to world stages. "Basketball as a sport has inspired me to be an exceptional athlete. It's allowed me to dream big and continually find ways to learn and grow," Patty said.

"But my love of basketball has come from the fact that it has brought me happiness, joy, health, education and knowledge, with greater appreciation and perspective on life. At the end of the day, a platform was created for me to carry and be seen as my true identity as an Australian, an Indigenous man of the land.

"When I combine those experiences, I become aware of the positive influence I can have on my own people in Australia who are continuously oppressed. It makes me want to work harder at finding ways to provide better opportunities to make a real impact on the lives of my people.

Indigenous youth are detained at a rate 23 times that of non-Indigenous young people. Currently, of the 10-13 year-olds incarcerated, Aboriginal and Torres Strait Islander children make up approximately 70 per cent of this younger age group.

"(These are) disturbing stats and we should feel responsible to take urgent and innovative actions to address this gross negligence occurring in the lives of young Indigenous people. Basketball will be the vehicle, and IBA will drive this vehicle to one day see more Indigenous Australians pulling on the green-and-gold for the Boomers or Opals. But if IBA can create the positive environment that allows my people to enjoy a healthy and safe life, to be accepted and participate in a society free from discrimination, then that's the real win for my people in this life."

The programmes delivered by IBA were the first of their kind in Australian sporting history, aimed at providing a consistent flow of Aboriginal and Torres Strait Islander players into elite basketball leagues in Australia and across the world, and into Australian junior and senior national teams.

The scope and breadth of Patty's IBA vision facilitated the targeting of community basketball competitions, national tournaments and development camps, complementing and supporting current Australian basketball systems. The focus was to provide better opportunities for Aboriginal and Torres Strait Islander youths to progress through those systems to the elite levels in the future.

The IBA's Indigenous Community Basketball League (ICBL) tipped off in 2021 and enjoyed its second season in 2022. Year One was delivered in eight regions around the country and recorded incredible participation numbers. ICBL Season Two again saw a comprehensive programme of matches and education in Darwin, Thursday Island, Cairns, Logan, Bendigo, Adelaide, Perth and Narromine. ICBL as a basketball competition, was dedicated to the development and capacity building of

Aboriginal and Torres Strait Islander talent — namely players, coaches, team managers and officials.

"Seeing the overwhelming response to last year's ICBL program only fuelled my desire to continue to find ways to provide opportunities and make a real impact on the lives of my people," Patty said as Season Two launched in February 2022. "IBA is our vehicle to make this possible. It's a basketball competition that goes way beyond the court, to encourage our young people to dream big, set goals and be inspired and motivated to chase their goals."

The ICBL's 2022 season culminated in the ground-breaking historic first National Indigenous Basketball Tournament (NIBT), a four-day event ahead-of-and-over-Easter at the Gold Coast Performance Centre and Runaway Bay Stadium. To the untrained eye, the Gold Coast Performance Centre may suggest an arts and entertainment facility but it is, in fact, one of Australia's most unique sporting precincts, Brendan Flynn its director.

Among his many roles in elite sport across Australia over four decades, Flynn was one of the architects behind the formation of the Women's National Basketball League and coach of the Australian Opals women's national team at the 1984 Los Angeles Olympic Games. The Gold Coast Performance Centre is unrivalled as a destination for the community, athletes, sporting teams and school groups to train, play and stay, accommodating athletics, beach volleyball, track and field, field sports, triathlon, hockey, and an Olympic-size swimming pool with the water set at 27-degrees, plus an indoor pool at a constant 31-degrees. The weights room/gym facility is second-to-none, as are the dining and conference areas. Accommodation is available in self-contained lodges that house up to 36 people. Runaway Basketball Stadium is just up the road.

Sally Phillips, IBA's General Manager of Strategic Initiatives, said one of Patty Mills' sponsors, Under Armour, provided all the uniforms and

Sport Australia gave a grant toward the cost of staging the historic, though one-year overdue NIBT. "Yes, COVID has a lot to answer for," Benny Mills reiterated on the NIBT's opening day as 160 Indigenous youths and 84 support staff representing Victoria, Western Australia, Northern Territory, South Australia, Torres Strait, New South Wales, Queensland North and Queensland South regions settled in at the Gold Coast.

Day One opened with a Junior NBA Training camp promoting standards of safe play while also delivering valuable training techniques and off-court life skills education. The eight boys and eight girls teams heard from various community leaders and elders from the IBA programme's core themes of people, identity and culture, education and health. These were invaluable life lessons devoted to being proud to be Indigenous, of being proud to "own your story" and recognising opportunities for success in the wider community. It was spell-binding stuff.

Games started on Good Friday after a culture-rich opening ceremony which included an inspirational video from Patty in Brooklyn. "Hello everyone. Patty Mills here," he said. "Just wanted to wish everyone that is competing in this year's NIBT the very best of luck. For me, I just wanted to say how proud I am of everyone that's been a part of IBA, from the RCs, to the volunteers, everyone that's made this vision come to life. For the kids, I hope that this has been a special place for you to be able to fulfil your potential on the basketball court, but also become aware of your own identity.

"And understand that it's about being proud of that, and using that as motivation to succeed in anything in life, not just basketball. And my last message is to take pride in representing your region. You've had many good weekends throughout the ICBL and now you have a chance to be able to represent your region, so take a lot of pride in that. You know this is about 'owning your story' and you have a great platform and a great opportunity to do that. So, that's it from me, here in Brooklyn, getting ready for a playoff series against the Boston Celtics. I just wanted to say, all the very best, have fun, and thank you to everyone that's been involved."

"We felt so lucky to receive that grant from Sport Australia," said Phillips, who previously was a WNBL star at Dandenong Rangers and Adelaide Lightning, before being Head of the Women's National Basketball League for Basketball Australia. Typically, BA was "very supportive" of the inaugural NIBT, but played no tangible role in any aspect of it. It is safe to say the event was funded by a certain Aussie guard playing in the NBA for Brooklyn.

Air fares, accommodation, uniforms and gear, plus a daily supply of fresh fruit and vegetables, meals and drinks… it quickly would have added up. "For this to be an annual event as we all want it to be, finding funding from non-Indigenous Australians and companies will be a key," Phillips said. The inaugural NIBT was supported by Sport Australia, Under Armour, leading Australian retailer Coles, publishing company Sony Music Publishing Australia, dedicated specialty officiating brands Ref Warehouse and ARCHER Officials, and sporting and leisure equipment giants, rebel.

"It was amazing to see the kids' faces when they were given their Under Armour gear or when they each were presented with their own Spalding basketball," Flynn said. As the Gold Coast Performance Centre director, and still with a keen eye for basketball talent, Flynn attended some of the match-day sessions. "They identified three or four kids as potential NBA or WNBA prospects. For the future of Indigenous sport, the sky is the limit."

The NIBT focus was on the 14-year-old age group. As Benny Mills explained: "We have had Michael Ahmatt, Danny (Morseu) and Patrick as Indigenous basketball Olympians," he said. "It's time for a few more, don't you think? So when you think about under 14s, how old will they be at Brisbane 2032?" Exactly the prime age to be representing the Boomers and Opals at those Olympic Games.

"The fact is, Patty should be knighted or given sainthood for doing this," Flynn said. "The young Indigenous kids (at the NIBT), their lives are changed forever. Some of them have never seen shoes before. Most of the kids have never flown in an aeroplane before, or never seen that amount of food before. The basketball is one aspect but their eyes are being opened to a world of possibilities." Flynn said the focus on 14 and under was important and the next logical step should be an Indigenous Centre of Excellence.

The historic and brilliant first staging of the NIBT was a huge success at every level but there was little time for Patty's parents to greatly enjoy the fruit of their labours, jumping quickly on a plane to the USA. No sooner had Benny and Yvonne landed in New York ahead of Brooklyn Nets' Game Three in the opening round of the Eastern Conference playoffs against Boston Celtics, than they were greeted by the news their son had won the NBA's 2021-22 Sportsmanship Award.

Named after Detroit Pistons' NBA champion, the Joe Dumars Trophy honours the player who most embodies the spirit of sportsmanship on and off the court. Nets coach Steve Nash broke the news to Patty with his team assembled, telling them the league had sent a video presentation they should now watch.

"Good sportsmanship is found in your attitudes," it began. "In the way you do things, in the smile you wear. And remember, if you're a good sport, everyone can enjoy the game better" it continued as old-time black-and-white footage dissolved into action of Patty on the court with the Nets.

Clear the video was revealing Patty had won the award, the team broke into spontaneous applause and support for the amazing Aussie guard as he grinned and accepted their plaudits. Hugged and feted by his teammates, a delighted Patty was handed the coveted award in a shape of a small, inscribed crystal basketball.

"I just wanna say we get to see Patty's sportsmanship every day," Nash told his team. "We get to see what type of character he is, what he brings to our group every day. But this is voted on by the league, the players — not media, no-one else. It's the players, your peers, so congratulations and thank you for everything you do for us." Then Nash added as a joke: "And you've got to carry it the whole day."

Mills was typically humbled by the award. "It was another one of those recognitions that you don't really set out to achieve in a lifetime," he said. "You just go about your day-to-day business and be who you are. But the recognition is cool. The coolest thing about it is that it is your peers, your teammates, the players you play against who vote. I guess it is a credit to my family, my parents, my upbringing and my culture specifically, and all the values that I have been taught growing up."

Sadly for the Nets, not enough of them actually bought into sportsmanship and the value of working together for a common goal. When Benny and Yvonne arrived in time for Game Three of their first round playoff series, the Nets already were down 0-2 to the Celtics. Those matches were in Boston, so there was some optimism Brooklyn could take the next two matches out at home and level the series.

Boston stole Game One with a Jayson Tatum spin to the hoop for the final 115-114 scoreline, Game Two a more regulation 114-107 Celtic success, albeit from a 17-point deficit. But with Ben Simmons staying in street clothes for the duration, even home in Brooklyn the Nets could not withstand the Green Machine, losing 103-109. Patty Mills saw sufficient daylight in Game Three to contribute 12 points but Game Four on Anzac Day was no different, Boston completing the only sweep of the 2022 first round with a 116-112 road win.

Starting the season among championship favourites, Brooklyn bowed out in the most unceremonious manner imaginable. It was an ignominious end, the sold-out crowd of 18,099 at Barclays Center watching as Tatum became a legitimate superstar, shining even brighter than Kevin Durant. After all the buzz Mills helped generate early in the season, it came steadily apart as Kyrie Irving, not suiting because of his refusal to take a COVID vaccination, returned to play 29 games.

That was on top of team disruptions caused by James Harden's trade demand, shooter and Mills-duplicate Seth Curry coming to Brooklyn in the deal which swapped Harden for Ben Simmons, and the latter's physical and mental woes. At a time when taking a leaf from Patty's sportsmanship and leadership examples should have been essential, this was a team so far from being on the same page as to being in different books.

"Patty Mills is my favourite international player," ESPN basketball commentator and former New York Knicks and Houston Rockets head coach Jeff Van Gundy declared in the wake of the Tokyo Games. "I don't think people realise — you can say 42 points, nine assists, right? So for NBA fans, they say 'yeah, guy has got 40.' You don't get 40 in a FIBA game, like *ever*. You just don't do that and particularly in a game that is going to be as hard-fought as that (medal) game.

"His uniqueness is his willingness to move for 40 minutes. He's in great condition, he knows how to play off the ball. And he's willing to do it longer than you're willing to guard him. Patty Mills is my favourite international player that I don't think so many people realise how great he was."

Patty Mills' greatness always has been about more than just basketball. "My family, my background, my family's background and what they went through, 100 per cent defines me, who I am," he says. "And being able to use those elements or characteristics or whatever it is to get by things or to do things or to achieve things, whatever, I think has gotten me to where I am today.

"My mother being a part of the Stolen Generation and my dad being from the Torres Strait, those two are both the Indigenous peoples of Australia, and that is my upbringing of who I am. But along with that comes a lot of great things, a lot of good things and cultural things, but obviously a lot of adversity as well. I think I've just gotten to the age where I've understood how to not only acknowledge it but teach and educate others.

"It's those interactions, when I go to communities and places that they would never think that I would go, nor other people, I think it's times like that they really understand — and I speak to them in language or whatever it may be — but it's those moments that they understand that I'm just like them. And I tell them I'm just like you, running around with holes in my shoes or no shoes on dirt or whatever it may be that they realise I'm just like them. And I think the more that I'm able to connect with them in that way, that automatically opens up the idea for them to think that: 'Well I can do it too, if he can.' And that's the message.

"I don't think I'm ever going to really understand how much impact I'm having. I mean, I think I know — I've been told that before, and I've been told that by Cathy Freeman, of all people. She said to me: 'I don't think you understand how much of an impact you have on Indigenous kids, but all Indigenous people.' And I guess I'm at the point now where I see myself as an ambassador for all Indigenous people throughout the world because they are the same battles, they are the same fights. And I've seen that and I've heard that from people all around the world and I think that's really unique and really special. That I have that opportunity to be able to then inspire all these other people from all around the world. I think it's important but I think it's special, yeah."

Signing a new two-year $USD14.5 million deal at Brooklyn Nets, Patty's multiple strengths are truly appreciated. He is the quintessential, once-in-a-lifetime Australian.

CHAPTER SEVENTEEN
CHANGING OF THE GUARD

All good things must come to an end and for Patty Mills, the end of the 2022 NBA season meant the chance to come home and replenish in Australia. But this was no ordinary trip back. The "Patty Mills 'Unearthed' Australia 2022 Tour" marked an ambitious homecoming for the four-time Olympian. Fans relished the opportunity to see and hear him in action, "up close and personal" through a series of on-court basketball camps and uncut conversations.

From September 5-21, he appeared at the Gold Coast, Logan, Sydney, Thursday Islands, Perth, Adelaide and Melbourne, hosting coaching clinics and sharing his experiences in Brisbane, Sydney, Perth and Melbourne via his "uncut and intimate conversations" to a spellbound audience. Called the "Speaking My Language – Patty In His Own Words", the engagements were an unqualified success. But when he returned to the NBA, the turmoil at Brooklyn Nets still was evident, Steve Nash fired as coach a mere seven games into the 2022-23 season with the win-loss record at 2-5. All the promise and excitement of what could be built in Brooklyn now was a thing of the past.

Nash was replaced by assistant coach Jacque Vaughn, who chose to downgrade Patty's role on the roster. "I've challenged him to be ready to play when he's called upon," Vaughn said. "He's gone multiple games without playing and still works every day… There's gonna be a playoff game where Patty is gonna have an impact because he's mentally and physically ready." But there was a hollowness about Vaughn's rhetoric. (Ironically Vaughn was sacked by the Nets 54 games into the 2023-24 season after a 50-point loss to Boston Celtics.)

After playing in 81 games of the previous season's 82, Patty was restricted to action in just 40 matches, his minutes plummeting from 29.1 to 14.2, his points average from 11.4 per game to 6.2, his lowest return since he averaged 5.1 points at San Antonio a decade earlier. But the Nets finished with a 45-37 record, one win better than in 2021-22, and their sixth place in the Eastern Conference meant they avoided the play-in tournament. It did not count for much though, Philadelphia 76ers sweeping Brooklyn 4-0 in their best-of-seven first round series. Patty played just five minutes in the playoff series loss and suited up to play just three of the last 24 games in the regular season. "My parents taught me that you don't sulk when you don't get court time. Just make the most of it when you do play," was Patty's ethos.

Unsurprisingly, on July 6, Patty and teammate Joe Harris were traded to the Houston Rockets and Detroit Pistons respectively, ostensibly so Brooklyn could unload their contracts. But that was just the beginning. Houston traded Patty on to Oklahoma City Thunder where there was excitement he would reunite with fellow Aussies Josh Giddey and Jack White. Giddey was a sensation at OKC in his 2021-22 debut and built on that in 2022-23 averaging 16.6 points, 7.9 rebounds and 6.2 assists. White was a peripheral member of the Denver Nuggets 2022-23 champion. Two Australians in the same NBA team had occurred previously, but three? However it was never to be.

Oklahoma City traded Mills to Atlanta Hawks, his fourth team in 10 days. Nothing could have prepared him for such an off-season. Meanwhile in Australia, the Boomers' squad of 18 players for the FIBA World Cup team to play in Okinawa, Japan, only was out-of-date on its player locations. The squad was Xavier Cooks (Washington Wizards), Dyson Daniels (New Orleans Pelicans), Matthew Dellavedova (Sacramento Kings), Dante Exum (Partizan Belgrade), Sam Froling (Illawarra Hawks), Josh Giddey (Oklahoma City Thunder), Chris

Goulding (Melbourne United), Josh Green (Dallas Mavericks), Joe Ingles (Milwaukee Bucks), Nick Kay (Shimane Susanoo Magic), Jock Landale (Phoenix Suns), Thon Maker (Fujian Sturgeons), Will McDowell-White (New Zealand Breakers), Patty Mills (Brooklyn Nets), Keanu Pinder (Perth Wildcats), Duop Reath (Al Riyadi Club Beirut), Matisse Thybulle (Portland Trailblazers), Jack White (Denver Nuggets).

The squad went into camp in Cairns from August 1-10, ahead of its Four Nations Warm-Up Tournament in Melbourne from August 14-17 against Brazil, Venezuela and South Sudan. It then would head to Tokyo for final preparations. Landale was playing some terrific basketball for Phoenix in its Western Conference semi final series and going to be a key player for the Boomers in Okinawa. National coach Brian Goorjian made Dellavedova and McDowell-White his final cuts, reducing the squad to 13. Only allowed to suit 12 at the Worlds, he kept an additional player due to injury concerns around Landale and Goulding, ahead of the exhibition matches in Melbourne.

Excitement in the wake of the Tokyo Olympics result only grew when the Boomers' opponents in Group E were revealed. Australia would need to negotiate the Japanese home crowd in Okinawa in its FIBA World Cup Group E where the Boomers also drew Germany and Finland for the right to advance. Germany, at #11, was their highest-ranked opponent, Finland at #24 and Japan #36. Goorjian's Boomers were ranked #3.

The bronze medal success at the Tokyo Olympic Games two years back was expected to act as a springboard for further medal podium visits by the Australian men's team. Group E was no so-called "Group of Death". Far from it. Maybe the "Group of Deaf" because any whining about this cluster of opponents needed to fall on deaf ears. With the top two teams in each group after intragroup play advancing to the Round of 16, the road ahead for the Australian team was paved with gold.

The World Cup from August 25 to September 10, presented Australia

Changing of the guard

with a fine opportunity to improve on its best result, fourth place in 2019. The warm-up series against Venezuela, Brazil and South Sudan was scheduled for Melbourne on August 14, 16 and 17 but did not go as planned. After dominating Venezuela 97-41, Australia followed up by suffering a stunning 86-90 reversal to Brazil.

"We started the game with an element of softness," Goorjian conceded. "We got really outhustled the first five-six minutes of the game. But, big picture, maybe a little punch in the face right now at this stage isn't a bad thing. Helps us back to the reality of how tough this is going to be.

"We came here to win the game, I coached the game on the sideline, I wasn't just moving bodies around, I was trying to win. That was disappointing but I now take a deep breath and does it help me with a few things moving forward? For sure. That next step to be the best in the world at something is really, really, difficult. The culture's been strong but let's see where we go now with a few punches in the face."

A potential knock-out blow was still to follow. While Australia beat South Sudan 88-67, the final team of 12 was decided during this match when Landale, in his first game back from injury, suffered a horrible setback. A shattered Landale, whose preparation was disrupted by problems with his right ankle, went over on his left ankle just five minutes into the Thursday night match. The Boomers flew out for Japan the next day, Landale only able to offer his heartfelt best wishes. There were truly only two players on this team Australia could not afford to lose – Patty Mills and Jock Landale. Despite the Boomers' brave face, the general consensus now was that gold would be very unlikely.

"My MRI results are back and I'll be good as gold. Nothing too serious, just gonna need a bit of time on this one. See you in a Houston Rockets jersey soon and a Boomers one come Paris 2024. Sitting here this morning knowing the Boomers are about to take off to Japan and I'm absolutely kicking myself I'm not right there beside them," Landale tweeted. "All the build up and preparation we go through as athletes just to have it yanked away 12 hours beforehand sucks."

If there was one national team the Boomers might have preferred to avoid to open their second stage of the FIBA World Cup in Manila, Philippines, it was Slovenia. Australia needed two wins to go through to the quarter-finals, having successfully qualified for the 2024 Paris Olympic Games during its intrapool stage. The Aussies consolidated their place at the Olympics with their 109-89 win over Japan, which, coupled with New Zealand's 74-83 loss to Greece in a rival pool, ensured the Boomers would be the World Cup's higher-placed Oceania Zone finisher. The first big goal at the World Cup, qualifying for the 2024 Paris Olympic Games, was a ticked box. But now Slovenian superstar Luka Doncic stood in Australia's way of advancing at the World Cup, the memory of the Boomers winning their historic first ever Olympic medal in Tokyo two years earlier over his European qualifier still a raw one.

The danger for the Aussies was how closely Slovenia had studied their form. Apart from the first quarter of the Boomers' opening intrapool game, when Finland on a high performed as if it was playing Game 7 of an NBA championship series, they had tentatively been negotiating a new phase in the team's evolution, the changing of the guard. Once Australia settled into its groove, with Patty Mills and Joe Ingles leading the way but Josh Giddey (14 points, 9 rebounds, 8 assists), Dante Exum, Xavier Cooks, Josh Green, Jack White, Nick Kay and Duop Reath all providing memorable moments, the Finnish contest was well and truly finished. Patty typically led the scoring in the 98-72 rout with 25 points at 50 per cent, plus eight rebounds, two assists and four steals.

An 8-0 start by Germany rocked the Boomers on their heels, coach Brian Goorjian dropping two F-bombs in his early "snap to it" timeout.

It worked too, Patty going off for 13 straight points in a 17-point half. Germany's star backcourt of Dennis Schroder (30 points at 53 per cent, 5-of-9 threes, 8 assists) and Maodo Lo (20 points at 67 per cent, 4-of-8 threes) though steadily carved up the Aussies' much vaunted defence. Both guards but particularly Schroder, exploited Australia's tactic of switching on everything, isolating and continually exploiting Kay on the pick-and-roll.

Kay was one of the Boomers' most hard-working and reliable players, but in no way could he contain Schroder on the drive or stepping back for a triple. And Germany executed the play as regular as clockwork. It was only Matisse Thybulle fighting over screens to prevent the defensive switch, that somewhat stymied Germany's offence, and a 22-13 third quarter by the Boomers in which Reath had eight points on two triples and a dunk, set up victory. Or so it seemed.

Another 10-0 German outburst to start the final quarter quickly erased Australia's 66-62 lead and while Giddey tied the game at 81-81, he split two free throws for 82-83. Two uncharacteristic turnovers by Mills, including one for the win after a timeout, proved critical, Germany adding two more points for a stunning victory. The Boomers pleaded for a foul call on Giddey's last-gasp heave with 0.2 of a second left. But such pleas were the real "Hail Mary". (It's Euro-centric FIBA. You're playing a European team. Foul or not, that won't be being reviewed. Other way around? Then, maybe.)

The 82-85 loss in which Patty again shone with 21 points at 64 per cent, five rebounds, six assists and a steal, meant no further margin for error. Host nation Japan, buoyed at coming from 18 down to defeat Finland, now loomed as a genuine threat to Australia's chances of advancing out of the group. But consecutive shot blocks by Reath in a 4-0 start showed Australia's intent, Giddey again superb and with it from tip-off. But this was arguably the best game Xavier Cooks ever played. While the then

Sydney Kings "big" was a dual NBL champion, an MVP winner and an athlete who now had wet his feet in the NBA, this was a whole new ball game. Blocking a shot at one end, running the lane to the hoop to take a pass from Ingles for a super slam, meant he too was up for this one.

His 24-point (at 60 per cent, 10 offensive rebounds) and 16-rebound double-double was one for the ages, especially considering this was the international level and just how much was at stake. Josh Green's insertion into the starting lineup also paid dividends, showing the Dallas Mavericks just how much his offensive talents were being wasted in the NBA – and his defensive work was exemplary.

The lead was quickly ballooning into deep double-digits in the second quarter, Nick Kay a factor and Dante Exum again showing how invaluable he was becoming for this team, the game appearing to be done and dusted at halftime, the Boomers ahead 57-35. Two fouls on Reath and one on Green in the first 11 seconds of the second half made it look very much that FIBA wanted to give the sold-out 10,000-plus home crowd something to cheer about. Australia though extended its lead to as many as 27 points before Japan came with a rush, Yuta Watanabe and Joshua Hawkinson problematic as Australia's great defence went out the window.

Japan clawed back to within 13, its zone defence also restricting the Boomers before some better ball movement and timely drives turned this back into a comfortable win. Goorjian shortened his rotation to nine – Jack White, Chris Goulding and Dyson Daniels only used very late - but his only form concern was with Thybulle, who for the first time appeared a little lost and unsure of his role now. The fact Japan's zone noticeably slowed the Aussie offence – and surely Goulding made this team as its three-point shooting zone-buster, yet his services were not sought – would be among the notes Slovenia should have taken from the Boomers' 109-89 victory. Patty had a quiet shooting night for 11 points, but dished nine assists.

Changing of the guard

If Australia continued to choose to defensively switch on every pick-and-roll – which the Boomers could when playing with a so-called "small ball" lineup – Slovenia no doubt would isolate Australia's bigs as Germany had, and some zone also would cause hiccups. That was, of course, unless those areas already were addressed during the Boomers few days without a scheduled match. Beating Slovenia, then Georgia simply were "musts" when their tournament shifted to Manila. Losing to Germany meant that result carried through to the second stage of the World Cup. To advance to the quarter-finals, Australia had to beat Slovenia and Georgia.

But the Slovenia match slipped from Australia's grasp quickly. As expected, Slovenia was fired up for this rematch of the bronze medal playoff in Tokyo and had Luka Doncic and athletic centre Mike Tobey setting a cracking pace. At the close of the first quarter, Slovenia led 28-18, forcing the Boomers into a game of catch-up. Josh Giddey led the way with 25 points at 61 per cent, plus eight rebounds and four assists. But his six turnovers were expensive. Patty Mills' 17 points included 3-of-4 triples, and his eight rebounds and three assists were invaluable. But Australia's only other reasonably reliable scoring avenue was Dante Exum who finished with 13 points. Slovenia's 91-80 success meant Australia had one match to go and its FIBA World Cup was prematurely over.

Goorjian said losses to Germany and Slovenia showed his side currently was a "step off" the teams contending for medals and his side's reaction under pressure against Slovenia showed more work was required. "Offensively, for us, when we play it with pace, when we move the ball and dribble it less we are a really good team," Goorjian said, before further observing the Boomers now were dribbling too much and had not moved the ball with their previous tenacity.

Australia beat Georgia 100-84 to end its disappointing campaign on a high, despite missing the chance to win a medal. Patty Mills led the side with 19 points, while Dante Exum added 18 and Duop Reath 16, including a perfect three-point shooting display of 3-of-3, as five Aussie players reached double figures in points.

"It's definitely a disappointing result (to leave the World Cup without a medal)," Mills said post-game on ESPN. "But it was important to us as a playing group that we came out and finished this thing right, finish with a win."

Giddey led the Boomers in scoring across the tournament, with 19.4 points per game, Patty next on 18.6. Only Exum also averaged double figures in points with 11.0. Stalwarts Ingles and Kay averaged 6.6 and 6.4 points respectively. Unlike the focused and fully committed Boomers of Tokyo, this now was most definitely a team in transition, with changing roles. There were several instances where the role breakdowns were apparent. Giddey and Cooks for example, in the extended Australian team ahead of Tokyo, now were significant contributors. Letting go of the baton can be a challenge. Goorjian, who took the 2023-24 season off from fulltime coaching to focus solely on Australia's quest in Paris, declared the road to the Olympic Games had begun, with more change imminent as the Boomers accommodated the next generation of players.

There was much to think about, although the three-point loss to Germany was given greater perspective when the Germans smacked Slovenia 100-71, eliminated the USA in a semi final and went on to win their historic first ever World Cup.

Patty Mills returned to the US, ready to play for coach Quin Snyder at the Atlanta Hawks. Snyder previously coached the Australian pair of Dante Exum and Joe Ingles at the Utah Jazz so already had an idea of the work ethic and attitude of Australian basketball players. After his depleted lineup lost a match against the Philadelphia 76ers, Snyder was moved to address Patty's contribution in his post-game press conference. "I think that's who he's been as far as the way that he plays," Snyder said.

"He puts a stamp on the game with his defence, with his activity, his energy, his voice. He's the epitome of stay ready. He hasn't been playing and then obviously gets an opportunity tonight. I thought that group changed the game when they came in the first quarter at the end there and really gave us a boost ... it's not easy to play against Patrick Beverly pressuring you 90 feet. But that's what Patty's done. I just have tremendous respect for him as a player and it is also reflective of who he is as a person and as a teammate."

Snyder said the work Patty puts in the gym is "unique" - to "always be ready" for a game - and also said that "you hear about that sometimes, it's very seldom that someone can actually handle their profession that way."

But his first season as a Hawk was having its ups and downs, the dreaded DNP-CD (Did Not Play-Coach's Decision) too regularly appearing on post-game stats sheets. Then he was embarrassed when the NBA announced its annual All Star Game balloting due to a bizarre mix-up. In a video he shared on his social media account, Patty revealed that the image used of him on the NBA's All Star voting page was incorrect. The photograph actually was of Atlanta Hawks teammate Wesley Matthews. Patty's video showed his live reaction to the blunder, shaking his head in disbelief with the caption: "All-Star voting off to a good start," with a laughing emoji.

Meanwhile in Australia, the Federal Government's plan to give First Nations people a Voice to Parliament was turned into a divisive political manipulation by the forces which opposed it ahead of the October 14 referendum. Patty Mills' impassioned and measured plea to fans, friends and anyone prepared to listen and educate themselves on the "Yes" referendum designed to give Aboriginal and Torres Strait Islanders a voice to parliament and Constitutional recognition, went unrequited. His explanation for the "If you don't know, vote no" Australians was simple. If you don't know, let me explain it to you.

"This weekend, one of the most controversial votes in Australian history is taking place," he said. "It does not need to be this difficult. It's simple. Let me break it down for you. Australia is voting on having a committee made of Aboriginal and Torres Strait Islander people to represent Aboriginal and Torres Strait Islander people on issues and policies that will affect Aboriginal and Torres Strait Islander people. This committee cannot make any new laws. They cannot control funding. They cannot sit in Houses of Parliament. They are only there to advise.

"The reason why this is so simple but so important is because we are voting on the referendum to update the constitution. Would you want a plumber or electrician to give advice on plumbing? Would you want a doctor or a mechanic giving advice on fixing your car? Would you want me or Ash Barty to give advice on tennis? It is simple. Get advice from the right people. Vote Yes."

The man who never lets Australia down sadly was let down by voters across Australia on October 14 when the No vote prevailed. Typically, he soldiered on. In January, Patty Mills was named as an inaugural recipient of an Australian Embassy Award for sport. The award recognised Mills' achievements as a leader in his sport and in proudly representing Australia on the international stage. There still was one more international stage to come. The 2024 Paris Olympics for Patty represents that last chance to improve on the bronze of Tokyo.

But of the eight teams to already qualify, namely host nation France, world champion Germany, runner-up Serbia, Canada, USA, Australia, Japan and South Sudan, right now most would only pencil in those last two national teams as likely Aussie wins. The remaining four spots in Paris will come out of the Qualifying Tournaments that will see Latvia, Lithuania, Italy, Spain, Montenegro, Greece, Georgia and Finland among

Changing of the guard

the European teams battling it out.

Then there's also Brazil, Puerto Rico, Dominican Republic, New Zealand, Egypt, Lebanon, Philippines, Mexico, Angola and Cote d'Ivoire. The conclusion that a medal of any colour will be anything but a cakewalk or some dream run for our "gold vibes only" men is an accurate one. That's not to say, by any stretch, they cannot do it. It's just a courtesy reminder Australia will not be the only country sending its best available 12, the USA also anxious to mount another "Redeem Team" assault. For Patty Mills and the Boomers, a return to the medal podium would be mission accomplished.

Leap year occurs every four years – in Olympic years – but February 29, 2024 would forever be memorable, sending shockwaves across Australian basketball. The Atlanta Hawks waived Patty Mills, the iconic figure of the Boomers without an NBA contract for the first time since 2009. Fears of what this might mean to Australia's hopes of medalling again in Paris saw some of the sport's biggest names offering advice on what his next course of action should be. Further opportunities would exist for Patty and the parting words of Atlanta Hawks coach Quin Snyder did his future prospects no harm.

It was "an absolute pleasure having the chance to coach him," Snyder said. "He's someone you're glad your paths crossed. I've been a fan of his from afar, a fan of the Boomers because of Joe Ingles, and I've followed him for a long time. Patty's the type of professional that you point to for how you handle everything across the board — the good times, the bad times, the successes, the failures. We're grateful that we had a chance to have him here for a short time and we wish him all the best."

As the shockwave swept over Australian basketball and Patty Mills' fans, it was his former teammate at Brooklyn Nets, a championship winner and league MVP in Kevin Durant who spoke publicly about the Boomers icon. Asked what impact Mills had on both the NBA and the international game, Durant replied: "Just a flat out legend for the Boomers. He has been a constant for that program since I've been in the league. They play with such a toughness and you know that comes from their best player, which is Patty.

"And then (to) have an opportunity to play with Patty for two years at Brooklyn, I see why he's become such a legend over there. He's so passionate about where he's from, he's so passionate about the culture itself and basketball. And he's an extremely hard worker whose journey should be spoken about with some of the best. He continues to push the game forward man, and inspire a lot of people. And that's what I love about this game."

The Hawks converted the contract of guard Trent Forrest, 25, from a two-way deal to a standard pact, Patty only hitting the court in 19 of Atlanta's 58 games. Consequently he was averaging a paltry 2.7 points, 1.1 rebounds and 10.6 minutes off the Hawks' bench, shooting 37.3 per cent from the floor and 38.2 from three-point range. For a frightening moment, it appeared Mills' 879 NBA games with the Portland Trail Blazers, San Antonio Spurs, Brooklyn Nets and Atlanta Hawks, averaging 8.9 points and 2.2 assists over that career, was over.

Temporarily.

"Excited about it. Again, at this time of year to be able to add somebody (who) has that much experience, playoff experience, winning experience, and he's a great teammate, he knows how to fit in. We just think he's another really good fit for a lot of different reasons. Stylistically, the way he plays, the way he competes, offensively he can create space, and his catch-and-shoot game, dribble hand-off game is something we already have in our system. And then his professionalism, his leadership, all of those things are 'add values' to what we have going. And also, we're just tired of being on the other side of him being a Heat killer, so if we can get him to join us, that's a really good thing. I have deep respect for him."

The speaker? Erik Spoelstra, head coach of the Miami Heat, the man who watched Game 5 of the 2014 NBA Finals turn into a San Antonio Spurs rout, Mills scoring 14 points in the third quarter to beat his ballclub 4-1 in the best-of-seven championship series. Fast-forward to a decade later and with Miami on a 35-26 win-loss record chasing an Eastern Conference playoff berth, Patty would be the perfect fit. Heat guard Tyler Herro was sidelined from February 23 with a knee injury, Josh Richardson (shoulder) out from February 11 and requiring surgery. Patty bringing his big-game experience and shot-making ability to the Heat was a win-win for both parties.

As always, he was gracious in his departure from the Hawks, posting on social media. "Thank you @ATLHawks for allowing me to be part of your organization. Although it was brief, I learned a lot and made relationships I'll always cherish. I hope I was able to make a positive impact on and off the court." The question now was only whether prolonged inactivity with Atlanta had diminished his skillset.

That minor concern immediately was erased when he entered Miami's match against Josh Giddey's Western Conference top seeded Oklahoma City Thunder and swished a trademark three-point basket from the top of the key. Mills continued to match his season-high points in his Heat debut, playing 16 minutes, immediately beyond the 10 minutes of daylight he averaged under Snyder at Atlanta. He made an impact too, with back-to-back three-pointers in just four minutes.

In a dazzling opening to his Heat career, Mills knocked down three triples at 75 per cent in his 13-point contribution - at an overall 71 per cent - to match his top score as a Hawk. Not a bad debut, Patty also grabbing two rebounds and finishing the game with a team-high plus/minus of +13. The plus-minus statistic measures a player's impact, represented by the difference between their team's total scoring versus their opponent's when the player is in the game.

"It was great to see him finally do it in a Heat uniform instead of against us," Spoelstra said. "We've seen that for too many years. You could see why he's been able to do what he does. He's ignitable, he's smart, he's been in a lot of very good systems so he knows how to fit in, even though he hasn't had a practice (with Miami). Fifteen years in, it's all the same kind of stuff. He can play his game. He helps our best players. He'll definitely add to our depth."

Though Miami lost to OKC 100-107, Mills understandably was relieved to again be in an environment where his skills were appreciated. "Anytime you get to have a chance to get on the floor is always good," he said. "Disappointing loss, we gave ourselves chances there." Not coming up with the 50-50 balls, a pregame topic, was a concern but Patty was thrilled to again be on the floor and contributing. "It's been great," he said of joining Miami. "In such a short amount of time, it's felt comfortable and it's actually felt a lot longer than what it has (been). I feel like I'm in a place where it's really valued for what I have to bring and I think it allows me to give much more of myself to a team, this locker-room, the organisation and to a culture. So it's been a very comforting last 48 hours."

Asked specifically how he saw himself fitting into the Heat structure, Mills said: "I think it's more of a mentality of 'whatever it takes' and just seeing the opportunity, your chances. The clear thing here is one goal and everyone being able to buy into that and do their part to be able to be the last team standing at the end of the day. So, whatever it takes, you go out there and try to do it."

In just his second Heat outing, Miami narrowly lost 108-110 to Washington Wizards. Patty played 14 minutes, hitting a three amid his seven-point tally and again with a team-high plus/minus rating of +9. The door to success and its adjacent road to Paris once again was ajar.

About the Author

Former News Corporation journalist and multiple award-winning sports writer Boti Nagy is a five-time nominee for Basketball Australia's Hall of Fame for his contribution to the sport, and was inducted last year into the Basketball SA Hall of Fame. He previously has written three critically-acclaimed books on basketball, *High Flyers*, *Mahervellous! The Brett Maher Story* and *A Type of Life*, his memoir in the sport.

Starting his career at the keyboard as a 15-year-old contributor to South Australia's weekly *Messenger* newspaper, Nagy secured a cadetship with News Corporation in 1974 and rapidly earnt a reputation for his accuracy, fearlessness and flair, setting a benchmark for those to follow as a 12-time winner of national Basketball Writer of the Year awards.

During his working life, he has covered Olympic Games and basketball World Championships, with the unique distinction of seeing every team since the launch of the National Basketball League in 1979 and the Women's NBL in 1981.